Images of Colonial India in British Writing

1757-1857

Images of Colonial India in British Writing

1757-1857

Sindhu Menon

Prestige

an international publishing house

Published by
PRESTIGE BOOKS
in association with
ASIA BOOK CLUB
3/28, East Patel Nagar
New Delhi 110 008
Ph. 9818755529
email: prestigebooks@gmail.com
website: asiabookclub.com
ISBN: 81-7851-033-2

Printed at Chaman Offset Press, New Delhi 110 002

Contents

for

My Father

who not only gave me life

but also made it

worth living

and to

the memory of

My Mother

Foreword

Dr. Sindhu Menon's scholarship is a rare combination of exceptional alertness to the insights of contemporary thought with a more than ordinary awareness of the wisdom she has received from a traditional background. This gives her study a wonderful balance. Her work, stemming from a doctoral dissertation she did under my supervision some years ago is about the Representation of India in British writing from roughly the Battle of Plassey in 1757 to the First War of Indian Independence (the British still call it the Great Indian Mutiny). In this work Dr Menon shows a healthy respect for the Work of Art as a finished product, an aesthetic artifact, a thing made, without sacrificing her freedom to see the Work as Text, Art as process, as communiqué, a thing said, as part of a larger discourse. Dr Menon is as interested in the structure of a Romantic Ode as she is in the undertext, the sub text and the over text of the Ode. This fusion of aesthetic concern with a sharp social and political concern is what I think makes Dr Menon a fine example of the representative Indian scholar, intellectually alive, but tempered with the restraint that comes from her *samskara.* Dr Menon is fully aware of the developments in Theory and she does use these insights in her work on the British image of India. In particular I find her creative use of Edward Said and her intuitive sympathy for the procedures of New Historicism, which she has fully internalized in her work to be excellent examples of how literary theory should be deployed in literary study. Theory is not an end in itself and Dr Menon has been able to use it with delicacy and tact.

Her main argument is that the monolithic status of the British Raj is questionable and she suggests that the Colossus was in fact riven with cracks, ruptures and gaps. This focus on the cracks is very much in the fine traditions of deconstructive literary criticism but what distinguishes Dr Menon's work is the almost seamless way in which she moves from theoretical insights to the actual consideration of literary texts. She moves effortlessly between texts ranging from Edmund Burke and William Jones to Wordsworth, Coleridge, Moore, Keats, Scott and many others seeing these varied writings as part of the literary and cultural discourse of the 100 years she has chosen to study. So a travel account exists cheek by jowl with a Romantic Ode and Dr Menon will give the same serious attention to both texts. She does this with a refreshing candour and with good humour, surely marks of a mature and sophisticated mind.

It is now some years since Sindhu Menon worked with me on this study for her Ph.D. I can still recall the feverish activity and the edgy and single-minded zeal with which Sindhu would pepper me with questions and clarifications and the speed with which she wrote her chapters. I often found it difficult to keep pace with her. Since then and now I see a more relaxed scholar, one who can take the longer view of things, and write in an expansive and elegant style. This finished work surpasses even my expectations. I can say with all the conviction at my command that there are very few scholars in India today who know as much about the Romantic age in England as Sindhu does. The work therefore is entirely welcome and will be an important intervention in Anglo Indian studies and in work on the Indo British Literary and Cultural encounter. I warmly commend this book to the reading public.

University of Hyderabad **Mohan Ramanan**

Acknowledgements

There are a number of scholars, teachers, colleagues, friends and others who helped me in preparing the present book. I express my gratitude to:

⊗ My Guru, Professor Mohan Ramanan. Thank you Sir, for your help, concern, encouragement, your valuable attention to details and your *incredible* store of patience;

⊗ Professor Viswanathan, for a series of interesting discussions and extremely useful suggestions;

⊗ Professor Sudhakar Marathe, for advice, interest, the occasional much-needed pulling up and for showing me that teaching and learning could be fun!

⊗ Dr. Tejaswini Niranjana, for making me approach my once-dreaded 'Theory' and learn to handle it;

⊗ Professor Alladi Uma, for making me realize my own blind spots and later on for showing me that one Platonic ideal—that of HOD—at least, could exist in reality!

⊗ Dr. Hoshang Merchant, for giving me a precious glimpse into what literary creation could be, other than 'research';

⊗ Professor Sachidananda Mohanty; for a stimulating M.A course: 'Literature against Itself', which enabled me to tackle and grasp many texts I would otherwise have dismissed as incomprehensible;

⊗ Professor P. Sailaja, for putting up with my frequent pure idiocy in language classes, and for recently discovered mutual interests which bolstered my confidence just when needed;

⊗ Professor Narayana Chandran, for setting THE standards;

⊗ Dr. M. Sridhar and Dr. K Suneetha Rani for their contributions to making my M.A years and initial research stages enjoyable and fruitful enough to inspire me to continue;

⊗ Mujeeb, Lavanya and Sunita, for ensuring that my feet stayed firmly on the ground;
⊗ Afeefa, for somehow intuitively sensing the times when I was insecure and almost always being the first one to offer a reassuring comment;
⊗ Anna and Nands for shared interests, books and trips;
⊗ Pramod and Murali, for literally shaming me into getting out of my stupor and finally get this book ready for publication;
⊗ The office staff of the English Department, University of Hyderabad and especially Mr. Murthy, for deciphering my scrawls and typing them up;
⊗ All my teachers at the English Department, St. Teresa's Convent, Kochi for fostering my love for literature and equipping me to go on;
⊗ Especially, Ms. Jayanthi and Ms. Aisha who made texts come 'alive' for me;
⊗ Professor Vimala Rao and Sindhu for so much, from books to food;
⊗ Professors Yadugiri and Drs. Ramadas Rao, Sarala, and Vaishali for making my sojourn at Bangalore University endurable;
⊗ Jayashankar uncle, for letting me raid his valuable private collection of rare books;
⊗ Sudha akka, Sowmya, Bharat and Meera for providing a home away from home whenever needed;
⊗ Viji, for a long friendship of a puzzling nature, as rewarding as it was complex;
⊗ Vidya, for somehow being there for me despite the miles between us;
⊗ Jai, for a unique friendship, wonderful as long as it lasted: the memories are still precious;
⊗ Rekha, Aruna, Angel and Sharmi for stimulating discussions and practical help;
⊗ Bindu and Sandhya for much more than I can put on paper;
⊗ Drs. Narasaiah and late Meenakshi for helping me stay physically alive during those critical writing blocks;

⊗ Gee—There is no way I could possibly thank you adequately. I survived;
⊗ Because of you and your faith in me;
⊗ Jean, Josephine and Annie for ensuring I had a link with Home;
⊗ Chitrakutty, for being my mentor, counsellor, friend and anchor in more ways than even you may have realized;
⊗ All my "Valiyachans", "Valiyammas" and cousins for their moral support;
⊗ My Grandparents for their blessings and affection;
⊗ Shreedeepa, for magically appearing at the very moment towards the finale of my labours, and being a friend, almost a soul-mate, just when I was in most desperate need of a friend;
⊗ A second dedication, almost for that special M.A batch of 2005-07 at UOH who helped to be finally fully convinced that my choice of teaching and research was the right one for me;
⊗ My Father, for living completely for me, for tolerating my worst tantrums, for always being there for me to lean on, for loving me so much that you almost forgot to live your life. "Achai", I realize now that you have already given me the equivalent of a million years of happiness!
⊗ Prestige Books, New Delhi, for bringing out the book expeditiously and elegantly;
⊗ Thank You God, for bringing me safely through what often seemed to be impermeable darkness. Thank You most of all for being there for me when I was too confused, upset, angry or foolish to even call out to you. This work **If** it contains anything worthwhile, is yours, Lord, I was merely the scribe.

Preface

This book concerns itself with the issue of representations of India in English texts produced during a particular period of the colonial era—1757-1857. The term Texts is employed very eclectically in the work, dealing with almost all available material, from Parliamentary speeches to Journals and epic poems.

A brief word of explanation regarding the double perspective that this book has adopted is necessary here: while it interprets the colonial representations, it also concentrates on presenting them to the reader almost in the frozen form of snapshots, which can be subjected to further analysis. These frozen images were merely the surface of the deeper stories of aggression, warfare, and violence inevitably associated with the colonial scenario. The readers' attention is drawn both to the claim of photographic reality the colonial writers made of their depictions of India as well as the inescapable history of warfare in which Indians were literally shot down by the guns of the colonisers. The surface calm of neatly arranged snapshots is disturbed through a process of analysis that brings out the turbulent history of violent colonial massacres; which are now being attempted to be concealed beneath the frozen images presented to us.

There is an attempt in the book to challenge the all-too easy solution found for the problem of colonial representations through an over valorization of ambivalence. While ambivalence is certainly present in colonial discourse, the argument that this weakened the edifice of empire is exaggerated. It is argued here that whatever the role of ambivalence was in theory, in practice, the Colossus of imperialism stood firm, helped perhaps rather than hindered, by the convenient concealment areas provided by the cracks created by the linguistic and psychological ambivalences built into the system.

Chapter I

Introduction: Surveying the Terrain

Something has been lost, but the representation is all we have.
Edward Said

A

This book examines various representations of India recorded in British texts produced between 1757 and 1857. No credence is given to the truth-value of these representations; they are not studied in the hope that they may reveal "facts" about India. This study endorses Stephen Greenblatt's modest avowal that "we can be certain only that European representations of the New World [read India in this context] tell us something about the European practice of representation" (1991: 7). It is precisely this analysis of representations *as* representations that is considered significant here. Any discipline which is even remotely connected with culture or even aesthetics cannot afford to neglect the brute presence of the representations themselves as distinct from questions of fidelity to some represented essence.

The intention is not to collapse the distinctions between reality and representation; assuming from a postcolonial perspective that the notion of reality is essential for praxis—but to emphasize the representations as distinct entities.

As Edward Said acknowledges in *Orientalism,* "There were—and are—cultures and nations whose location is in the East and their lives, histories and customs have a brute reality obviously greater than anything that could be said about them in the West" (1978: 5). This present study is not engaged with the representations themselves alone but also with the discursive networks they formed by their interlinkages with each other, where they "refer to, reproduce e, counter and build on one another" (Teltscher 1997: 3). As our grasp on "reality" seems to grow increasingly tenuous with each new theoretical innovation, the assumption that representations take on a reality of their own, for each interpretative community[1] gains in significance.

This book is largely contained within an Indo-British framework and for illustrative analysis uses representations generated by the colonial encounter between India and Britain. However, the analysis does draw upon and benefit from theoretical considerations of the colonial paradigm as a whole. For Britain, one of the foremost powers of the colonial era, the Orient was most closely associated with India.

A reference to the "inscrutable Orient" may conjure up images of Communist Chinese generals or sinister Arab chieftains in present-day America. But, Britain's collective unconscious may even now respond with a vague picture of imperial splendour in India. If such is likely to be the case today, one can imagine the charge the word India and its conceptual underpinnings must have generated in an age where imperial annexations were carried on in an aura of adventure which had not yet been dimmed by the forces of bureaucratization. It is no exaggeration to state that British writers[2] at one time or another, have used in connection with India nearly all the conventional connotations associated by the "West" with the "East."

A conceptual clarification regarding the validity of this signifier—the East/Orient—is necessary at this point. Raymond Schwab begins his monumental work *The Oriental Renaissance* with the very pertinent question:

> Sometimes qualified by near or far, sometimes identified with Oceania or Africa when not associated with Russia or Spain, the concept of Orient has come full circle. Since the world is round, what can this word mean? (1984: 3)

Quite evidently, there is no geographically accurate answer to this question. Indeed, it is an irony of history that a word which carries so little actual geographical sense as "the Orient" has acquired so much ideological baggage over the centuries that clarifications are almost rendered either impossible or useless. Ludicrous as the situation is, even "Orientals" now perceive themselves as "Oriental" which is an evident anomaly. However, the atlas as of now is West-centred and as long as this is so, the concepts associated with the terms the "Orient" or the "East" are unlikely to shed any of their semantic ballast. Perhaps the only solution is to put forward as a prerequisite the awareness that "this word [the East] and its synonym, the Orient . . . are words merely relative" (Leask 1993: 2).

The basic aim of this analysis (theoretically structured as it is around a postcolonial perspective) is not merely to enumerate or even elaborately describe colonial representations. Still less does it intend to triumphantly expose colonial (mis)representations and recover the "true," the "real" India. As Homi Bhabha remarks:

> The stereotype is not a simplification because it is false representation of a given reality. It is a simplification because it is an arrested, fixated form of representation that in denying the play of difference [that the negation through the other permits] constitutes a problem for the representation of the subject in signification of psychic and social relations. (1994: 75)

This study therefore has no intention of correcting (mis)representtations, even assuming that such an act was possible in absolute terms. Rather, the attempt is to see the confines within which these representational strategies operated, the forces which went into their production and the products they themselves generated in turn.[3] The study tries to uncover and examine the areas of semantic fluidity where (though the representations do not intersect with a "reality") at least the interpretative and representational models achieve a structural dynamism as opposed to a colonially constructed static essentiallism.[4]

This agenda may be criticized as having been overworked already. Indeed, it may be seen as a process of being "excessively preoccupied with the master's concerns" (Minh-Ha 1995: 261). Such an argument is based on the assumption that a concentration by erstwhile-colonized people on colonial strategies will lead only to an endless repetition of those very essentialising differentiations which were the foundations and justifications of colonial racism. This, it has been argued, is mere pandering to the social neuroses of the theoretically self-flagellating "guilty" West.[5]

Such an argument is valid in so far as any researcher who attempts to trace (as opposed to construct) either colonial or resistance strategies (of which representation is a major one) will have to confront these questions posed by Said in *After the Last Sky:*

> Why this absence? Did we never care about ourselves? How did we register the passing of time, the product of our work, the changes in our history? While "they" were travelling and observing, writing studies and novels, what were "we" doing? (1993: 96)

As of now, it has to be admitted that the possible answers to these questions still lie mainly in documentation of the local and not in speculation or interpretation based on texts emanating from the colonial metropolis. However, there is always the possibility that we *may* encounter areas where apparently no self-representation exists, or at the very least, is not preserved. Even more pertinent is the subtle danger that we may end up foisting our own postcolonial consciousness onto such chronologically distant voids. Even if we grant that local documentation and subsequent interpretation is *the* radical area, it does not necessarily follow that preceding areas have been totally and unproblematically exhausted. The bottom line on an interpretation of colonial representations may well be only the further exposure of the already exposed imperial edifice. But the newer and subtle layers of discursivity within this structure which are discovered as a result of each variation of perspective can be dismissed only at a considerably high price. The possibilities of what "we" can find out about what 'they" have said about us have not been exhausted precisely because far too much of that task also, until very recently was left to "them" by "us."

This is especially true in the case of India as is proved by frequent attempts to invest representations of India with a truth value not generally associated in contemporary theoretical parlance with the constructions of Orientalism. This tendency is well exemplified by a statement taken from John Drew's *India and the Romantic Imagination:*

> The main difference between the idealization of India and the idealization of other cultures is that the idealization of India happens to accord with Indian conceptions. In other cases, the projections are fanciful, in the case of India authentic. (1987: 153)

Such arguments appear to be desperate efforts to sustain the authenticity of Orientalism after it has already been demolished. The problem with Drew's theory, of course, is that the Indian conceptions, with which he claims that western projections accord, are, in this context, themselves interpretations and representations transmitted through western observers.

These representations were only too often integral parts of involved strategies of control. Almost without exception, they were implicitly if not explicitly, implicated in the colonial paradigm of power and control. But even if we consider representations merely and solely as aids to strategic control, surely any attempt at unravelling these strategies must begin with the representations themselves.

The significance of these representations as cultural (and in many cases, literary) artifacts also merits consideration. The fields of culture and aesthetics were the areas where these representations attained most of their individual identity and the relative autonomy provided by these spaces needs to be taken into account. The reference to relative autonomy, emphatically does *not* suggest that artistic or aesthetic merit can in some way "make up" for intolerance or racism. There is no conception that "art could redeem the nightmare of history." (Greenblatt 1991: 25). However, this analysis does insist on the idea that a category of art and the aesthetic does exist and that it does function (of course, in conjunction with constructed standards) to induce often positive responses, while the opinions and ideology conveyed in the work may be resented and rejected. This conviction is a sounding board against which individual works are studied, even as the common discourse they all shared in is kept to the foreground. Differences between representations almost identical at first sight, are often to be found in questions of genre, form, market trends and aesthetic orientations and not in conscious ideological commitments alone.

To avoid the complexity of the representations in their complete context will lead to an unacceptable essentialisation and simplification. If we adopt an attitude of total dismissiveness or hostility without scrutiny to all British representations of India, by labelling them as purely imperialist or racist, we will be simultaneously denying India's contribution as an idea at least to movements which have been rendered globally significant by the vicissitudes of history. In effect, this would amount to ignoring the value of the *idea* of the Orient which was at least a mental entity with solid historical consequences.

We should indeed combat theories similar to that put forward by Mannoni in *Prospero and Caliban,* which, quite apart from the fact of colonization, saddles all colonized people with an inherent dependency complex, which makes colonization inevitable. We can deny with all possible emphasis that an India ever existed which corresponded exactly to either James Mill's condemnations or Shelley's idealizations.

But we would have to carry this attitude to an exaggerated and undesirable all-encompassing level to argue that British Romantic/ Imperial representations do not affect us either as Indians or as humans because they lack "authenticity." This concept is well stressed by Frantz Fanon (who certainly cannot be accused of sycophancy to Western Imperialists) in his *Black Skin, White Masks:*

> The Negro, however sincere, is the slave of the past. Nonetheless, I am a man and in this sense the Peloponnesian War is as much mine as the invention of the compass. (1968: 225)

This is not to call for a liberal humanist universalism. But it still has to be accepted here that research which seeks only to reiterate and reinforce these boundaries will do nothing but ossify existing structures. Transcendence as such is an idealistic term with few claims or chances of being accepted today. However, attempts at crossing boundaries while retaining self-identity are necessary processes even if they remain at the stage of attempts alone. In the course of this activity one may at least discover new traversable cracks and fissures which serve to further expose the myth of colonial discourse structures as impermeable monoliths.

This study argues that the notion of imperial edifices being either impermeable or monolithic by nature is but a convenient myth. The shades of variation found among contemporary representations clearly show that we are dealing not with a uniform monolithic structure, but rather with a collage or jigsaw puzzle where the faultlines remain visible despite the surface appearance of a wholeness. Homi Bhabha's project, which refers to the deep ambivalences locked into the apparent universal fixities of colonialist epistemology, is a launching pad for pursuing this argument.

Bhabha speaks of the location of native resistance in the fissures of colonial discourse[6] and argues that not only native resistance but creative (perhaps unconscious) ambivalences of the writers themselves are also located in such gaps and problematic spaces.

Strategic textual discourses of control *cannot* totally succeed in their project of glossing over history. There are bound to be, as inevitable adjuncts of discursivity itself, lacunae where more dynamic versions of the process inscribe themselves. However, it *remains to be seen whether these ambivalences "weakened" the colonial structure in any way.* Their *presence* of course, is undeniable.

A picture of the imposing and mostly strategically successful imperial technique of colonial self-projection which *appears* solidly strong and unitary is presented by Gauri Viswanathan in her *Masks of Conquest.* She refers to the policy of English literature being used in India to present an ideal picture of European identity as opposed to the actual imperial selves who carried on the work of colonialism. She remarks:

> The English literary text, functioning as a surrogate Englishman in his highest and most perfect state, becomes a mask for economic exploitation, successfully camouflaging the material and the cul-

> tural activities of the colonizer. . . . The split between the material and the cultural practices of colonialism is nowhere sharper than in the progressive refinement of the rapacious, exploitative and ruthless actor of history into the reflexive subject of literature. (1989: 20-21)

Viswanathan's basic argument is that English literature functions as a discourse which provides the "natives" with an ideal picture of the colonial rulers.[7] This book takes this particular concept on board, but further argues that such an intention was not confined to literature in a narrow sense alone, but to all textual productions of the colonial discourses. Also, to render the colonizer as an idealised figure, a less-than-idealized version of the colonized had also to be produced simultaneously. This factor gives rise to the dual proposition that representations of the colony/colonized play an important role in the idealization process which was also part of the self-justifying and self-convincing strategies within the imperial centres themselves.

This analysis does attempt to examine the structurally imposing edifice of British textual representations in its deployment of representation to idealize colonial activities. But, more significantly, in a deviation from Viswanathan, the argument follows that the idealization project was not totally successful. It searches for those ambivalences which may reveal a *momentary* weakening (or, at the very least, the ontological inherent instability) of the binaries which sustained colonialism. To a large extent, such moments are co-opted back into the structure of the dominating discourse. But this option is neither total nor unproblematic and the gaps remain to remind us of the constructed and supplementary[8] nature of the narrative of colonial representation. It is indeed true that many of these moments have to be teased out (involving an occasional reading against the grain) but they nevertheless exist. They are the potential sources of a relieving conviction that no discourse of domination or oppression, however strongly built up or fortified, can be so successful as to be unchallengeable. This is not intended to suggest a search for inherent instabilities within the "negative" representations. There will be tenuous spaces which can accommodate both the resistance of the oppressed and the internal contradictions within the oppressors themselves. These spaces ensure that neither discourse becomes monolithic; they carry the possibilities of both opposition and self-questioning within their confines. They thereby indicate that there is scope for a creative dismantling, which is not intended to serve as an apology for Empire, but to indicate that the rhetorical edifice was inherently hollow and unable on its own to withstand scrutiny. The concept is that this hollowness is not a postcolonial creation but rather an evident aspect which (though almost always unarticulated) forced the proponents of Empire to overkill and overstatement.

The years 1757 and 1857 are selected as the boundary lines in this study. The battle of Plassey (1757) which helped British territorial power to come solidly into its own in India and the 1857 revolt[9] which hastened the end of the East India Company's direct rule are important landmarks in the history of early British colonialism in India.

Plassey was not merely a British military triumph; it held emotional significance of a much greater nature. As Martin Green remarks: "Plassey began a new era for the world because it marked the triumph of Europe over India [Asia]. Every European afterwards felt himself bigger" (1980: 35).

It was the West's victory over Asia that was signalled, and this induced both a superiority complex as well as a "tolerance" mainly based on complacency. It was only after 1857 when the natives stopped "falling on their faces and worshipping the gun" and in a conjunction of the two motifs (superior military power and submissive native) "himself fired a gun" (Green 1980: 80) that the rhetorical complacence set in tune after Plassey began to produce discordant notes. Jingoism and racism were, of course, always present, but as Patrick Brantlinger remarks, the pre-1857 attitude was one of a "relatively naive racism" (1988: 39). It is this naiveté which vanished after 1857 when complacency was no longer a viable choice. The foundations of imperial discourse had been shaken and a harder, more uncompromising and more "scientific" racism was necessary to keep the imperial and colonial projects moving. It is possible to find traces of a modest epistemological break in the colonial discourse on India which distinguishes the pre-1857 representations and responses from the post-Mutiny pronouncements. We may identify a "discontinuity" in the Foucaultian sense, as reflected in the question:

> How is that at certain moments and in certain orders of knowledge there are these sudden take offs, these hastenings of evolution, these transformations which fail to correspond to the calm, continuist image that is normally accredited? (Foucault 1984: 54)

Such a hastening of evolution can be seen in the increasingly racist and strident representations of India after 1857. This is not to deny either that there were versions of these traits in earlier periods or that there was a type of linear advance in attitudes and their expressions. Rather, attention is called to both "the sharp lines of discursive discontinuity and the longer lines of continuity in non-discursive *practices*" and to how these can result in obtaining "a more flexible grid of interpretation with which to approach relations of knowledge and power" (my italics).[10] While praxis, concrete action, does progress in a reasonably continuist schema, the discourses which engender them show a distinct discontinuity as "modifications in the rules of formation of statements which are accepted as scientifically true" (Foucault 1984: 54).

During the early stages of imperial annexation which are covered by this study, the full force of racism and officialdom had not yet totally crystallized into a well-established and scientifically bolstered ideology of Empire.

The texts produced in this period admit of illuminating contradictions and (as befits the productions of a formative period) are full of varied and individualistic responses to India. It was the period of "the Nabob" as opposed to the "Sahib"[11] who dominated the later periods. The individual perceptions of scholarly Orientalists, hard headed imperialists, Utilitarian reformers, Romantic visionaries and Evangelical missionaries, all entered into the construction of a complex network of British attitudes to India. All these perspectives were to a great extent, subsumed in self-righteous anger after the 1857 revolt. Richard Frere wrote in

1868: "You can have little idea how much India is altered. The sympathy which Englishmen felt for the natives has changed to a general feeling of repugnance—instead of a general feeling of content with their Indian lot" (qtd. Stanford 1968: 2)

This analysis does not agree that the "repugnance" mentioned above did not exist before and appeared as a direct effect of 1857. But, it does take into consideration the prominent rhetorical shift which allowed such feelings to be more openly articulated after 1857. This change of the discursive framework has been employed as the basis of value judgments by some critics:

> Compared with the men who were to follow them, those terrible Christian heroes of the Victorian era, preoccupied with the state of their souls and almost bent under the weight of their righteousness, the men who built the empire are much more attractive. (Edwardes 1968: 237)

This analysis does not consciously attempt such value judgments, but the fact that the Nabob *did* differ from the Sahib is part of the premises of the study.

The commercial profit motif, so essential to any colonial[12] enterprise occupies a centrestage position during this early period as well as in the later heyday of the Raj. However, especially during the earlier phase, the theme of profit co-existed with an equally romantic conception of India as a succession of exotic pageants.

There also existed the trope of India as the Promised Land, as the goal of a successful spiritual Odyssey. At the same time the notion of the Empire as "civilizing mission" which necessarily presented India as the negative pole of a benighted/ enlightened binarism was also making its presence felt. Besides these, we cannot overlook those who urged expansion for the sole sake of imperial grandeur and the Utilitarians who saw India as a convenient laboratory to try out their doctrines of reform.

Profit, Romantic Pageantry, Philosophical Idealization, Utilitarianism, Evangelicalism and Total Imperialism—these concepts are in no way monolithic or hermetic. Many sub-divisions and gradations are possible within each category. As parts of an interlinked group, these concepts cover the gamut of the images of India recorded by early imperial Britain. All these concepts contributed significantly to the construction of the British colonial archives. They merit equal consideration without any hierarchical privileging of one over the other. The political and ideological discourses underlying the texts which illustrate the concepts are considered in their corporate selves. However, a basic intention of this project is to foreground the individual material texts without either blurring the text-context distinction or losing sight of the importance of context. An analysis based on a reading and an interpretative technique contained within individual texts is followed, but as a matter of course it constantly enters the larger social text.

It is perhaps a sign of the "excessive"[13] nature of the post-colonial theoretical scenario that so much of justification appears necessary for a project which does not intend to outrightly condemn all offshoots of the imperial enterprise as solely and totally imperialistic. A firm conviction that any more rigidity conferred upon obviously constructed national boundaries (and therefore by implication, on national attitúdes) will lead only to a dead end for analysis forms the final ideological foundation of this project.

B

This section discusses the theoretical underpinnings of the project and briefly surveys the work already done in this area. The trope propounded in Frederick Jameson's The *Political Unconscious* of the theorization of the "simultaneous Utopian and ideological dimensions of culture" (1981: 9) is prominent in this analysis. Jameson urges a search

> through and beyond the demonstration of the instrumental function of a given cultural object, to project its simultaneously Utopian power as the symbolic affirmation of a specific historical and class form of a collective unity. (1981: 291)

Jameson, is of course arguing from a Marxist perspective which is not adopted here. But the basic concept that the work of culture/ art though definitely ideological and over-determined could still retain a "desire-to-Utopia"[14] in its very existence is accepted as being of primary significance.

This analysis disagrees with many specific arguments of individual postcolonial critics. But their works have been invaluable in providing both a starting point and scope for an occasional oppositional stance. In this project Frantz Fanon is taken as the ideal example of the earlier generation of postcolonial critics, who, while maintaining a high level of intellectual subtlety, still insisted on linking their theories to practical everyday manifestations of the process of decolonization. Evidently, he sought to dismantle and set aside the European intellectual traditions[15] in which it is possible to see later theorists such as Gayatri Spivak and Homi Bhabha as deeply imbricated.

In fact Fanon goes so far as to urge the colonized people to forget Europe altogether, to ignore it and get on with their lives. This is indeed, a tempting suggestion—since we cannot contemplate oriental aggression to seek retrospective vengeance—it seems exceedingly sensible to ignore Europe, to stop imitating Europe and to carve out new paths. Fanon views the energy and enthusiasm spent on justifications, denunciations and exclamations against Europe as so much waste. The more strident and more situated within European boundaries these processes are, the more easily are they co-opted by the system, reducing their radical potential and even giving the colonialist a complacent delusion of liberalism. Fanon remarks:

> Stinging denunciations, the exposing of distressing conditions and passions which find their outlet in expression are in fact assimilated by the occupying power in a cathartic process. To aid such processes is in a certain sense to avoid their dramatization and to clear the atmosphere. (1977: 251)

Indeed the colonial powers have easily managed to pat themselves on the back for having "brought about," by their own liberal efforts, the natives' progress to a stage where they can actually articulate protest. This rhetoric is exemplified by Macaulay in his 1837 statement that the day of a separation between England and India "would be the proudest day in English history" (qtd. Bearce 1961: 163) for England would then have succeeded in raising India to the level of being able to handle self-government. Of course, this rhetoric is bolstered by the conviction that there were still "miles to go" before this liberal goal could be attained and that any immediate talk of Indian freedom would be drastically premature.

Given the way in which the most vehement, the most anguished protests are treated by the imperial powers as an ideal reason to smile paternally, it is certainly tempting to follow Fanon's advice and stop squandering time and energy on such a process. It does seen sensible to suggest that once the actual colonial presence is got rid of, the earlier colonized people should get on with their lives without being intimidated by Europe's shadow over their shoulders till all eternity.

However, even if economic realities did not make such a stance isolationist and virtually impossible, the very nature of the colonial paradigm itself impels us to go back ceaselessly over its records. These have been so subtly disseminated and internalized that an analytic dismantling becomes almost an individual necessity for each aware member of a colonized race. The colonial relation did not confine itself to economics, it insisted on imposing itself on the cultures, and traditions and even the thoughts of those it ruled over.[16]

The miasma of colonially inflicted "absolute truths" has penetrated deep into the "native" psyche, rendering either a complex mimicry or an analytical deconstructive stance towards colonial verities essential for a recovery of self-respect. The attempt to mimic Europe would obviously reduce the "Third World" to a mere echo, an unsubstantial shadow. The path consistent with dignity would be that of continually exposing the colonial paradigm, *while not allowing it to dictate the terms of existence any longer.*

This book's interest to continue dealing with the colonial paradigm is not intended to effect a dismantling—which will circularly lead back to the liberal humanist claim that the Indian, for example, is "as good as" the Englishman. That is a position within which the basic framework of colonial binaries is accepted. And, it is also true that synthesis or compromise almost always means accepting dominant values at the cost of repressing or negating subaltern traditions. Hence, there is no demand made here that one puts history aside and tries to be "objective." As Fanon points out: "For the native, objectivity is always directed against him" (1977: 61).

The attempt made in this analysis is not, therefore, to achieve a fabled objectivity. However, it does operate on the premise that the rifts in the colonial discourse—which *admitted* of both native resistance and ambivalences from the "home" side itself—*must be* attended to if we are to overcome the deadening binarism of colonial oppression/native reaction, which predetermines its adherents' movements in never-ending vicious cycles. [The *effect* of these ambivalences, it must be repeated, is taken up for later analysis] Retrospective revenge and slavish mimicry are both repetitive acts whose time as productive action is past. What remains is to understand and articulate as frequently as possible, from as many geographical locales as possible, the sham (yet powerful) framework of the colonial enterprise. This, however is advisable in only as much as it can enable us to put the edifice behind us—a necessary presence, a reminder—but not necessarily foregrounded. If this work is partly carried out in the erstwhile colonial metropolitan cities also, so much the better. Such a process does not mean that "natives" can stop producing their own critique—that process has to go on incessantly. The native critics should not end with a flourishing rhetorical shout that "they" were racist, inhuman, cruel, frauds *et al*. These issues are no longer seriously questioned at a theoretical level, no matter what private prejudices may continue to be. The concentration has to be on analysis rather than on rhetorical denunciation. In the context of such an analysis, Edward Said's seminal project in *Orientalism* is of paramount importance. Said's argument that the Orient was a constructed (and not a "natural") entity, as well as his insistence on representations *as* representations are especially significant (1978: 5, 272). Said is on firm ground when he points out that the compact body of Orientalist thought *governs* what can be said about the Orient. But there seems to be a touch of overkill in the generalizing statement: "Every European, in what he could say about the orient was consequently a racist, an imperialist and almost totally ethnocentric" (1978: 204). This amounts to submitting to Orientalism completely, making escape or overcoming impossible, even unthinkable. Said, in fact refers to "the internal consistency of Orientalism" (1978: 5) and the "sheer knitted together strength of Orientalism" (1978: 6). This concept of an impermeable Orientalist structure has been demolished by critics like Homi Bhabha, who have shown it to be a very fissured terrain indeed. The "strength" is certainly there, it is the "knitted together" part that is problematic.

Said himself makes the point that the individual does have a role, dominated as one is by Orientalism, the surrender is not always necessarily uniform. In *Culture and Imperialism,* Said enunciates this concept with great precision:

> I do not believe that authors are *mechanically determined* by ideology, class or economic history, but authors are. I also believe very much in the history of their societies, *shaping and shaped* by that history and their social experiences in different measure. (1986: xxiv, my italics)

The concept of over-determination can of course be accepted, but it is also necessary to keep in mind Said's caution against "mechanical" determinism. In *Orientalism* itself, Said emphasizes the agency of the individual[17] and refers to the Orientalist paradigm as "a dynamic exchange between individual authors and the large political concerns shaped by the great empires" (1978: 15). The emphasis is on "dynamic" as opposed to inert or static predetermination. The gross political reality is now clearly evident, attention has to be paid to the details, which are "profoundly worked over and modulated" (Said 1978: 15).

This analysis is keenly interested in the moments "before the labels take over."[18] The two-fold idea is to show that the imperial discourse was fractured not only by outside resistance, but from within too and also to show that there were moments which, if they were (though, they *could* not be) traced back and developed fully could have produced a rather different scenario from the existing one. These are not 'Utopian' moments and often they contribute subtly and dangerously to the structure. Of course, *if* they had been developed—but then they were not.

This perspective is accepted in the present project; the representations are analyzed in their own right, leaving the vexed question of correspondence to reality temporarily aside. This shelving is meant to assist concentration on the readily available entities—the representations.

This project tacitly accepts Stephen Greenblatt's formulation of representation in *Marvellous Possessions* where he argues that it would be a "theoretical mistake and a practical blunder to collapse the distinction between representation and reality, but at the same time we cannot keep them isolated from one another. They are locked together in an uneasy marriage in a world without ecstatic union or divorce" (1991: 7).

Greenblatt's emphasis on those moments which indicate the uncertainty in the colonial edifice is significant. "In a dark time, the awareness of a contradiction is carried precisely in the small textual resistances—a kind of imagined possibility, a dream of equity" (1991: 65). These textual resistances do not, in most cases have a redeeming function, but they do serve as unravelling entities within the colonial paradigm. It is precisely these textual resistances/defences that are focused on in this analysis. Greenblatt is dealing with the rhetoric associated with Columbus' discovery of America, but some of his formulations are quite applicable to the Indo-British colonial framework also. He refers to the "fantastic representation of authoritative certainty in the face of spectacular ignorance" (1991: 90). This description can easily be applied to many assertions of the British colonizers in India and it is in opposition to these complacent "verities" that textual resistances have to be sought for.

Rana Kabbani, in *Imperial Fictions* has documented the trope of exotic eastern pageantry. The notion of the seductive and often dangerous power of the East (dealt with by Kabbani in the context of Arabia) provides the basis for obsessive accounts of voluptuous pageantry as seen, for example, in the anthropological writings of Richard Burton. As Said points out in *Orientalism*: "The Orient was almost a European invention and had been since antiquity a place of romance, exotic beings, haunting memories and landscapes, remarkable experiences" (1978: 1). This concept is graphically presented by Kabbani also. The specific example used is Egypt, but India could easily be substituted in this particular formulation:

> For Antony, the East arrived in Cleopatra's barge. It was a mixture of new delights: the pomp of pageant, the smell of perfume and incense, the luxurious brocades that shimmered in the sun and most notably, *the woman herself*—queen, love object, mistress and despot—was the East, the Orient created for the Western gaze. (1988: 22, my italics)

Such pageantry in India was regarded on some rare occasions (rare in the pre-1857 period) as too outlandish and even repellent. But, in general terms, there was a prominent aspect of awed fascination with the unknown Other as against a consciously acquired and nurtured contempt displayed by the later Raj writers.

Several documentary and informative works—Raymond Schwab's *The Oriental Renaissance,* Michael Edwardes' *British India: 1772-1947,* and *Glorious Sahibs,* Robert Sencourt's *India in English Literature,* Martin Green's *Dreams of Adventure, Deeds of Empire* and Hugh Ridley's *Images of Imperial Rule*—have proved extremely useful in laying the foundations of this analysis. Schwab's *The Oriental Renaissance,* especially, is an important source text. However, Schwab clearly places British imperialism in a relation of secondary importance to that of Europe as a whole. The present study primarily focuses on British Orientalism even as it makes use of Schwab's insights.

Michael H. Fisher's *The Politics of the British Annexation of India 1757-1857* and Eric Stokes' *The English Utilitarians and India* provides a historical perspective for this study. George Bearce, in *British Attitudes to India, 1784-1858* surveys the period stressing the texts less than their underlying discourses. This project foregrounds the individual material text for analysis.

K.K. Dyson's *A Various Universe* and Dodwell's *Nabobs of Madras* have functioned as signposts leading up to important records.

The theme of a spiritual Utopia in India is developed by John Drew in *India and the Romantic Imagination* where he asserts that "In matters pertaining to India, the *Bhagavat Gita* is to be preferred to the Mutiny records as a Bible" (1987: 294). He proceeds to extract every possible ounce of spiritual idealization that can be found in British representations of India, to such an extent that India finally becomes only an image, a mere shadowy background for Western philosophical self-realization:

> The Indian setting of Shelley's *Prometheus Unbound*, faintly discernible as an ultimate veil, serves to indicate that what might pass for an Indian influence is a recognition within the Imagination of India as an appropriate image for that mystical imageless state for which the Imagination is itself but an image. (1987: 281)

This is carrying idealization too far indeed. Starting from a philosophical concept, Drew proceeds to deny any existence whatsoever to India by itself, which becomes merely a rhetorical figure in the Western Romantic Imagination. In fact Drew falls straight into the trap Said cautions us about in *Orientalism* of concluding that "the Orient" was "essentially an idea or a Western creation with no corresponding reality" (1978: 5). In the present study, spiritualization of India is but one trope among many others equally significant and has no claims to exclusive authenticity. Also, Drew's work is mainly concerned with tracing subtle hints of an "Indian influence" on "major" Romantic writers. This analysis considers the major Romantics in detail but highlights the Indian dimension in "popular" writers (Southey, Moore and Scott for example) also.

Patrick Brantlinger in *Rule of Darkness* examines the presence of empire in relation to Victorian literature. The main motifs of imperialism analyzed by Brantlinger, such as the civilizing mission, a racially motivated concept of the survival of the fittest and imperialism as a set of attitudes governing all aspects of culture is similar in many ways to the use made in the Romantic period of the imperial theme. This analysis intersects with Brantlinger's project when he claims that "it is worthwhile noting that even at the height of the rule of darkness, alternative, anti-imperialistic visions of our common life together were available" (1988: 16). Of course, they generally stayed at the level of vision. Brantlinger provides specific examples—Hobson, William Morris and Olive Schreiner—of individuals, who he argues, held this alternative vision aloft. This study does not go so far in as much as no one person is exempted from the discourse of imperialism and presented as the proud torch bearer of a new paradigm. But, within the imperial discourse itself, the project searches for signs of the germination of a different (*not necessarily "positive"*) vision from the dominating one.

John Barrell's *The Infection of Thomas De Quincey: A Psychopathology of Imperialism*, Nigel Leask's *Anxieties of Empire: British Romantic Writers and the East* and Kate Teltscher's *India Inscribed*—recent works which testify to a renewed interest in the area—are either less concerned with the specific Indian situation (as against the Orient as a whole) or deal with European imperialism in general (and not just with the British aspect). The present project is contained to a great extent within the Indo-British framework though attention is paid to the imperial paradigm as a whole when necessary. An important concept borrowed from Barrell is his formulation of the This/That and the Other triad which allowed 'The Other" itself to be subdivided into a not-so-other "That" and an Absolute Other both opposed to the Self as "This." Barrell points out that this method worked so as to set the whole of the colonizing race, irrespective of class or gender differences (This vs. That) in opposition to the Orient as the Absolute Other. Also, within the Empire itself, the "Otherness" of the Other is graded so as to play off Muslim against Hindu or Sikh against Muslim. This trope provides a vivid perspective for understanding the occasional sudden shifts between avowed Otherness and near acceptance seen in many textual representations of India.

Nigel Leask and Kate Teltscher, to a large extent, cover the same area included in this study, in so far as they regard the Imperial discourse as cracked from the inside and seek to analyze these cracked spaces. But as Leask's title *Anxieties of Empire* indicates, he deals almost exclusively with the effect that the fear of corruption (physical, mental or moral) emanating from the Orient had on the imperial edifice. These fears, though significant, did not, in the final analysis lead to any serious thoughts of not retaining the Empire. Besides, the stress on anxieties leads Leask to totally ignore the many moments of complacence in the texts he is analyzing. This analysis, while it examines the fissures in the imperial discourse, does so with the conviction that the anxieties and even the alternative visions were mainly rhetorical (the value of rhetoric as rhetoric is acknowledged) and not possessed of practical power to shake the complacency of Empire.

C

This project lays no claim to exhaustiveness, considering the immense amount of extant material. However, a conscious attempt has been made to maintain an eclectic attitude with regard to the texts selected for analysis.

Some of the scholarly essays of Sir William Jones and other Orientalists,[19] published in the *Asiatic Researches* are included, as also are the Parliamentary Speeches (the language is often unparliamentary!) of Edmund Burke which relate to Indian affairs. James Mill's monumental *History of British India* and other Histories by Robert Orme, Alexander Dow and William Robertson are examined. The published letters, journals and memoirs of Eliza Fay, Emily Eden and James Forbes, among others, are taken up for analysis. The Indian motif in the "major" Romantic poets—Blake, Wordsworth, Coleridge, Byron, Shelley and Keats—is dealt with individually. Detailed analysis is undertaken of some full scale "Indian" works such as Robert Southey's *The Curse of Kehama,* Thomas Moore's *Lalla Rookh* and Sir Walter Scott's *The Surgeon's Daughter*. It needs to be repeated that the above list is in no way exhaustive since an Oriental/Indian element pervaded literally most aspects of discourse in the given period. However, it is hoped that the wide range of disciplines from which the materials for analysis have been selected confers on these primary sources a representative character, sufficient for working purposes at least.

This study consists of six chapters apart from the Introduction and Conclusion. After the Introduction, Chapter 2 deals with the historical background and surveys the various attitudes and their intersections, which are illustrated by the representations in the texts discussed in the later chapters.

Chapter 3 primarily considers the essays of Sir William Jones and the speeches of Edmund Burke. Certain essays and dissertations by other Orientalists who were contemporaries of Burke and Jones are also examined.

Chapter 4 deals with representative texts selected from the many Histories of India produced during the period. The most prominent text is James Mill's *History of British India* written from a Utilitarian perspective. As counterpoints, the Histories by Dow, Robertson and Orme, all Conservative writers, are also analyzed.

In Chapter 5, the genres of travel writing, letters, journals and memoirs are dealt with. This, in many ways, is the most inclusive chapter, since efforts have been made to include as much of the voluminous available material as possible. These supposedly "amateur" productions are analyzed with the same rigour that is applied to the more "scholarly" texts and this often yields up surprisingly relevant results.

Chapter 6 analyses a few full-scale works on India. The dominant motif of India in these works, the interpretations placed by the writers on their Indian material and the reception accorded to these oriental works are taken into consideration.

Chapter 7 undertakes an intensive study of the "major" poets of the period. The Indian motifs in their works as well as traces of an Indian "influence" are isolated and analyzed. Not just their poetry, but occasional prose pieces, published correspondence and Notebooks are used for analysis. Of course, the span of attention paid to each of these poets varies with the magnitude or otherwise of the Indian dimension in their works. For example, Wordsworth, though definitely affected by the imperial programme has very little to say about India as such. Shelley, on the other hand shows such an attraction to the trope of India that he has been referred to as "completely Indian" by Edgar Quinet (qtd. Schwab 1984: 63).

Section A of the Conclusion briefly recapitulates the arguments in the earlier chapters with emphasis on the ambivalences discovered in the analyzed texts. In Section B, the *effect* of this ambivalence is tackled. Gaps, silences, ambivalences—these have been traced in all the texts examined. But their *effect,* it is tentatively argued, was not always to "weaken" the structure. The colonial edifice did fail to be monolithic, but what exactly did that failure imply? There is an attempt to answer this question or at least problematize the issue throughout the book.

NOTES

1. The concept of interpretative communities is borrowed from Stanley Fish.
2. The term "writers" here does not refer solely to those who wrote "literature" in its exclusive sense. It incorporates as many as possible of those individuals who produced textual records of the colonial project.
3. "Representations are not only products, but also producers, capable of decisively altering the very forces that brought them into being" (Greenblatt 1991: 6).
4. The tension set up in an analysis of a poem by Wordsworth in Chapter 7 where his accepted image as a "Nature Poet" clashes with his evident relief that his daughter was born in the midst of "Culture" (clearly opposed to nature) is an example of the dynamism referred to in this context.
5. This argument is vividly articulated in Harish Trivedi's *Colonial Transactions* where we (the ex-colonized) are advised not to "follow the postcolonial liberal guilty West" (1993: 20) and instead to investigate the "assimilative or subversive strategies through which we coped with their Orientalisms" (1993: 20). It has to be said, however, that the very absence of a postcolonial "guilt" on the part of the erstwhile colonized people will enable them to function from a perspective different from that of the West.

6. This notion is clearly explicated in Bhabha's "Signs Taken for Wonders" where he remarks that "the place of difference and otherness or the space of the adversarial is never entirely on the outside or implacably oppositional. It is a pressure and a presence that acts constantly if unevenly), along the entire boundary of authorization" (1994: 109).
7. "The Englishman, actively participating in the cruder realities of conquest, commercial aggrandizement and disciplinary management of the natives blends into the rarefied, more exalted image of the Englishman as *producer* of the knowledge that empowers him to conquer, appropriate and manage in the first place" (Viswanathan 1989: 20).
8. The concept of supplement is adapted from Jacques Derrida's formulation in *Of Grammatology:* "As substitute it is not simply added to the positivity of a presence. It produces no relief, its place is assigned in the structure by the mark of an emptiness" (1967: 145).
9. The "Sepoy Mutiny" is of course the dismissive term used by the British historians. In Nationalist accounts, the reference is to the "First War of Indian Independence." Editorial comment of Paul Rabinow in his "Introduction" to *The Foucault Reader* (1984: 9).
10. The distinction between Nabobs and Sahibs is based partly on the concepts illustrated by Michael Edwardes in *The Nabobs at Home* (1957) and *The Sahibs and the Lotus* (1968). But while Edwardes places the transformation of the Nabob into the Sahib around the time of Warren Hastings' impeachment, this study regards the Sahibs as coming into their own only after the 1857 revolt. The terms Nabobs and Sahibs are used here as a "shorthand" to convey entire mindsets towards India. The Nabobs represent the ostentatious pre-Mutiny period, where their attitudes to India, though complex enough, were not often tinged with hate. The later Sahibs despite their paternalism also had the wariness of the native induced by the hate- and revenge-filled Mutiny epoch.
11. The word "colonial" is deliberately used here instead of "imperial." This indicates that while spokesmen of imperial grandeur often urged imperialism for imperialism's sake even at the cost of financial setbacks, the actual physical act of colonization was securely tied to economic considerations.
12. The concept of "excess" has been aggressively employed as positive empowerment by Bill Ashcroft in the essay "Excess: Post-

colonialism and the Verandahs of Meaning." The adjectives he applies to postcolonial criticism are "too much, too long, too paranoid . . . too . . . excessive" (1994: 33). Excess is here visualized as an indication of postcolonial exuberance.

13. The neologism "desire-to-Utopia" is formed on the same pattern as the "will-to-power."
14. "Leave this Europe, where they are never done talking of Man yet murder men wherever they find them. Look at them today swaying between atomic and spiritual disintegration. We have better things to do than follow that Europe" (Fanon 1977: 25).
15. As Fanon points out in *The Wretched of the Earth,* colonialism is never content with possessing economic control. "It turns to the past of the oppressed people and distorts, disfigures and destroys it" (1977: 169).
16. "I do believe in the determining imprint of individual writers upon the otherwise anonymous collective body of texts constituting a discursive formation like Orientalism" (Said 1978: 23).
17. The phrase "before the labels take over" is taken from Said's description in *Orientalism* of Marx's reaction to imperialism in India. While arguing that in the final analysis even Marx prefers to stand safely in an "Orientalized Orient," Said points out: "that Marx was still able to sense some fellow feeling, to identify even a little with poor Asia suggests that something happened before the labels took over. It is as if the individual mind could find a pre-collective, pre-official individuality in Asia—find and give in to its pressure upon his emotions, feelings, senses—only to give it up when he confronted a more formidable censor in the very vocabulary he found himself forced to employ" (1978: 255).
18. For example, Charles Wilkins, Colebrooke and H.H. Wilson.

Chapter 2

The Zeitgeist: The Historical, Social and Political Scenario

Our King has all the Indies in his arms
And more and richer when he strains that lady.

(Shakespeare, *Henry VIII)*

This chapter is divided into three sections—Section A deals with early (pre-1757) Western representations of India, Section B sketches the process of the British East India Company's annexations and achievement of political power in India during the period 1757-1857; and Section C discusses the then prevalent ideological trends influencing representations of India. In Section A, major European representations of India during the classical and medieval periods are examined, but within these most attention is focused on early *British* representations. In Section B, along with a chronological tracing of the increasing British political and military power, those textual representations of the period, which are too slight for individual study, are also considered. The obvious omission of certain major texts in this section exists because they are reserved for later detailed analysis. The discussion of the ideological trends is intended to foreground both the many strands of thought and also the basic attitudes and assumptions they shared in common. The chapter as a whole serves as a background against which detailed analysis of individual texts can be carried out.

A

Representations of India in the Western world have a history, which can be traced back beyond even Alexander's invasion in 327 B.C. Indeed, Alexander's conquest itself is engraved on a palimpsest which already bore the mark of the mythical invasion of India by Bacchus, the Greek God of wine. The earliest reference to an Indian influence in classical Europe can be found in the tradition that Pythagoras (500 B.C.) had visited India and learnt there the concept of metempsychosis.

When we approach historical records from the mysteries of myth, we find that the earliest surviving Western representation of India is to be found in Herodotus (480-425 B.C.). Herodotus' representation of India is subordinated to his main theme of the struggle between Persia/East and Greece/West. The factual knowledge, if any, which he had of India seemed to be limited to only that part which formed a Satrapy of the Persian Empire. He refers to such curiosities as gold-digging ants (1954: 54-56) and to the incredibly wealthy and populous nature of India. These are rendered possible by the positioning of India on the limits of the "human world" which gives it the potential for being convincingly a land of marvellous possibilities. At the same time Herodotus also lays the foundation for a study of Asian society, which is represented as functioning on fundamentally different basic principles from those of Greece.

Hippocrates (460 B.C.) puts forward a certain proposition, which later formed the core of a particularly dominant political theory about India. He takes the "despotism" of Indian/Asian rulers for granted, as also an inherent servility in the people and argues that the climatic conditions as well as established false principles were ontologically conducive for this state of affairs (qtd. Embree 1989: 62). A somewhat different perspective is to be found in the fragments preserved of a later writer Ctesais (416-398 B.C.) who praises the justice of the Indian kings and idealizes India to present a Utopian picture (qtd. Embree 1989: 70). It should be kept in mind at this stage that during the early period surveyed in this chapter India and Asia were to a large extent interchangeable names in the West.

With Megasthenese, who was the envoy of Seleucas Nikator (Alexander's successor) to the court of Chandragupta Maurya, we have direct observations in the place of derivations from vague second-hand accounts. He gives an account of Brahmins and Fakeers, mentions the holy river Ganges and attempts some description of the flora and fauna of the land. He also has fabulous stories like that of "two cubits long flying serpents" (Megasthenese 1877: 56). Also, he was the first Western writer to state explicitly the thesis that the crown owned all property in India and that no private person could own land. This was later used as an explanation for "Oriental Despotism."

A later Greek writer, Philostratus, uses these early records as source materials in his *Life of Appolonius of Tyana.* The journey of Appolonius to India (now generally seen as fictional) bears a close resemblance to the travelogues of earlier Greek writers. The kings of Taxila are presented in this work as "Philosopher Kings" living in quiet simplicity and a glowing account is given of King Porus. The wisdom of Indian government is made use of here to criticize the West (qtd. Sedlar 1980: 190-98). This was as popular a usage as that which treated the East as apology for western institutions. In either case, the effect was generally to set up and enforce the East as the "Other," the binary opposite of the West.

A Greek historian of the second century A.D., Arrian[1] made use of the accounts of Nearchus and Onesicritus (both of whom accompanied Alexander on his journey to India). About eight centuries after Megasthenese, Cosmos Indicopelustus (who was in India from A.D. 535 to A.D. 547) wrote *Topographia Christiana, which* provided much information on trading routes and facilities. This was also developed further in the *Periplus of the Erythraean Sea* (75-901 A.D.), which provided a detailed account of the trading ports of India and also the social Organization (Periplus: 1875). Also, as Sedlar points out, India's contribution to the philosophies of many of the so-called Christian heresies was immense (1980: 208).

In the Middle Ages, occasional travellers made their way to India. A typical example is that of Bishop Jordanus in India about 1323. Another important landmark is *The Travels of Sir John Mandeville* (originally written around 1357 and later translated into English). The author stresses the myth of a fabulously wealthy India: "the beste and the most precyiouse dyamaundes bene in India" (1921: 97). He also refers to the Prester John figure—"the grete emperor of Ynde" (1921: 103).

Apart from this translated version of Mandeville's travels, English literature, at this period has few significant references to India. Most prominent among those references which do exist are the *Gestes of Alexander* (early fifteenth century) and the *Romance of King Alysander* written in a Southern dialect nearly a hundred years later (Qtd. Sencourt 1990). Chaucer's work composed during this period shows little reference to India—"the great Emeritus, King of Inde" in the "Knighte's Tale" and a mention of "Ynde" in the "Squire's Tale" are all.

Travellers from countries other than Britain had been making visits to India and recording their experiences ever since Vasco Da Gama's successful trip in 1498. An important literary presentation of Gama's trip can be found in Camoens' *Luciad* (written in 1592).[2] The prosperity of India is indicated by a verse speech he gives to the Zamorin (Ruler of Calicut):

> But should you have the wish in merchandise
> With us to trade, this fertile land is blessed. . . .
> Of rubies rare, and diamonds we're possessed
> In heaps, nor deem these boasts or idle vaunts,
> Our rich and ample store by far exceeds your wants.
>
> (Qtd. Oaten 1901: 73)

Marco Polo, in the late thirteenth century travelled to China and visited India by way of Sumatra. He refers to religious rites as well as commercial matters and his narrative is a valuable source for information on early South India (Polo 1961). Early during the fifteenth century, the Italian Nicolo Conti and the Russian Athanasius Nikitin had visited India by the overland route and recorded their impressions. In a bout of intolerance, Nikitin remarks of the inhabitants of Bidar: "All are black and wicked and the women all harlots or witches and they destroy their masters by poison" (qtd. Oaten 1901: 41).

Conti, on the other hand generally does not give vent to such splenetic remarks. When describing the rite of sati or the King's Harem, he certainly intended to be "diverting" by representing the exotic, but there is no sharp or direct condemnation by tone" (qtd. Kaul 1997: 63-64).

Ludovico Di Varthema, who was in India around 1502, asserts that though the inhabitants were not Christians, if they were but baptised, their numerous good works would ensure their salvation. At the same time he also refers to the custom of wife sharing and to what he sees as the almost frightening sexual aggressiveness of the native women (Varthema 1974: 203).

Apart from these travellers, a large number of missionaries—Francis Xavier and Roberto de Nobili being ideal examples—visited India. Though the Emperor Akbar received them with keen intellectual curiosity and courtesy, nothing very concrete was really achieved by way of proselytizing.

The first Englishman[3] who is known to have visited India was Thomas Stephens, who came to Goa in 1579 and became Rector of the Jesuit College in Salsette. His letters, which aroused great curiosity among his countrymen, are related only to Goa. Ralph Fitch, a London merchant who has left significant records about the cultural and religious practices of the Indians followed Stephens in 1583. In 1599 John Mildenhall visited the Court of Akbar and made him presents, but serious interaction was to a great extent foiled by the Portuguese.

During the Elizabethan age,[4] we find only a few scattered references to India in British literature. These are not of any great significance, though they do indicate that the distant land of India was gradually gaining a symbolic status within the British imagination. The major impression left by India at this stage seems to be one of unbounded material prosperity. This, combined with the immense distance of India from the European metropolis, gave the land just the right aura of exoticism to make it suitable for evocative literary usage.

During the Jacobean period in English history, Sir Thomas Roe visited the Court of Jehangir as an official ambassador from the King of England. His Commission read: "Our true and undoubted attorney, Procreator, Legatee and Ambassador to that high and mighty monarch, the Great Mogoor, King of the oriental Indyes, of Condahy, of Chismer and of Corosan" (qtd. Oaten

1991: 39). In 1609, William Hawkins had arrived at the court of Jehangir and been treated as an interesting visitor. But he had been unable to achieve anything concrete in the way of treaties or concessions. It was after this that Roe was sent as an official accredited Ambassador in 1615. But even he could manage no official treaty between King James and Jehangir.

In 1616, the noted eccentric, Thomas Coryat was also in India. He scandalized Roe by addressing a flattering Persian ode to the Emperor and accepting a thrown-down gift of hundred rupees. Another of his escapades was to shout out in the native tongue at the time of prayer that Mohammad was an imposter. In this context, E.F. Oaten remarks that only his reputed madness saved him from the wrath of the people. Perhaps it is also possible to imagine that hospitality if not tolerance had something to do with it; the records do not indicate any occasion, when, in these early stages, the natives unleashed any "Oriental fury" on the western visitors.

Other representations of India in English during this period include those by Edward Terry, William Methold and William Bruton. All these writers have recorded their impressions of India, touching the areas of administration, jurisprudence, and religious customs.

In the latter half of the seventeenth century, the most prominent western visitors to India were not British, but the Frenchmen Tavernier and Bernier. Tavernier published his *Six Voyages* in 1676 and Bernier's *History* was published in 1670. Prominent British travellers during this period are John Fryer (1673), Ovington (1689) and Hamilton (between 1688 and 1723) who have all left lengthy accounts of their Indian experiences. These early records do treat India as "different," but it is not really shown as the kind of difference which automatically produces contempt. The experiences were felt to be strange and inassimilable, but the necessity of peaceful trade if nothing else seems to have kept the comments and conclusions within bounds.

During this period, the western visitors were hardly treated as objects of veneration by the Indians. Indeed, the situation is drastically different; as Pere Calmette (writing in the late seventeenth century) remarks: "In the interior, a white man hardly as yet escapes public ridicule" (qtd. Fisher 1996: 15). This indicates a rather different scenario from the one presented by O. Mannoni in *Prospero and Caliban* where the native's dependency complex induces submission at first sight to the white men.

A merchant expedition sent to Bengal in 1632, records that they were "fain to kiss the Nawab's feet" and considered it a good bargain if trade would thereby prosper (qtd. Oaten 1991: 174). Even in the early eighteenth century (indeed almost up to Plassey in 1757) the British representatives in India were quite literally "kowtowing" the Indian rulers. Three letters of John Russell in the early eighteenth century indicate this trend. In 1711, Russell writes to the Viceroy of Bengal, Azimus-Shah-Khan: "with the humblest submission . . . dedicating at your feet the life wholly dedicated to your service . . . present this petition after kissing the ground on which treads the greatest and most powerful prince." In a 1713 letter to Jahandar Shah, Russell declares that his forehead was to be considered as the tip of the Emperor's shoe. Writing in 1713 to Emperor Faroukshihsiar, Russell presented himself as "the smallest particle of sand . . . with his forehead at your command rubbed on the ground . . . and giving reverence due from a slave . . . to your throne which is the seat of miracles" (qtd. Fisher 1996: 14). Just as the period between 1757-1857 was the age of the Nabob, and that between 1857-1947 was dominated by the figure of the Sahib, during the period between the establishment of the British East India Company (1600) to the Battle of Plassey (1757) we see the figure of the Trader, acknowledging (rather hypocritically perhaps, but nevertheless acknowledging) the sovereignty of the Indian rulers and taking their claims to magnificence and reverence at their own estimation.

The main note sounded by the travellers of this period in their representation of India is one of luxury and riches, so much so that the chaplain Edward Terry begins to wonder if he has painted too rosy a picture altogether. So, to counterbalance this, he comes up with the argument:

> Lest this remote country should seem like an earthly paradise without any discommodities, very great was the danger there from lions, tigers, and jackals in the rivers from crocodiles and on the land from snakes and other venomous and pernicious beasts. (Qtd. Forster 1921: 123)

This does sound like special pleading; his own description so far has been enough to produce a picture of Utopia, and all that Terry can come up with to post against this is that the wild animals there are dangerous!

Both Roe and Hawkins refer to Indians as "faithlesse"—an obvious result of being often frustrated in their ambassadorial activities. However, they do not stop begging for the favours of the "faithlesse" sovereign of this "faithlesse" people and they also go into raptures while describing the luxuries of the East.

One of the closest approaches to a racism which breeds a superiority complex is to be found in the records of Sir Thomas Herbert (1634) who refers to "the stinking weeds of cursed Heathenism" and describes the Zamorin as "a naked Negro, but as proud as Lucifer" (qtd. Sencourt 1990: 118). Both religious and colour prejudice can be seen here. But, it should be remembered in this context that the British during this time had no great idea of coming over and changing or salvaging India; nor did critical portraits dampen their ardour for the riches of the East. They were quite prepared to treat and trade with "cursed heathens" if necessary.

The presence of India appears to be slightly more prominent in the literature of this period when compared to the Elizabethan Age. Walter Mountfort wrote a play (unpublished) titled *The Launchinge of the Mary or the Seaman's Honest Wife* directly related to the voyages of the East India Company. We can find some references to India in Milton's *Paradise Lost* and in Dryden's *Hind and the Panther.* Dryden's 1675 play *Aurengzebe* has an Indian setting and characters, though he changes history beyond recognition, for example investing Shah Jahan's chief queen with an incestuous passion for Aurengzebe and making Shah Jahan lust after his son's fiancée. Even more significant in this context is Dryden's 1673 play *Amboyna* which specifically deals with the struggles between the Dutch and British East India Companies; a strong piece of anti-Dutch propaganda. The dying hero of the play, an official of the East India Company, speaks as follows:

> Tell my friends, I died so as became a Christian and a
> Man, give to my brave Employers of the East India Company.
> The last remembrance of my faithful service
> Tell them I seal that service with my blood.
> And dying wish to all their factories.
> And all the famous merchants of our Isle
> That wealth which their generous Industry deserves.
>
> (Dryden 1961: 97)

Obviously, by this time, the trade in India was a cause to die for, a noble enough cause to provide martyrdom. We can see the Romance earlier attached to religious causes here shifting smoothly to commercial operations.

Also significant are the researches of John Marshall in Indian philosophy published in 1674 as *Dialogue with a Brahman on the Origin of the World.* In this work Indian philosophy is treated at a very superficial and simplified level, but it is not ridiculed or contemptuously pushed aside. During Queen Anne's reign we find references to India scattered in different genres: Gay's *Beggar's Opera,* an epitaph by Pope, a religious treatise by Isaac Watts. Later works which refer to India begin to talk of the Nabob and often use this perspective, as can be seen in the texts of the later 18th century; the period following the victory at Plassey

B

This section examines the annexations of the East India Company and its gradual achievement of political power in India during the period 1757-1857. That century saw the company serially annex or else extend its indirect rule over most of the Indian states—a far cry from the few factories and trading posts it possessed before 1757. The first region in India over which the Company gained administrative control was Bengal. The British army under Robert Clive defeated the Nawab of Bengal Siraj-ud-

Dulla at the Battle of Plassey in 1757 and put a puppet of their own choice, Mir Jafar, on the throne. To show his gratitude Mir Jafar paid a large sum of money to the Company and also ceded to its rule the vast area referred to as the "Twenty Four Parganas."

Later, Mir Kasim, with whom again the British quarrelled on the issue of trade permits, replaced Mir Jafar. Mir Kasim was deposed and Mir Jafar reinstalled as Nawab. The then Mughal Emperor, Shah Alam and the Nawab of Oudh, Shuja-ud-Doula joined hands with the deposed Mir Kasim and met the British troops in the battle of Buxar in 1764. The Company won the war and the Emperor came over to the British side while Oudh had to sign a treaty of submission. After the death of Mir Jafar in 1765, his son was elevated to the throne, but by this time all power in Bengal was concentrated in the Company's hands. Shah Alam, by the treaty of Allahabad also handed over the sovereignty of Bengal, Bihar and Orissa to the British.

Though the Nawab of the Carnatic was officially deposed only in 1801, from 1765 onwards, the Company had de facto control over his domains in South India. In 1766, the Company received the vast tract known as 'the Northern Sarkars' from the Nizam of Hyderabad. In a much criticized action, Warren Hastings in 1773 captured the province of Rohilkhand, erstwhile ruled by independent tribes and also interfered in the government of the province of Benares, which in fact if not in appearance was brought under British rule.

The later Governor-Generals in India, during the process of their annexations, had to fight three major wars with the Marathas and four with the Mysore Sultans—Hyder Ali and Tipu. The first Maratha war, fought during Warren Hastings' time, ended in 1782 on terms favourable to the British. Lord Wellesley superintended the second Maratha war (1802-4) and the third war was fought during the administration of Lord Hastings. Both these wars went in favour of the Company and Maratha power was totally crushed and considerable territory annexed.

The four Mysore wars were also finally beneficial to the British though they had to sue for peace in the initial stages. After Hyder Ali and Tipu Sultan were both dead, their territories were brought under British domination. Cornwallis also annexed Malabar in South India following the Third Mysore War.

Wellesley, the Governor-General from 1796 to 1805, brought many provinces under the indirect control of the Company through the Subsidiary System, which consisted of the native ruler paying large amounts to maintain a force of Company troops in his territory and allowing the Company to dictate his foreign policy. Tanjore, Surat and the Carnatic were important areas where the Subsidiary System was enforced.

As a result of the Nepal war under Lord Hastings, the Company annexed Simla and the first Burmese war conducted under Lord Amherst brought in Assam and Nagaland. William Bentinck mainly maintained a policy of non-interference, but Cachar and Coorg were annexed during his tenure; 1828-1835. In 1843 Sir Charles Napier conquered and annexed Sind and the Punjab, which had earlier flourished independently under Ranjeet Singh, was annexed in 1849. The Governor-Generalship of Dalhousie (1843-56) saw a stream of annexations mainly through the Doctrine of Lapse, according to which the succession of any province where the contemporary ruler did not have direct male issue "lapsed" to the Company. Using this doctrine, Satara was annexed in 1841, Jaipur and Sambhalpur in 1849, Udaipur in 1851, Jhansi in 1853 and Nagpur in 1854. Berar was annexed in 1853 through military force.

The last major annexation, that of Oudh, took place in 1856, after a long and chequered relationship. Since after the Mutiny in 1857, the British tried to prop up the remaining Indian rulers as faithful allies, the annexation of Oudh may be considered the final major annexation and Dalhousie's period both the most prolific and conclusive for territorial expansion.

The process of annexation was not, by any standards, a seamless linear project. While the "men-on-the-spot" in India generally regarded annexation in a favourable light, as pertaining to imperial grandeur, the Company Authorities back in Britain, were more often than not apprehensive about large-scale acquisitions. Company records and correspondence provide interesting pictures of how India and her politics were viewed in the metropolitan centres of Britain and how their relationships with the distant colony were constructed.

Even as Clive's exploits at Plassey were being glorified, it was possible to trace dissenting voices. Horace Walpole in 1764 writes:

> Lord Clive has been suddenly nominated by the East India Company to the Empire of Bengal, where Dupleix has taught all our merchants to effect to be King making Earls of Warwick and where the chief things they have made are blunders and confusion. It is amazing that their usurpations have not taught the Indians union, discipline and courage—we are governing nations to which it takes a year to send our orders. (Qtd. Fisher 1996: 14)

Obviously, the suggestion is that "merchants" would do well to stick to trade and not attempt administration, where all they can achieve are "blunders and confusion." The Indians need to be *taught* "union, discipline and courage" indeed, but it is not the Company's job to do that. The economic motive was predominant in these early stages and the most ardent advocates of expansion had to provide reasons based on economic factors if these ideas were to be countenanced.

In the beginning at least, the Company was not interested in annexation for empire's sake. Pitt's India Act, 1784, contained the following specific clause:

> Whereas to pursue schemes of conquest and extension of domination in India are measures repugnant to the wish, honour and policy of this nation; the Governor-General and his Council are not, without the express authority of the Court of directors or the Select Committee to declare wars or commence hostilities or enter into any treaty for making war against any of the country princes or states in India. (qtd. Mahajan 1969: 80)

In keeping with this policy, we find even as late as 1803, the Governor-General Wellesley, referring to the pacific Directors of the East India Company as "a pack of narrow-minded old women." As Fisher points out, many of the Company officials in India regarded, "London as betraying the Company itself by not proving worthy of its conquests, because London was trying to hold back the Company in its expansion across and rule over India" (Fisher 1996: 28). Even on those occasions where the Company itself did not oppose expansion, British national interests were rarely associated with those of the Company.

A letter written by Clive to the then Prime Minister, William Pitt in 1759 and Pitt's reply clearly indicate the two different paradigms both were speaking from. Clive's letter indicates a desire for imperial expansion, but he is careful to curb his enthusiasm and concentrate on solid economic arguments to further his cause. Obviously, even this strategy was not very successful since Pitt did not send a favourable reply. Clive writes:

> I have represented in the strongest terms the expediency of sending out and keeping up constantly such a force [in India] as will enable us to embrace the first opportunity of further aggrandizing ourselves; and I dare pronounce from a thorough knowledge of this country's government and of the genius of the people . . . that such an opportunity will soon offer. . . . Musselmans are so little influenced by gratitude that should he [Nawab of Bengal] ever think it his interest to break with us, the obligations he owes us would prove no restraint. . . . The natives themselves have no attachment whatsoever to particular princes and . . . they would rejoin in so happy an exchange as that of a mild for a despotic government. . . . Now, I leave you to judge whether an income of two millions sterling yearly, with the possession of three provinces abounding in the most valuable productions of nature and of art be an object deserving the public attention. This project may be brought about without draining the mother country. . . . A small force from home will be sufficient as we always make sure of any number we please of black troops . . . who will readily enter into our service. (qtd. in Fisher 1996: 61-63)

Pitt's reply to Clive's secretary who delivered this letter was that while it was *possible* to annex Bengal, it would not be *wise* to do so. So large an increase in revenues to either the Company or the crown would "endanger" our liberties "by concentrating too much financial power in certain hands. Pitt also remarked: "it was not probable that Clive would be succeeded by people equal to the task" (qtd. Fisher 1996: 60). During this early period, the

British policy framers were not thinking in terms of "the White Man's Burden," the superiority of the West is indeed accepted; but there is no desperate eagerness to civilize dark areas. Both the opponents and defenders of political expansion based their arguments on economic foundations.

Interestingly, even the men on the spot did not favour expansion. Their attitudes varied according to changing circumstances since there was no official monolithic policy of annexation. Clive himself, *after* the annexation of Bengal, writes to the Company Directors in a tone very different from that he had used when writing to Pitt:

> To go further, is in my opinion a scheme so extravagantly ambitious and absurd, that no Governor and Council can adopt it, unless the whole system of the Company's interest first be entirely new modelled . . . by grasping at more, you endanger the safety of those immense revenues and that well founded power which you now enjoy. (qtd. Mahajan 1969: 51)

The arguments both for and against annexation, even when voiced by the same person, finally come down to economic terms. Even when the Company later changed its stand and began to advocate annexation, the underlying reasons were mainly related to trade and commerce. Of course, this was rarely openly admitted and the authorities made a literal parade of liberal, progressive and "just" reasons for expansion. As will be seen, further Governor-Generals with imperial ambitions had no difficulty in producing any type of reason that was required of them. They constructed their images of India and Indians in such a way that these representations would be more than sufficient and satisfactory justifications *after* the act of annexation.

In the earliest stages of annexations, British officials themselves often pointed out in clear terms that the claim that Company rule was "good" for the natives was largely fictitious. In 1769, Bucher, the British Resident at Murshidabad, wrote:

> It must give pain to an Englishman to have reason to think that since the accession of the Company to the Diwani; the condition of the people of this country has been worse than it was before; and

> yet I am afraid that the fact is quite undoubted. The fine country which flourished under the despotic and arbitrary government is verging towards its ruin, while the English have really so great a share in the administration. (qtd. Mahajan 1969: 49-50)

Such admissions grew rare as the urge for expansion increased. Yet, it is worthwhile to note that the discourse did, at a certain stage provide spaces where such comments could be inscribed. It would not be an exaggeration to claim that an uneasy awareness that such an assessment could be true led the Company officials to insist on *the appearance* at least of just and fair proceedings, which made the native appear to not only request but indeed clamour for British rule.

Writing not in a postcolonial context, but as early as 1867, James Hutton remarks: "In India, indeed, the 'outraged people' have never proved very clamorous for absorption into the British Empire, apparently preferring to endure any amount of oppression under a ruler of their own race and religion, to being transferred to the tender mercies of the infidel and the alien" (qtd. Fisher 1996: 186). This conclusion is justified by the fact that those officials who insist that Indians badly wanted to be absorbed into British rule produce no positive records. They merely "speak for" the Indians and expect their voices to be accepted as authentic. For example, William Bentinck justified the Company's annexation of Coorg in 1834 by unilaterally proclaiming "it is the unanimous wish of the inhabitants of Coorg to be taken under the protection of the British Government" (qtd. Fisher 1996: 21). The only proof given for this "unanimous desire" is Bentinck's proclamation itself which is thus to be accepted as its own guarantee.

Sheridan, speaking on the fourth day of the impeachment of Warren Hastings, makes the point that to be handed over to British authority was more a source of terror to the natives than anything else. The attendants of the Begums of Oudh, after having been scourged, put in irons and starved, to make them reveal their mistresses' secret treasure are given a "threat of a curious nature":

> After being confined in Fyzabad, after being double ironed at Lucknow, after being publicly scourged—now comes the climax, the threat that they would be sent—where? To Chunar Gaur. They are given four days' notice that they would be sent into a British fort—into pure British custody . . . we will send you from this place into custody purely British and think what your situation will be then. (qtd. Carnall 1989: 20)

Sheridan emphasizes the point that it was unutterably disgraceful to the British image in India that their name and power be used as terrorizing agents. Under the circumstances, he seems to indicate, it is difficult to conceive of Indians, on any occasion where they could possibly act as free agents, actually begging to be absorbed into British territory. Nevertheless, "the clamour of the natives" was, for a considerable period, used as the primary justification for annexation and absorption.

When this argument simply could not be serviceably used any longer, the officials turned to other justifications. Obviously, it was not enough to just march in and annex territory on the basis of military superiority, "just" causes had to be stated, at least retrospectively. Indeed, it had to be asserted that the British were by no means the only or even chief ones benefitting from expansion, the natives also gained as much if not more. Indeed, Wellesley went so far as to state that annexation benefitted even the deposed native rulers since they were thereby relieved of their debts and the burdens of administration! (qtd. Fisher 1996: 29)

A letter from Malcolm to the Peshwa, Baji Rao II, urging him to submit to British annexation and willingly abdicate, is notable for its incredible sophistry:

> The tribe to which your highness belongs has been celebrated in all ages for its courage. Brahmin women have burnt themselves upon the funeral pyres of their husbands. Men have thrown themselves from precipices to propitiate the deity for themselves or to avert misfortune from their families. The sacrifice demanded from you, is in fact only the resignation of a power which you do not possess and which you can never hope to regain. You are called upon for no such great effort. (qtd. Edwardes 1968: 183)

Abdication is presented as an act of courage. And what is even more ironic is that the instances of courage—Sati and self-sacrifice—held up, as examples to the Peshwa are those very practices, which later Evangelists were to thunder against. Though employed for utilitarian purposes, the conceptual register in this context indicates a certain ambivalence—these Indian customs were at the same time examples of mental courage and also indications of a lack of "progressive" civilization. These concepts were used in turn, each being foregrounded as the occasion demanded, but within the paradigm they coexisted uneasily.

The other prominent argument was of course that of the inherent superiority of the British systems as opposed to native ones. The "incapacity" of the native rulers was stressed so that the annexations could be justified, primarily to an audience at Home, which at any rate was not too impressed with the economic connotations of annexation. This rhetoric, later having taken on the guise of self-evident fact was used directly to the Indian rulers themselves. In a Report of a meeting between Bentinck and the rulers of Oudh, Bentinck is shown as saying:

> Wherever the country of rulers bound to the British Government by treaty has been taken possession of directly by act of aggression on our part, the annexation has always been justified; upon the ground of the disorders which prevailed and the unfitness of the native government to conduct affairs and their failure to establish a proper systematic Government that should be a source of happiness and contentment to the people. (qtd. Fisher 1996: 20)

The justification here becomes fact, yet it is to be remembered that in the first instance, it *was* justification; that an excuse, however inadequate was felt to be necessary. In direct progress from this stage, we see the range of the arguments expanding. In the case of Oudh, the territory in question was at least bound to the Company by treaty. By the time of Dalhousie, the justification is broadened so as to extend to independent provinces also. In addition to an undoubted superiority of administration, annexation was justified also as practical and administrative consolidation, this being the argument likely to carry most weight with the Directors at Home. In 1848, Dalhousie wrote, in response to his critics:

> I cannot conceive it possible for anyone to dispute the policy of taking advantage of every *just* opportunity which presents itself for consolidating the territories that already belong to us, by taking possession of states which may lapse in the midst of them; for this getting rid of these petty intervening principalities, which may be made a *means of annoyance*, but which can never, I venture to think, be *a source of strength* for adding to the resources of the public treasury and for extending the uniform application of the system of government to those whose best interest, we sincerely believe will be promoted thereby. (qtd. Fisher 1996: 23, my italics)

The fact that there were critics of imperialism, who for purely practical reasons at least, sought to curb expansion, also needs to be accentuated. Economic arguments had to be put forward to counter this attitude. But, at the same time, the fiction of a "just" cause had to be kept up, incongruous though it appears among the other pragmatic arguments. Obviously a continued murmuring of the "just cause" clause served as a lullaby to soothe some conscientious doubts, which were existing, though mainly regarded only for their nuisance value.

To this preoccupation with recording (at least after the act) "just causes," we may apply Stephen Greenblatt's formulation of "linguistic actions performed entirely for a world elsewhere," other than on the site of performance (1991: 56). Greenblatt records Columbus's account of his taking possession of America on behalf of the Spanish Crown. With regard to the natives who were around at the moment of the declaration of appropriation, Columbus remarks, "no opposition was offered to me" (qtd. Greenblatt 1991: 52). Obviously the natives, under the circumstances—a speech act in an unknown tongue and incomprehensible visual signs—could not be capable of either assenting or contradicting. But within the formalism of the act, all that matters was that there was no opposition, the question of *why* this was so is not permitted to arise. It is possible, of course, to argue from this linguistic formalism "words do not matter, that language is a mere screen for the brutality of power." But the absurd declaration of Columbus is also "a sign of ethical reservation" (Greenblatt 1991: 64-65), a kind of textual resistance which demanded at least the appearance of legality and justice. Within the colonial context in India, a retrospective justification seems to have been necessary on the same principles—a justification which is not actually intended for the affected natives, but for a world elsewhere, the observers at "Home." Obviously the concepts of equity, fair play or justice were overlooked in *colonial practice,* but they had to figure rhetorically in statements of *colonial theory,* which reveal their own absurdity and strain the semantic resources of the language to an almost unbearable degree.

By the 1840s the attitudes of the Company Directors with regard to expansion in India had undergone considerable changes. Far from acting as a brake on the Governor-Generals's imperialism, they started advocating a policy of aggression. The major factor in this, of course was that the economic benefits, which could accrue from expansion, now began to appear in larger than life proportions. An 1841 letter from the Directors to the Governor-General touches both on this economic factor and the constant preoccupation with the "justness" of expansion. The Company in this letter, urged the Governor-General not to abandon "any just and honourable accession of territory or revenue which could be had . . . by annexing states into British control" (qtd. Fisher 1996: 71).

This change in the metropolitan attitude, was reflected prominently in the discourse of expansion articulated by the men on the spot in India. Sir Charles Napier, who spearheaded the annexation of Sind could confidently write in his diary: "How is all this to end? We have no right to seize Sind, yet we shall do so, and a very advantageous, useful, humane piece of rascality it will be" (qtd. Fisher 1996: 236). Despite its surface wry honesty, the notion of "justice" is not abandoned here, only concealed. In view of the changed atmosphere, Napier could speak of annexation as a "piece of rascality," but he could not leave it at that. It had to be characterised as "useful, advantageous and humane," the last adjective at least referring specifically to the supposed betterment accruing to the natives from British rule. Advantageous" and "useful," seem to refer to British interests, contrasting rather too obviously to the supposed "humanness" of the action. In the large major annexation before 1857, that of Oudh, we can see an uneasy juxtaposition of grimly pragmatic assertions with convoluted attempts at ethical sophistry with which to justify expansion. No rhetoric was at this period specifically "wasted" on the natives themselves. Colonel Sleeman, requesting (in effect, commanding) the King of Oudh to dismiss an official not preferred by the Company does not even bother to argue that the man is guilty of something. He merely states that "there is no necessity to prove his guilt, as the appointment imposed on him is not his Jageer or hereditary property. Therefore, it is not necessary at the time of his dismissal to investigate the proofs" (qtd. Fisher 1996: 268-69).

At the same time in explanation of the actual act of annexation, Dalhousie had to write, in quasi-religious terms: "The British Government would be guilty in the sight of God and man, if it were any longer to aid in sustaining by its countenance, an administration fraught with suffering to millions" (qtd. Mahajan 1969: 204).

Obviously, the imperialists fully understood the unequal nature of the terrain where they rehearsed their policies and politics. But in their discourse, they maintained the fiction of imperialism as "just" procedure and even heavenly mandate. This rhetoric cannot stand up to a cross checking with the contemporary documents (those addressed to the natives and those circulated among the actual expansionists themselves) which reveal, in explicit terms, the arbitrary and fundamentally economically motivated nature of expansion. The highly poised rhetoric loses its effect from such contradictions, which reveal clearly that on most occasions, the perpetrators of imperialism did not actually believe their own rhetorical flourishes. However, as will be seen, the rhetoric was as necessary on a psychological level as military might was on a practical level. The contradictions weaken the imperial edifice as a construction if it is examined in retrospect.

But at the time of construction, they functioned as essential constituents of the structure.

C

In this section, the ideological trends, which influenced early British attitudes to India, are examined. The major trends analyzed here are a paternalistic spirit of Conservatism, Utilitarianism, Evangelicalism, Commercialism, "pure" Imperialism and Romanticism. The two ostensibly opposed political theories, which influenced early British rule in India, were Conservatism and Utilitarianism. Indologist expertise was generally allied to Conservatism, while Utilitarianism offered its services to the Whig trends of reform. In the early stages of expansion, it did appear as if Conservatism was in possession of the upper hand. During Clive's tenure, for example, the British were far more concerned with commercial and military activities than with the subtleties of administration or reforms. Eric Stokes in *English Utilitarians and India* points out that even when the British had to fashion an administrative machinery of their own, they continued for quite a long period to regard themselves as inheritors; rather than innovators, as the revivers of a decayed system and not as the vanguard of a new one. A conscious attempt from London, under the Lord North ministry to introduce English principles in India was strongly resisted by Warren Hastings, who argued in favour of preserving Indian society and its institutions against what many viewed as the anglicizing 'danger.'

The Conservatives firmly upheld a belief in the necessity and sanctity of permanent institutions, established by tradition. Indologist research into Vedic society provided the picture of a highly institutionalized and traditional society, which was duly eulogized. Edmund Burke, in the course of his opening speech during the impeachment of Warren Hastings emphasized this view: "Faults, this nation [India] may have. But, God forbid we should pass judgment upon people who formed their laws and institutions prior to our insect origins of yesterday" (Burke 1987: I 41). He repeats the point in a later speech: "Let me remind your Lordships that the people of India lived under the settled laws to which I had referred you, and that these laws were formed whilst we, I may say were in the forest; certainly before we knew what technical jurisprudence was" (Burke 1987: II 5). Since Burke functioned as the very embodiment of Conservative philosophy, his testimony may be accepted for the apparent reverence bestowed by the Conservatives on an "ancient" India as a result of which they opposed overt Anglicization of India.

The Annual Register, which presented the Conservative viewpoints, gives a laudatory account of Hyder Ali in a 1783 issue:

> Hyder Ally [sic] was undoubtedly one of the greatest princes, as well as the greatest warrior that India has ever produced. His mind was so vast and comprehensive as at once to reach to and embrace all the parts of war and government. If he was not a legislator he had, however, the merit of establishing, so mild and equitable a system of government that the new subjects of so many countries were not only attached to his person in a most extraordinary degree but the neighbouring nations showed on every occasion their wishes to come under his protection. . . . He might profitably have been considered as one of the first politicians of his day, *whether in Europe or in Asia.* (qtd. Bearce 1961: 14-15, my italics)

This report, which showed one of Britain's most indomitable foes not as a benighted native, but as a formidable warrior and statesman bolstered up the argument that India had reached a level of development which rendered Anglicization superfluous and unnecessary. The phrase "one of the foremost politicians in Europe or in Asia" has to be foregrounded in a discussion of the Conservative principle. In the first place, the argument ran, India had developed according to its own natural genius. In the second place, these developments, at least in the case of particular individuals were formidable, even when compared to *European* achievements.

With regard to the natural genius of the Indian people, William Robertson, the Conservative historian writes: "under a form of government which paid such attention to all the different orders of which society is composed, particularly to the cultivators of the soil, it is not wonderful that the ancients should describe the Indians as a most happy race of men and that the most intelligent modern observers should celebrate the equity, the humanity and the mildness of the Indian policy" (Robertson 1981: 268). The argument is that the Indians have, using traditional and gradual steps, devised the best possible institutions for their own government. It is to be noted that the Conservatives do not suggest that the empire be given up. It is up to the British to see that India is governed properly, but, from the Conservative perspective, the tools should be used for this process by British administrators, but they ought to be Indian in origin and nature.

Despite a conviction of the necessity of continued British rule, the Conservatives did attempt to dispel ignorance and prejudice regarding India. James Cumming, senior official at Company Headquarters and a staunch Conservative sharply criticizes certain British tendencies, which were undermining the traditional institutions of India. He accuses the British of not being content with making their fortunes in India, but also insisting on "indulging their national bigotry and pride and their learned vanity." He finds deplorable the prejudiced attitude, which allows British reformers to turn to the people of India and say:

> You are all a parcel of poor, ignorant, semi-barbarians; you do not even understand your own language and system as well as we enlightened Englishmen who have been at regular grammar schools. . . . We have studied jurisprudence and history and political economy. We will show you how to administer justice in India and how to conduct its internal government. (qtd. Bearce 1961: 31-33)

Given that the principal aim of British rule was to govern India pragmatically, with an eye on benefits for Britain, philosophical Conservatism did not have much of a chance of becoming the paramount ideology. The Reformers and Utilitarians very often succeeded in making the Conservative view of India appear totally reactionary and opposed to both British and Indian interests accusing it of preventing modernization and progress. Though traces of paternalist Conservatism did continue to exist, the tide of Anglicization surged forward during the tenures of Cornwallis and Wellesley. On a surface level at least, it is possible to claim that Utilitarian and Reformist tendencies were able to supersede Conservatism. Of course, a closer examination of the underlying similarities between these two ostensibly opposed ideologies reveal that any perfect binary opposition set up between them is a facile construct. Nevertheless, it is important to remember that Reformist and Utilitarian attitudes to India defined themselves against Conservatism.

Unlike the Conservatives who were attracted to the traditions of ancient India, the Utilitarians and Reformers presented Indian culture as primitive, immoral and rude. They adopted a dismissive attitude towards Indologist claims on behalf of Indian culture. The Utilitarians were intimately connected with Indian affairs—in 1819, James Mill and later, his son J.S. Mill were in the executive management of the East India Company. Jeremy Bentham, the "founder" of Utilitarianism cherished an ambition to be the lawgiver of India and had taken considerable efforts to formulate a suitable legal code for India. Eric Stokes points out that Bentham's essay "On the Influence of Time and Place in Matters of Legislation" was composed with the objective of considering what modifications, if any were required in order to transplant his legal system to Bengal (Stokes 1982: 49). The Utilitarians primarily regarded India as raw material waiting to be shaped by the colonizers, as the ideal laboratory for trying out Utilitarian doctrines, without too much domestic protest against experimentation.

Liberal reformers normally recommended that in the interests of good government India should have western political institutions, such as a Legislative Assembly. James Mill, representing the Utilitarian viewpoint did not endorse this argument. In an *Edinburgh Review* article of 1810, he argued instead:

> The stage of civilization and the moral and political situation in which the people of India are placed, render the establishment of legislative assemblies impracticable. A simple form of arbitrary government, tempered by European honour and European intelligence is the only form, which is now fit for Hindustan. (qtd. Bearce 1961: 68)

Thus Mill recommended an authoritarian British government in India as the best possible system. Other reformers, following the trope, which presented India as the benighted Other of civilized Europe, often came around to this view. The "upliftment" of India took on the aspects of a mission and some officials at least were imbued with a crusading zeal for reform.

This reformist spirit, together with a total lack of understanding of Indian customs, often produced an effect of unintentional comedy. W.H. Carey records that the first Chief Justice of the Calcutta Court, contemplating the bare legs and feet of the natives who gathered to welcome him, remarked to a colleague: "See, brother, the wretched victims of tyranny. The Crown Court was surely not established before it was needed. I trust it will not have been in operation six months before we shall see these poor creatures comfortably clothed in shoes and stockings" (Carey 1980: 78). It is tempting indeed to speculate on how beneficial exactly this reform would have been and how the Justice proposed to bring it into effect.

On the surface of it, the Utilitarians and Reformist Liberals were as staunch supporters of the Anglicization (in varying degrees) of India as the Conservatives were its opponents. The Conservatives, helped by Indologist research placed ancient India on a pedestal, while the Utilitarians dragged it down as far as possible. Yet, despite this apparent polarity, the two groups were in some ways merely positioned on two sides of the same coin.

Both ideologies emphasize "ancient" India, either to glorify or degrade India as such. Contemporary India did not enter the picture so prominently, and was mainly a backdrop on to which the differing conceptions of ancient India could be projected. Along with the glories of Indian tradition, the Conservatives also emphasized a certain unchangeability of Indian society. This procedure successfully denied much importance to Indian history between the Vedic Age and the age of colonization, except perhaps as an unfortunate interlude. Many Conservatives and Indologists—Burke and Jones are prime examples—thereby managed to reconcile a genuine respect for India's past, with a patronizing attitude towards contemporary India, which helped to sanctify the imperial mission.

While deriding Indologist claims for Indian culture, the Utilitarians conveniently accepted the Indologist idea of the "permanency" of Indian institutions—a process, which they regarded as akin to stagnation. James Mill insists that whatever crude institutions India may have developed at one stage, they were later allowed to stagnate beyond redemption. He regards India as not having changed or evolved in any significant way since despotic rulers opposed change and prevented the country from entering the mainstream of world history as Europe had done. He argues:

> [From] the writings of the Greeks, the conclusion has been drawn that the Hindus at the time of Alexander's invasion were in a state of manners, systems and knowledge, exactly the same with that in which they were discovered by the nations of modern Europe, nor is there any reason for differing widely from this opinion. Their annals from that era till the period of the Mahometan conquests at least are a blank. (Mill 1978: 120)

The language and the tone as well as the intended effect may be different. But basically, Mill and the Conservatives argue that India has not changed much from Alexander's conquest to the British one. Neither Conservatives nor the Utilitarians were too appreciative of contemporary India; the former regarded it as having lapsed from an original purity and the latter as the natural evolutionary stage from an already degraded past. Either way, the imperial mission was justified by a construct of India, which as Said puts it in *Orientalism* served for "dominating, restructuring and having authority" (1978: 3) over the country.

The Utilitarians and the Reformers openly advocated varying degrees of Anglicization, which in fact meant total British control. The Conservatives stressed the need for preserving Indian institutions, but also implied a convoluted theory, which could be a forerunner of Kipling's concept of the "White Man's Burden." According to this theory, the tools of government in India ought to be Indian and not British, but since contemporary Indians were incapable of "good" self-government, it was up to the

British paternalists to see that these tools were used properly. This concept is presented in William Jones' "Hymn to Ganga." In the "Argument" to the poem, it is stated that the Hymn is "feigned to have been the work of a Brahmin in an early age of Hindu antiquity, who by a prophetical spirit discerns the toleration and equity of the British government and concludes with a prayer for good laws well administered" (Jones 1976: XII 322). The concluding lines of the poem are:

> Nor frown;, dread Goddess on a peerless race
> With liberal heart and martial grace
> Wafted from colder isles remote
> As they preserve our laws and bid our terror cease
> So be *their* darling laws preserv'd in wealth, in joy, in peace.
>
> (Jones 1976: XII 333, my italics)

The Conservative argument encapsulated here is that the *British* rulers are responsible for "preserving" *Indian* laws. In short, if Indian laws are to be successfully implemented *or* if India is to be anglicised, the Empire has to continue, what is more, it has to continue for the benefit of the Indians themselves. The Conservatives and the liberal Reformist categories melt into each other, sliding as it were, to fit into mutual areas of ambiguity to provide a surface concrete substratum, at least ideologically, for continued imperialism. As will be seen in the chapters dealing with representative figures like Burke and Mill, internal contradictions abound in these ideologies. However, what is most significant is that these, far from being weakening fissures, were paradoxically the essential components, which allowed both respect for tradition and liberalism to coalesce into a support for Empire.

This leads us directly to that ideological strand which may be referred to as "pure" Imperialism, which by its less subtle and more overt presence exposes the contradictions in both the Conservative and Utilitarian arguments. George Bearce remarks that Britain had no specific philosopher of imperialism and that imperial attitudes more often came from policies and action than a comprehensive statement of theory (Bearce 1961: 35). Ignorance, prejudice, national pride and a Romantic attraction to grandeur contributed to the desire to maintain and expand the Indian Empire even at high economic and moral prices.

The spirit of imperialism as seen after the impeachment of Warren Hastings was in some ways different from what had gone before. To a certain extent, it was a reaction against the stereotypical "Nabob" represented by men like Clive and Hastings. A major fear of the Conservatives in Britain was that the British officials who went out to India might end up corrupted by India. There was a fundamental conflict between the *noveau riche* Nabobs, allied to the rising commercial classes and the traditional land owning elite of Britain.

Samuel Foote's 1772 play *The Nabob* dealt with the exposure and discomfiture of the Nabob Sir Mathew Mite. Robert Sencourt points out: "the type was at once familiar and thoroughly unpopular" (1990: 210). Mite's leading character traits are ostentation and unscrupulousness and with the wealth of India, he has also brought to Britain the vices of India. The subtitle of the play *The Asiatic Plunderer* is evocative of Burke's fulminations against Warren Hastings. The author refers to the notion of "geographical morality" when he asks, "Why rob the Indian and not call it theft?"

After the East India Company itself was arraigned in the person of Warren Hastings, the attitude prevailing was one against Nabobism. The new officials were not encouraged to become Indian in any way and they were expected to continue imperialism while also demonstrating British martial and moral superiority. However, though the Nabob's parade of irritating ostentation in Britain may have been reduced, it seems that imperial grandeur and ostentation increased proportionately in India itself. From the earliest period, Company agents in India had insisted upon pomp and splendour as the best method of overawing the natives and ensuring their subjection. The Rev. Mr. Anderson's account of the pomp of the President of the Calcutta Fort indicates the extent of this ostentation:

> He had a standard-bearer and bodyguard, composed of a sergeant and a double file of English soldiers. Forty natives also attended him. At dinner each course was ushered in by a sound of trumpets

> and his ears were regaled by a band of music. Whenever he left his private rooms, he was preceded by his attendants with silver wands. On great occasions when he issued from the factory, he appeared on rose back or in a grand palanquin or a coach drawn by milk white oxen. Led horses with silver bridles followed and an umbrella of state was carried before him. (Qtd. Carey 1980: 17)

The conviction that ostentation was necessary to overawe the natives continued even after the impeachment of Warren Hastings. The "new" imperialism, at least till 1857, ensured to a certain extent that displays of Nabobism were subdued at "Home" but they certainly flourished in India. The chief officials in the colony were beginning to identify themselves with legendary military conquerors and explicitly put forward this identification as sufficient justification for their ornate mode of living. Wellesley's friend Lord Valentia justifies the Governor-General's costly construction of a magnificent residence in Calcutta on these grounds:

> The sums expended upon it have been considered as extravagant by those who carry European ideas and European economy into Asia, but they ought to remember that India is a country of splendour, of extravagance and of outward appearances, that the Head of a mighty Empire ought to conform himself to the prejudices of the country he rules over, and that the British, in particular ought to emulate the splendid works of the House of Timour [sic]. (qtd. Bearce 1961: 47)

Both the Conservative and the Reformist philosophies had opposed the idea that the British officers should become Indianised in any way. The Reformers, of course, were for Anglicization of the natives themselves. The Conservatives, while they considered that Indian traditions should be preserved, desired the British rulers to remain as father figures above these traditions, applying them to individual cases with unbiased minds and just hands. But, the ground realities of imperialism were viewed with regard to British prejudices as to what "native prejudices" were. The Indians were depicted by British observers as wanting/ needing pomp and spectacle and British imperialists, when accused of "going native" often retorted that they were merely catering to native prejudices so as to keep the Empire going. A close examination reveals that in this argument the British position was logically untenable from either side.

If they claimed that their ostentation and aggression were only to impress the natives, then in effect, it meant that Britain had not succeeded in "reforming" India and that native inclinations still dictated the style of government. On the other hand, if at all "Nabobism" was presented as inherently luxurious and enjoyable, then the process of Indianisation was complete; India, as feared by many, had succeeded, with her indolence and luxury, in corrupting the representatives of the temperate West. Caught in this double bind, it was no wonder that formal theorizing of Empire was not carried beyond a certain dangerous frontier in this period. Yet, the double vision was necessary—so that ostentation could be attacked and defended simultaneously, while imperialism continued its progress.

In effect, the theory of Empire was constantly trying to reconcile the irreconcilable and it was when confronted by this aspect that many officials argued that Empire was an entity in itself almost free of human constraints. In the *Political History of India,* Sir John Malcolm argues: "Empire is a substance which has hitherto defied and will always defy the power of man to fix in any desired shape. It is mutable, from causes beyond the control of human wisdom" (Malcolm 1826: 19). This, then, is what a large part of the early theory with a pro-Empire slant comes down to—a quasi mystical system which is dependent on both contradictions and a willing blindness to these—even while dealing in them—to maintain its coherence.

The point is not so much that this detached concept of Empire is not tenable, as that in the early stages the proponents of Empire could not provide a more factual basis for their arguments, despite their conviction of the superiority of Western rational Empiricism. Considering the evidence we have of the immense amount of planning and deliberation that went into the construction of Empire, it is possible to firmly agree with Edward Said when he argues that "By the beginning of World War I, Europe and America held 85% of the earth's surface in some sort of colonial subjection. This, I hasten to add, *did not happen in a fit of absent minded whimsy or as a result of a distracted shopping spree*" (Said 1990: 71, my italics). Indeed, Empire was planned and constructed, but the constructing blocks were illogical and ill assorted enough to force the makers themselves to cast a mystifying veil of rhetoric over the entire process. But, as I have been arguing, this rhetoric as well as the gaps, which it covered up, were, paradoxically, not just gaps but *necessary* constituents of the construction also.

Dreams of Imperial grandeur, it has to be remembered, did not devalue the important motif of commercial aggrandizement and profit. As discussed in Section B, the officers in India had in most cases to put forward sound economic reasons to justify their political actions. Indeed, during the early period, the East India Company was divided over the question of whether to concentrate on its commercial or its political functions. In the initial stages at least, the Directors of the Company held that costly wars were quite incompatible with successful trade, and tried to curb the imperial ambitions of some Governor-Generals. The Company, however, was not the sole arbitrator of British economic interests in India. In his *John Company at Work,* Holden Furber reveals "a much more complex pattern of British economic interests in India, including an extremely vigorous private sector operating in the interests of the Company's monopoly" and suggests a number of links between the economic contact between India and the West and the rise of British Imperialism (Furber 1948: 321).

Changes in the political situation also often led to drastic changes in economic policy. For instance, before the conquest of Malabar, the Company had been trying every way in its power to force the natives to sell them pepper at reduced prices. When they obtained sovereignty, however, the entire picture changed and it was argued that it was in their interest now, not to reduce, but to raise the price as much as possible, as long as there were foreign competitors to purchase it. At the same time as demonstrated by Pamela Nightingale, it was the question of the monopoly of the pepper trade and the stiff economic competition offered by the French from Mahe that led to the annexation of Malabar in the first place (Nightingale 1970). Economic and imperial interests thus functioned hand in hand and it was a very small minority of staunch pseudo-imperialists who could put forward plans for expansion without listing corresponding economic advantages. There were, of course, some individuals like Charles Grant who argued that the joint prosperity of both Britain and India had to be the chief goal of imperial economic policy. However, in most cases, the imperial power was used to safeguard British interests rather than Indian ones.

It was argued that only under British rule could the Indians develop sufficient taste and achieve enough prosperity to buy British goods and so be a flourishing market for private trade. At the same time, immediate economic gains would not be possible if a large share of the profits were to be invested back in India itself and the shareholders demanded quick returns. Within this double bind, it is not surprising that while imperial rhetoric catered to the theme of India's economic resurgence, imperial policy often pursued British interests at the cost of injuries to the Indian economy. The end result was that the concept of India as a market for British goods was gradually shaded off into the picture of India as a source provider and the British interests were declared paramount. An appeal made by a British silk industry worker to maintain protection of British interests encapsulates this attitude:

> I certainly pity the East India labourer, but at the same time, I have a greater feeling for my own family. I think it is wrong to sacrifice the comforts of my own family for the sake of East India labourers because his condition happens to be worse than mine [sic]. (Qtd. Bearce 1961: 216)

Obviously such a paramount position of British interests could be maintained only if the British possessed the necessary political power to enforce it. Beneath the grand rhetoric of paternalist imperialism, the profit motif stands firmly entrenched. Though it is not possible to specifically attest cause and effect relations for each particular case, it is still necessary to regard commerce and Empire as symbiotic processes.

With regard to religion, two distinct strains of thought prevailed with regards to India in this early period of imperialism. The first trend was a Romantic idealization of India as a spiritual Utopia, the Promised Land. This motif has been thoroughly examined by John Drew in his *India and the Romantic Imagination.* Traces of this attitude can be seen in the philosophy of Coleridge and the work of certain Indologists. However later in life, Coleridge rejects his earlier fascination with Indian philosophy and even attacks it fiercely from the point of view of a committed Christian apologist. Even those Indologists, who spoke passionately about the glory of Indian culture, insisted on the supremacy of Christianity as the only "revealed" religion. However, a lofty idea of Indian philosophy did work on the Romantic imagination for a while, and not all authors labelled Indian thought as "monstrous" as Southey does in the Preface to his *Curse of Kehama.*

This attitude, however, did not have much influence on imperial policy or practice in India and is to be traced mainly in works of the imagination. The real struggle over religion was between the missionaries who wished to convert the "benighted" Indians and those imperialists who feared that missionary "interference" may disturb the smooth process of administration and trade. The major question debated was whether Christianity would help or hinder the process of imperial rule. The early missionaries received little encouragement from the Company, officials and on occasion were even actively discouraged. To counter this attitude, committed Evangelists like Grant and Wilberforce formulated arguments, which sought to prove that conversion would actually be beneficial to the Empire. Grant stated that "by planting our language our knowledge and our religion in our Asiatic territories, we shall put a great work beyond the reach of any contingencies, we shall probably have wedded the inhabitants of those territories to this country" (qtd. Bearce 1961: 62). Claudius Buchanan also argued that Christianity could strengthen the Empire because "there can never be confidence, freedom and affection between the people and their sovereigns where there exists a difference of religion" (qtd. Bearce 1961: 83). Just as Imperialism had to be justified by economic arguments, missionary work had to be justified through imperialistic arguments.

It was the missionary impulse which produced the darkest pictures of India. Wilberforce declared in 1813 that "our religion is sublime, pure and beneficent, theirs is mean, licentious and cruel" (qtd. Bearce 1961: 82). Most missionary travel accounts and records of the time indulge in gruesome descriptions of Indian religion, apparently on the principle that the worse these pictures appeared, the more zealous would be the support for Evangelical activity. However, even if we grant that a few missionaries were sincere in their desire to spread the gospel, it is evident that those who actually, politically governed India were not at this stage too concerned about the soul of the Indian. The "Nabob" was far more concerned with "oriental luxury" and with providing a reasonably strong administration; it was only much later that we have "Christian administrators" like those shown in W.D. Arnold's *Oakfield,* who agonize over the spiritual fate of both Indians and of Britons in India. It is safe to say that despite the many pious proclamations of deliverance through Christianity, the missionary impulse would not have been encouraged, if it had not proved that it was at least not actively opposed to imperialism.

The common purpose of the ideological stands so far discussed was the—preferably profitable—perpetuation of Empire. It now remains for us to see the implications of the presence of these ideologies in the discourse of Romanticism. On the one hand, Indological research and Conservative thought helped to propagate the notion of India as an idyllic, "natural" counterpoint to a corrupt and mechanical Europe. "Ancient India became a sort of Utopia for the Romantic Imagination." (Tharu and Lalitha 1991: 43). Shelley's *Alastor,* set in Kashmir, and Moore's *Lalla Rookh* furnish us with excellent examples of how India is seen as an idealized locale, an earthly version of Paradise and Eden. Raymond Schwab links imperial advancement and related the idealization with the overturning of individual bondage to rationality" which constructs the "Romantic Sublime."

> It was logically inevitable that a civilization believing itself unique would find itself drowned in the sum total of civilizations, just as personal boundaries would be swamped by over-flowing mobs and dislocations of the rational.[5] All this together was called Romanticism, and it produced through its many re-creations of the past, the present that propels us forward. (Schwab 1984: 16)

This idealized India, however, co-existed with a Gothic version well illustrated by Southey's *Curse of Kehama.* The origin of such grotesque and fearsome conceptions of India can be traced back to Utilitarian and Evangelical attempts to debunk Indian culture. James Mill, in his *History* bluntly states:

> No people, however, rude and ignorant whatsoever who have been so far advanced as to leave us memorials of their thoughts in writing have ever drawn a more gross and disgusting picture of the universe than what is presented in the writings of the Hindus. In their conception, no coherence, wisdom or beauty ever appears; all is disorder, corporal passion, violence and deformity. (1978: I 187)

The Gothic aspect of the Romantic imagination, with its fascination for the unknown, especially in its more outlandish versions avidly seized on this particular attitude towards representing India. We see in the Romantic paradigm a compromise being delicately maintained between the duality of an Edenic India inhabited by "noble savages" and an effectively thrilling horror chamber inhabited by unpredictable barbarians, who worshipped monstrous Gods. Individual accounts shade off from one perspective to the other without much concern for internal coherence—and ironically, perhaps this contributes to a kind of stability for the overall structure.

The images of India, finally delivered up by both Conservatism and Utilitarianism, as well as the conviction shared by both that imperialism should continue, were appropriated by Romanticism/ Gothicism and covered over with flashes of brilliant imagery, which enhanced the "effect." These aesthetic Romantic depictions of India, in turn, fed back into the ideological and administrative processes, and the cycle continued unbroken; hiding its inconsistencies through calculated silence or overpowering rhetoric.

NOTES

1. An interesting comment of Arrian's: "Nor do the Indians consider it any disgrace for a lady to grant her favours for an elephant, but it is regarded as a high compliment to the sex that their charms should be deemed worth an elephant" (1877: 222).
2. *The Roterio Viagem de Vasco Da Gama* is the only extant eyewitness account we have of Gama's visit to India. The authorship is attributed to a fellow sailor. The sailors mistake temples for churches (1998: 30), the perfidy of Arab rivals is referred to (32) and the Malabar people are described as untrustworthy and lazy" (34). [References taken from a Malayalam translation of the original. English translations mine.]
3. *The Anglo Saxon Chronicle* mentions Sigehelm, who is supposed to have been sent to India during the time of King Alfred. If true, this would make him the first British visitor to India, but we have no records like those left by Stephens. (1962: 73)
4. R.C. Banerjee has recorded twenty references to India in Shakespeare (1964: 67-75).
5. Goethe's lines:

   Would thou the young year's blossom, the fruits of its decline
   And all by which the soul is charmed, enraptured, feasted, fed?
   Would thou the earth and heaven itself in one sole name combine?
   I name thee, Shakuntala, and all at once is said! (1964: 168)

   exemplify the sheer power and charge this discovery of the East had.

Chapter 3

Reluctant Fathers: Conservatives and Orientalists

If we are not able to contrive some method of governing India well which will not of necessity become the means of governing Great Britain ill, a ground is laid for their eternal separation, but none for sacrificing the people of that country to our constitution.

Edmund Burke

This statement made by Burke, before the Parliament in 1783, was perhaps the closest Britons had come in that century to at least a consideration of relinquishing Empire as a solution to the problems caused by imperial expansion. In 1775, speaking with regard to the American colonies, Burke himself had remarked that one of the alternatives suggested had been that of "giving up the colonies, but it met so slight a reception that I do not think myself obliged to dwell a great while upon it." Even though the Indian and the American contexts were widely separated, much must still have happened between 1775 and 1783 to render possible a public statement that there *were* circumstances under which the giving up of imperial domination could be a practical possibility. It is of course true that Burke's main concern here is with the fear that the Indian connection may lead to Britain being governed ill—the fear of "Nabobism." However, it is worth noting that, generally speaking, nearly all British commentators on India of this period—Indologists or Anglicists, Conservatives or Utilitarians—usually concurred on the perpetuity, or at least the very long life of Empire. Even later writers like Macaulay who took the possible ending of Empire into consideration set that event in the dim and distant future. Under these circumstances, Burke's assumption that "governing well" was a necessary part of the right to govern, without which Empire ought not to be continued and that Indians should not be "sacrificed" to the British Constitution attains considerable significance. His very use of the term "sacrificed" instead of "salvaged" or "saved" marks a perspective, which however tentatively, took the Indian side of affairs into consideration.

The notion of abandoning Empire however is somewhat of an exception in Burke's discourse, let alone in the Conservative policy as a whole. Indeed, Burke qualifies his assertion immediately with the statement: "I am, however, far from being persuaded that any such incompatibility of interest does in fact exist. On the contrary, I am certain that every means effectual to preserve India from oppression is a guard to preserve the British Constitution from its worst corruption" (Burke 1963: 369). However, it is valid to keep the fact that such a concept—giving up of Empire—had been tentatively articulated by an arch Conservative at the background of an analysis of the Conservative and Indological discourse on India.

In this chapter, the "Indian" writings of Edmund Burke and of the noted Indologist Sir William Jones are examined in some detail. References are also made to certain statements of Warren Hastings—official patron of early Indological studies and also target of Burke's vehement accusations of despotism and corruption—and to some other Indologists whose works were published in the *Asiatic Researches*. Emphasis is laid on the fact that just as many Utilitarian reformers and Evangelists failed in maintaining logical coherence in their vituperations on India, the Conservatives and Indologists who avowedly eulogized Ancient India while supporting Empire could not erect a flawless rhetorical edifice either. By the very nature of their overtly "pro-Indian" stand, the gaps perceived in this discourse are mostly of a nature that could simplistically be referred to as "anti-Indian." More important than the nature of these contradictions is the fact that they internally fragment Conservative/Indological discourse. But though rendered vulnerable to easy *rhetorical* deconstruction the discourse retains its potential for pragmatic application and *practical* success.

A

Edmund Burke is today regarded as one of the most important patriarchs of modern Conservatism. Anthony Quinton indicates his importance with the remark that one can define "the Conservativeness of a position in terms of its closeness to the convictions of Burke" (qtd. Carnall 1989: 76). The fact that Burke functioned as the very embodiment of Conservative philosophy is quite significant from the perspective of his deep involvement in Indian affairs also. Respect for tradition, and a conviction that—as Burke puts it in *Reflections on the Revolution in France*—"in what we improve, we are never wholly new" (Burke 1963: 439) were hallmarks of the Conservative tradition. The Conservatives therefore, supported by Indological research, strenuously opposed the Anglicization of India. Conservative suspicion of rootless innovation as such was a strong factor in Burke's demand for the preservation of Indian institutions. "I feel an insuperable reluctance in giving my hand to destroy any established institution of government upon a theory, however plausible it may be" (Burke 1963: 372). Once Indological research had demonstrated that India *did* have traditions worth considering, the Conservatives were at hand to argue that these traditions should not be swept aside.

In relation to Indian affairs, Burke is chiefly remembered as the most ardent prosecutor in the impeachment of the Governor-General Warren Hastings. The valourization of this particular role is understandable when we consider that more than three quarters of Burke's writings on India consist of speeches made during the impeachment. However, Burke's relation with India cannot be confined to just the impeachment. The *Ninth Report on the Affairs of India* presented before the British parliament in 1783 was written by Burke, and in it he strongly advocated reform of the East India Company's government of its Indian territories. Most of the 1783 East India Bill, which sought to regulate the affairs of the Company was authored by Burke and he defended it in a famous speech in the House of Commons on December 1, 1783.

Rather ironically, Burke's initial involvement with India was seen in attitudes favourable to the East India Company. In 1767 and 1773, he defended the Company from ministerial supervision. Indeed, he was thought of as so well disposed to the Company that an offer was made to him to be Chairman of a committee of supervisors appointed by the Company to go out to India and reorganize the administration. Ultimately Burke rejected this offer, but it is still significant to note that he figured among the number of prominent figures who were offered or solicited Indian Employment. Closer examination of Indian affairs led Burke in 1783 to conclude that there were great abuses in the Company's administration of India. From this period he urged Parliamentary control more vehemently than he had ever opposed ministerial supervision, maintaining his stand even against initial accusations of opportunism and inconsistency.

In the *Ninth Report* (June 25, 1783) itself, Burke flatly stated that the East India Company had followed "principles of policy and courses of conduct by which the natives of all ranks and orders were reduced to a state of depression and misery" (1963: 341). He was firmly against Anglicization and condemned all attempts to "administer justice in the remotest part of Hindostan as if it was a province of Great Britain" (1963: 346). Even in purely pragmatic terms, he insists that "the prosperity of the natives must be previously secured, before any profit whatsoever from them is attempted" (1963: 355).

While defending the 1783 East India Bill, Burke speaks in detail of the responsibility entailed by Empire. This doctrine as expounded by the Conservative Burke is both similar to and different from the "civilizing mission" of imperialism as spread by the Reformers and the Evangelists. The similarities between these attitudes will be considered in due course, the present emphasis is on the differences they displayed.

Burke did urge reform most zealously, but it was reform of the British system that he demanded, not of Indian entities. India, he argued, was already civilized:

> This multitude of men does not consist of an abject and barbarous populace; much less of gangs of savages. . . . But of a people for ages civilized and cultivated—cultivated by all the arts of polished life while we were yet in the woods. (Burke 1963: 374)

This is Burke's fullest articulation of the theme of a pre-colonially civilized India, to which he returns again and again during the course of his impeachment speeches. In governing such a nation, the first care of the British should be, Burke argued, not to overthrow, but to preserve the existing institutions and the second to tactfully employ the instruments made available readymade to their hands by Indian tradition.

Even among the Conservatives who argued for Indian culture and the continuance of Indian institutions, Burke was regarded as somewhat singular for his personal sympathy towards Indians. Will Burke, Edmund Burke's cousin who had held office in India, found Burke's Indian sympathies quite incomprehensible. He wrote to Burke's son that he could not "for the soul of me, feel as Edmund does about the Black primates" (qtd. Carnall 1989: 64). Burke himself was only too aware that such attitudes were unfortunately widespread among his contemporaries. One of his constant complaints was with regard to the lack of sympathy of the British public for the Indian natives. He draws analogies of India with certain European situations in the hope that "India might be approximated in order to awaken something of sympathy for the unfortunate natives, of which I am afraid we are not perfectly susceptible whilst we look at this very remote object through a false and cloudy medium" (Burke 1963: 375).

Burke seems to have felt that he was standing as a defender of humanism against what he saw as the prevailing tide of a subtle racism. He vehemently asserts in a letter that he has "no party in the business [the impeachment] but among a set of people who have none of your roses and lilies in their faces, but who are the images of the great pattern as you and I. I know what I am doing, whether the white people like it or not" (qtd. Carnall 1989: 64). However, under the effect of Burke's comparatively liberal rhetoric, we should not lose sight of the fact that *if well carried out,* he considered paternalistic imperialism not only as justified, but also as desirable.

In his opening speech during the impeachment, Burke takes the concept of Britain's paternalistic responsibility to her Indian subjects as the keynote. Earlier on, in his defence of the East India Bill, Burke had already stated, "it is our protection that destroys India" (1963: 376). He accused England of abdicating her responsibilities in India:

> Every other conqueror of every other description has left some monument either of state or of beneficence behind him. Were we to be driven out of India today, nothing would remain to tell that it had been possessed during the inglorious period of our domination by anything better than the orang-outang or the tiger. (1963: 377)

Amidst any amount of rhetoric Burke still makes the commercial basis of Britain's imperial enterprise very clear. He refers to the East India Company as "a state in the guise of a merchant" (1963: 394)—notably, not the other way around. In the *Ninth Report,* he had gone so far as to state: "If it can be proved that the Company have acted wisely, prudently and frugally as merchants, I shall pass by the whole mass of their enormities as statesmen" (1963: 380). He proceeds to demonstrate at length that not even as merchants have the East India Company acted in a successful or commendable fashion.

Very importantly, Burke also firmly opposes the concept of Oriental despotism, on which much of Hastings' defence was based and which indeed had sustained many past and future appropriations of India:

> He [Hastings] pleads that he did govern on arbitrary and despotic, and as he supposes, Oriental principles, he lays it down as a rule that despotism is the genuine constitution of India. But nothing is more false than that despotism is the real constitution of any country in Asia. . . . It is certainly not true of any Mohammedan constitution. . . . That the people of Asia have no laws, rights or liberty is a doctrine that wickedly is sought to be here disseminated through this country. But I again assert that every Mohammedan government is by its principles a government of law. (1963: 396-99)

This was a proposition of singular importance, considering that one of the most fixed stereotypes with regard to the East was that of Oriental Despotism. Indological studies join hands with Conservatism here, as Burke refers to his personal study of the Koran and texts of Mohammedan jurisprudence (translated by Indologist scholars) as the basis for his arguments. Burke opposes this knowledge as a corrective to Hastings' "man on-the-spot" arguments.

After he has disproved, to his own satisfaction, the truth-value claims of a theory of Oriental despotism, Burke proceeds to make his pleas for India, based on a concept of universal, "natural" laws, principles and values. An inherent invalidity of arbitrary power and the fundamental nature of value-based laws were the cardinal tenets of Burke's argument. In general and all-encompassing terms, he asserts that Hastings' claims to arbitrary power were null and void. From this perspective, Burke also takes strong exception to what he describes as Hastings' concept of "geographical morality." The defence for Hastings had indicated that actions in Asia do not always bear the same meanings that they would bear in Europe. Burke repudiates this argument forcefully:

> My Lords, we positively deny that principle. . . . The laws of morality are the same everywhere and there is no action . . . of extortion, of peculation, of bribery and of oppression in England, that it is not an act of bribery, extortion, peculation and oppression in Europe, Asia, Africa and all the world over. (1963: 395-96)

Burke insists upon the achievements of Indian Culture and the significance of the laws they had codified at a time when Britons were unlettered and uncivilized. He shows the courage of his convictions by declaring that far from being "inferior beings" the Indians were as much, if not more, sensitive, refined, as worthy of respect, as the English gentry. He proceeds to illustrate this comparison by asserting that the "situation in which an English citizen of Mr. Hastings' description should domineer over the vizier of the Mughal Emperor and give the law to the first persons in his dominions" was as unthinkable as "the Lords of England having their property seized by a delegate from Lucknow and their pedigree being tried by any court of Adawlet in Hindostan" (1963: 413).

Such a comparison between Indian and British gentry, institutions and customs, which insisted on their essential equality, is indeed commendable. If on occasion, Burke *does* refer to the "native rabble," we should perhaps place more emphasis on the second word and regard it as but a further extension of his Conservatism, which insisted on traditional rights and entrenched privileges. At least towards a native elite, towards the "better class" of natives, Burke was liberally disposed in his avowed stance. He deserves full credit for openly asserting that Indians were not to be treated as some strange species, but were equal members of the human race with undeniable rights and privileges.

Such then is the generally accepted picture of Burke in relation to Indian affairs—the Conservative defender of established traditions, the liberal humanist spokesman of the rights of a racial Other and the staunch opponent of corruption and oppression. There is a great deal of factual evidence for this picture, but it is not a complete portrayal, nor does it tell the whole truth. Several aspects of Burke's (admittedly powerful) rhetoric have been overlooked or bypassed in constructing such a portrait. Nor do these aspects belong to a class that demands a great deal of textual excavation to be brought out. They exist side by side with Burke's well-known and oft-quoted statements, within the same speeches and writings. If we regard the generally accepted version of Burke's discourse as a coherent text, these aspects appear as the gaps in that text—and ironically they provide the space required for the rhetorical maneuvering needed to make the overt portrayal practicable.

Primarily, these "gaps" consist of certain essentialisations of India and Indians, which certainly merit the appellation of ethnocentric if not racist. They are all the more significant inasmuch as they are allowed to enter the discourse, even though their effect on a surface level is to reduce the force and validity of the central argument. Of secondary importance is a certain "Anxiety of Empire" (to borrow Nigel Leask's phrase) in Burke, a fear that the Indian connection would shatter the fabric of British society. This aspect is here examined first, before the more complex area of Burke's stereotyping of India is analyzed.

In many parts of Burke's writings, we can trace manifestations of a fear that corruption, disease and "filth" (all somehow associated with India) would be let loose on Britain's shores resulting in anarchy and chaos. As an ardent Conservative, nothing could be more repugnant to Burke than the idea of the corrupt *noveau riche* Englishmen from India eroding the traditional foundations of British society. This fear of empire in Burke has of course been noticed and studied before. What has not been much considered is the way in which a slippage in Burke's discourse laid the responsibility of India-related British corruption not on the corrupt officials but on India itself—a classic instance of blaming the victim.

In his "Second Letter to Sir Hercules Languishe on the Catholic Question," Burke lists out the principles of Protestant Ascendancy in Ireland, Jacobinism being the worst (qtd. Carnall 1989: 58). In another letter written a year later, Indianism had advanced up the scale of infamy and replaced Jacobinism as the greatest evil. "Our government and our laws are beset by two different enemies which are sapping its foundations—Indianism and Jacobinism. Of these, I am sure, that the first is the hardest to deal with and the worst by far" (qtd. Carnall 1989: 59). By "Indianism" Burke obviously meant a corrupt and oppressive system of government in India, with Warren Hastings as the presiding evil genius and which was in imminent danger of spilling over into the sacred precincts of the British metropolis.

Interestingly, apart from a few central characters—of whom, Hastings was the prime example for Burke—who were inherently corrupt, Burke regarded the British administrators of India as more ignorant than evil intentioned.[1] Significantly jeopardizing his own case against Hastings, Burke fervently argued that there was inborn corruption in India among the natives which automatically corrupted young and inexperienced administrators sent from Britain:

> The banyan extorts, robs, plunders and then gives him [the British administrator) just what share of the spoil he pleases to . . . while we are here boasting of the British power in the East, we are in perhaps more than half our service nothing but the inferior, miserable instruments of the tyranny which the lowest part of the natives of India exercise. (1987: 134)

This note of "inscrutable Orientals" cleverly manipulating unsuspecting and well-intentioned British officers for their own ends has been sounded in fiction often enough. But Burke here presents it as fact—the vivid description given by Burke of the blandishments of a Debi Singh whom Hastings was accused of favouring could have fitted perfectly into an Evangelical script intended to whip up missionary fervour against India. Debi Singh is described as the "great magician" who entices his British employers with the "torpid blandishments of Asia" and watches his chance to carry "points of shameful enormity" with the "duped young men, rather careless and inexperienced than intentionally corrupt" (Burke 1987: I 178).

Many of those who heard Burke may have wondered what exactly Hastings was being accused of, when the natives themselves were so irredeemably corrupt and vicious. These inconsistencies may be explained away as rhetorical necessities, perhaps. That is, Burke extols Indians when he needs to condemn Hastings and degrades them when the intention is to condemn Hastings' native allies. But the overwhelming fear that the administration of India could prove self-destructive for Britain points to a dread in Burke of India itself as a terrifying and unknown entity, the Other, in fact, with which Britain was not equipped to cope.

In a lengthy passage, Burke sets forth his fear that the foundations of Britain's polity and society, indeed the very fibre of national character itself would end up being destroyed because of her Indian connection. At this point, India is *not* regarded sympathetically as a country that had to be protected as she was suffering the excesses of a corrupt administration, but as an active principle that in itself was the root cause of the corruption. The prosecution of Hastings is referred to as "a great censorial prosecution for the purpose of preserving the manners, characteristics and virtues of the people of England" (1987: I 448). The British people, says Burke, are in danger of giving up their characteristic virtues to "become a nation of liars, concealers, forgers and dissemblers, in one word, a people of Banyans" [sic] (1987: I 449). This paranoia reaches its apotheosis when he claims: "Today, the Commons of Great Britain prosecute the delinquents of India. Tomorrow, the delinquents of India may be the Commons of Great Britain" (1987: I 450). Of course, a Conservative Burke has nothing bad to say about the Aristocracy, Indian or British. But his comments on the "Banias" and the "rabble" are scathing indeed. Burke's professed empathy for the Indians becomes very suspect when we consider the fact that his worst fear was that Britons might turn into a "people of Banyans." Surely it is not possible to display such ill concealed contempt for a people while totally subscribing to the rhetorical eulogies and sympathy simultaneously bestowed on them.

It now remains to examine certain fundamentally prejudiced generalizations of India and Indians that make their appearance in Burke's rhetoric on a reasonably regular basis. Burke attributes the fact that Indian accomplices are less easily detected than white men to this reason: "The Banyan escapes in the night of his complexion" (1987: 1 36). The Hindus are referred to as "the aboriginal people of India who are the softest in their manners of any of the human race, approaching almost to feminine tenderness . . . these people are of all nations the most unalliable [sic] to any other part of mankind" (1987: I 43). The dark, feminine and unsociable Hindu is one of the most enduring stereotypes of Orientalism, and Burke's avowed liberality does not function as enough reason to gloss over the fact that he did subscribe to the stereotype.

Burke's long dissection of the "essential character of any Hindu Banyan" is astonishing in its all-encompassing sweep. It can be compared with, in fact even identified with Macaulay's racist sneer at Hindus in general and Bengalis in particular. It is surprising that such an accomplished orator as Burke did not realize the weakening effect such damaging descriptions could have on his own case against Hastings. The description:

> My Lords, a Gentoo Banyan is a little lower, a little more penurious, a little more exacting; a little more cunning and a little more money making than a Jew. . . . There is not a Jew that is so crafty, so much an usurer, so skilful to turn money to profit and so resolved not to give any money but for a profit as a Gentoo broker of the class I have mentioned. (1987: II 393)

The Jew and the "Gentoo" are placed firmly within the pigeon holes created for them and there is no display of relativism or even tolerance to alleviate this effect.

Burke also enforces the concept of the never-ending, never-changing tenacity of ancient India. "The Indians held on in an uniform tenor for a duration commensurate to all the empires with which history has made us acquainted, and they still exist in a green old age, with all the reverence of antiquity and with all the passion they have against novelty and change" (Burke 1987: II 47). It is particularly self-defeating to argue for the unchanging and *unchangeable* nature of India, when the whole of one's argument is built up around the proposal that devastating changes have been brought about there. This is in fact an excellent illustration of the *historicizing* and also *simultaneously naturalizing* paradox on which the Orientalist archive seems to have precariously balanced itself.

In the course of Burke's eloquence, distinctions are pointed out between the "essential" natures of "white men" and "natives." It must be recorded to Burke's credit that his essentializations of his countrymen are by no means totally approving. However, that still does not validate statements on human nature couched in absolute terms, which admit of no exceptions:

> The white men are loose and licentious; they are apt to have resentments and to be bold in revenging them. The black men are very secret and mysterious; they are not apt to have very quick resentments, they have not the same liberty and boldness of Europeans and they have fears too for themselves. (1987: I 35)

This statement serves to establish the Britons and the Indians almost as polar opposites by nature, a situation that renders even understanding well nigh impossible. Even more startling is it to see Burke endorsing in advance the view Kipling was later to formulate about the meeting of the races. After all his pleading for equal and dignified treatment for the Indians, it is unexpected to find Burke suddenly asserting, with great eloquence that "never the twain shall meet." He does not envisage, at this point even the exception provided by Kipling, or a benevolent ruler-ruled relationship or the tentative fellowship proposed by E.M. Forster, but insists that the *only* possible relation between these races was one based on money and money alone:

> I do not suppose either generosity, friendship or even communication can exist between white men and black; no, their colours are not more averse than their characters and tempers. . . . *It is a money dealing and a money dealing only that can exist between them*. . . . There is no friendship between these people, when black men give money to a white man, it is a bribe and when money is given to a black man, he is only a sharer in infamous profits. (1987: II 430, my italics)

Burke envisages a situation where friendship or fellowships are myths; and the racial gulf unbridgeable. He stands revealed as implicated in the "imperfect sympathy" he accuses the administrators of displaying towards India. Indeed, what understanding—except perhaps that of rhetoric or of so-called "objective" treatises—is possible in relation to a people, with whom, despite a shared humanity, fellowship is not just difficult, but insistently impossible?

During the later speeches of the impeachment, Burke moves very far away from his early declaration that there were conditions under which a cessation of Empire should be contemplated. At this stage Burke clearly asserts the political principle of long possession conferring legitimacy. "There is a sacred veil to be drawn around the beginnings of all governments. Ours in India had an origin like those which time has sanctified by obscurity" (1987: II 60). We have indeed come full circle here; the imperial mission now has the legitimacy to continue.

It has been indicated in the previous chapter that in the final analysis, different strands of ideologies combined together to ensure that the Empire could continue. The emphasis here is not on the fact that the Conservative doctrine also contributed to Empire—that is now accepted without much contradiction. The aspect foregrounded is the internal inconsistency between what subscribers to the ideology—here represented by Burke—avowed that they were saying and what they actually said. And these inconsistencies, with hindsight show us a rhetorical weakening—albeit a paradoxical one, as at the moment of use, they made the rhetoric possible.

The discourse of Conservatism in its fractured form may resemble Utilitarian or Reformist principles to some extent. But, as will be shown in the following chapter, the discourse of Utilitarianism itself was not free from these inconsistencies. The question therefore is not so much that of a resemblance or divergence between the various discourses, as that whether the separate strands were able to maintain logical coherence within themselves, and remain at least rhetorically moored to their acknowledged basic principles. As far as the case of philosophical Conservatism—represented by Burke, as related to India—is conceived, we may conclude that its tenets were more often than not self-contradictory and even mutually exclusive. What we see in Burke's speeches is an extremely complicated attempt to balance the conservative principle of respect for tradition anywhere, with tacit support for the imperial project and a covert conviction of European—at least of all "good" Europeans'—superiority. Of course, this intellectual balancing was very necessary—pure conservatism could not support empire and pure mercenary colonialism could not attack corruption. A perfect example of logical inconsistency, even incongruity, functioning for an emotional and practical advantage is to be seen at this juncture.

It remains to be seen if the discourse of Indological scholarship—which was one of the staunchest allies of Conservatism—was any more logical in its stances. The next section of this chapter examines this area, with special emphasis on the works of Sir William Jones—probably the Indologist par excellence.

References are also made to other well-known contemporary Indologists—Charles Wilkins, H.T. Colebroke and H.H. Wilson, as well as to "missionary Orientalists" like William Ward and Carey. The focus will be on how the Indologist discourse, obviously intended to know more about India, and if possible to improve its image, despite some success in these areas, in a way dug its own grave by narrowing the bounds of its subject and subjected itself to render service for the cause of Imperialism. Though the avowed link of most Indology was with Conservatism, it can be seen that Reformism and Utilitarianism were able to trace the gaps in its rhetoric and to co-opt these to their own purposes. None of this is intended to detract from the Herculean labour or immense scholarship of many Indologists. But as Jones himself admits, "pure" scholarship (supposing that chimera to possess a fleeting existence) was impossible "among Europeans resident in India, where every individual is a man of business in the civil or military state" (*Asiatic Researches*: I i) (from now on referred to as *AR* in parenthetical references).

B

It is my ambition to know India better than any other European ever knew it.

Sir William Jones

Born on 28 September 1746, William Jones had exhibited signs of an extraordinary capacity for linguistic and literary activity from an early age. At fifteen, he had published poems in Greek and he translated the Persian poet Hafiz into English verse at sixteen. In 1768, he translated the Persian *History of Nadirshah* and produced a Persian Grammar in 1771. Before he left England for India in 1783, Jones was already proficient in Arabic, Hebrew and Persian; he was "also a poet, a jurist, a polyhistor, a classicist and an indefatigable scholar" (Said 1978: 77).

The rise of Jones' fame as a linguist and Orientalist coincided with the extension of the East India Company's commercial activities in India into political and administrative ones. Jones, a lawyer by profession, represented an ideal combination of the legal expertise and linguistic competence required to cope with the increasing complexities of Indian administration. Not surprisingly, he was offered a judgeship, in India and accepting it, arrived in Bengal in 1783.

There can be no doubt that Jones looked forward with a scholar's keen interest to his tenure in India. His memorandum entitled "The Objects of Enquiry during my Residence in Asia" (Jones 1976: I 97) consisting of sixteen items with regard to practically every branch of knowledge is a sufficient indication of this. However, we are not to suppose that a quixotic idealism bereft of practical considerations led Jones to India. Indeed he avows quite candidly that he must be "twenty years in England before I can save as much as in India, I might easily in five or six" (*Ibid.* 33). An assessment of Jones' complex motives, ranging from the desire for knowledge, altruism and that for profit can be fairly constructed based on his letter (March 17, 1782) to Burke, where he expresses his eagerness to go to India, to mitigate the misery of Indians, to purchase oriental books and manuscripts and to earn enough to live independently in England (*Ibid.* 45).

The period when Jones arrived in India was remarkably appropriate for the evolution of Indological studies into a vigorous academic discipline. Raymond Schwab remarks, "the decisive period in Indian studies began with the arrival of English civil servants in Calcutta around 1780, who, supported by the Governor Warren Hastings began an extraordinary undertaking" (1984: 33). The demands of administration required a heightened awareness of India, the Governor was firmly traditionalist and opposed to Anglicization and the Civil service included erudite linguists and scholars like Wilkins and Colebrooke. The stage was set for the crystallization of individual discourses on India into an academic field. "Fact finding teams were now encouraged, which could provide conclusive results more quickly, than individual efforts, however talented" (*Ibid.*). An initial step in this direction was taken with the Organization of the Asiatic Society in Bengal on January 15, 1784. Jones was the moving and sustaining spirit behind this undertaking, for which reason, and for his numerous individual research contributions, he has been called the "Father of Indology."

As it was resolved to conduct the Asiatic Society on the pattern of the Royal Society at London, of which the King was patron, the Governor-General Hastings and his Councillors were formally requested to accept the role of patrons. A favourable answer was returned in due course.

It is interesting to note the connections Jones, the founder of the Society had with both Hastings and Hastings' chief accuser, Burke. As Hastings "seemed, in his private station the first liberal promoter of useful knowledge in Bengal, and especially in Persian and Sanskrit literature" (AR: I v), he was requested to accept the title of President of the Asiatic Society. Hastings declined in a letter where he acknowledged the offer as an honour conferred on him. He also recommended Jones as the best President, as "the Gentleman whose genius formed the institution and is most capable of conducting it to the attainment of the great and splendid functions of the foundation" (*Ibid.* vi). In addition to these initial contacts, Hastings maintained a close relationship with the Society, and with Indological studies, by sending interesting information when it came his way and by writing the Preface for Wilkins' translation of the *Bhagavat Geetha* [sic].

With Burke, Jones had maintained a friendly relationship in England and Burke had assisted Jones in his thwarted attempt to enter Parliament. Even before he had set foot in India, Jones was recognized as a high authority on that country and Burke inviting him to discuss the Bengal Bill, wrote in 1782: "The natives of the East, to whose literature you have done so much justice are particularly under your protection for their rights" (qtd. Mukherjee 1987: 45). As far as an interest in the traditions of India and their preservation are concerned we are able to trace similarities between Burke and Hastings—though Hastings was the better informed and Burke the more passionate.

In the first four volumes of the *Asiatic Researches* (the official organ of the Asiatic Society, which started publication in 1788) the vast majority of articles consist of Jones' famous Anniversary Discourses and other essays. The widely varying interest indicated by the topics considered in these works show the extreme catholicity of Jones' taste. As Schwab remarks: "Jones was interested in everything, uncovering and compiling information in many fields; Indian chronology, literature, music, fauna and flora. He discovered and guided others to the summits of poetry and philosophy, though the study of local law alone seemed to him entirely serious" (1984: 36).

In his "Preliminary Discourse" delivered to the Society, Jones expressed his great delight in finding himself among so vast an *unexplored* field as "Asia, which has ever been esteemed the nurse of sciences, the inventress of delightful and useful arts, the scene of glorious actions, fertile in the productions of human genius, abounding in natural wonders and infinitely diversified in the forms of religion and government in the laws, manners, customs and languages as well as in the features and complexions of men" (*AR*: I vi). The scholar's eagerness and curiosity to launch into this unexplored field and acquire knowledge is almost palpable. The question of whether "any number of learned natives are to be enrolled as members of the Society" is raised in this issue, but is left to be resolved after further discussions. After these introductory remarks, the discourse is concerned with the orthography of Asian words. Jones evolves a system for transliterating Sanskrit characters that has not fallen into disuse even today. In the "Second Anniversary Discourse" (*AR*: I 335-42) Asia is presented as a handmaid to a sovereign Europe, but it is nonetheless stressed that Asiatics should not be condemned, "from whose researches into nature, works of art and inventions of fancy, many valuable hints may be derived for our own improvement and also advantage" (*Ibid*. 336). A general survey of Indian literature and Indian progress in the various sciences is undertaken in this discourse.

The "Third Anniversary Discourse," titled "On the Hindus" and the next few discourses deal with different people of Asia—the Hindus, the Chinese, Arabs and Tartars etc. For present purposes (in relation to India) the discourse on the Hindus is the most significant. Here, Jones pays a compliment to the structure of the Sanskrit language: "The Sanskrit, whatever be its antiquity, is of a wonderful structure, more perfect than the Greek, more copious than the Latin and more exquisitely refined than either, yet . . . no philologist could examine them all three without believing them to have sprung from some common source, which perhaps no longer exists" (*Ibid.* 349).

This interest in establishing "common sources" is a primary concern of Jones. This will be examined later in greater detail. He also puts forward the argument that the Hindus were from early ages a "commercial people" no matter how sedentary they appear at the present moment, and also quotes Greek writers to the effect that the "Indians were the wisest of nations" (*Ibid.* 353).

Three "inventions"—"the method of instructing through apologues, the decimal scale and the game of chess"—are specifically laid to the Hindus' credit and Hindu literature is also commended, with "their lighter poems" being "lively and elegant, their epics, magnificent and sublime in the extreme" (*Ibid.* 354). The general conclusion drawn is that "nor can we reasonably doubt how degenerate and abased so ever the Hindus may now appear, that in some early age they were splendid in arts and arms, happy in government, wise in legislation and eminent in various knowledges" (*Ibid.* 347). Much more remains to be said about this positing of a "Golden Age" but at present, it is sufficient to remark that such a concession was made to the now "abased Hindu."

The Eleventh (and final) Anniversary Discourse (*AR*: IV 151-57) deals with "The Philosophy of the Asiatics." Here Jones remarks that more of a successful research than expected could be carried out in fragments of ancient Indian literature. He also expresses a hope that Hindu philosophy may be made available through accepted translations since "one correct version of any celebrated Hindu work would be of greater value than all the dissertations or essays that could be composed on the same subject" (*Ibid.* 154). Jones discusses the doctrine of the Vedanta on the existence of matter and asserts that as a system based on purest devotion, "nothing could be further removed from impiety" (*Ibid.* 155). He adds that many of the moral principles found in the Gospels can be found in the Hindu scriptures also, and that even part of the Newtonian concepts can be found in the Vedas and the Sufi texts. The expression in Indian scriptures of an all-powerful spirit, which is addressed in "pious and sublime terms," is commended heartily through parallels with Western doctrines.

Apart from the Anniversary Discourses, Jones also published in the *Asiatic Researches* essays, among others on Indian chronology, Gods, music, plants and mystical poetry. In the essay entitled "On the Gods of Greece, Italy and India," an attempt is made to draw parallels between deities worshipped in all three countries. Jones delves deep into mythology and fable to identify the members of the pantheons with each other, mainly based on similarity of names (sometimes forced) and one primary attribute in each case. He provides eloquent descriptions of Hindu divinities that were to have considerable circulation among his contemporary Romantic poets; Shelley and Southey being prime examples. While advancing parallels between the Gods, Jones leaves the question of influence undecided: "which was the original system and which the copy, I will not presume to decide . . . neither the Asiatic nor the European system has any simplicity and both are so complex, not to say absurd; however, internalized with the beautiful and the sublime, that the honour, such as it is, of the invention cannot be allotted to either with tolerable certainty" (*AR*: I 229).

The Indian zodiac is credited with original development as not borrowed either from the Arabs or the Greeks (*AR*: II 228). The Hindu musical modes are analyzed in detail in an essay that attempts a comparison between the tonal systems of Indian and Western music (*AR*: III 55-93). Jones' somewhat bowdlerized translation of the *Gita Govinda* is appended to an essay on the "Mystical Poetry of the Persians and the Hindus" (*Ibid.* 165).

Apart from these works published in the *Asiatic Researches*, Jones' translation of Kalidasa's *Shakuntala* (*Sacontala* in Jones' version) and the *Manu Smriti* are of primary significance. The translation of *Shakuntala* was published in 1789 and was reprinted five times between 1790 and 1807, while the *Laws of Manu* (also known as *The Institutes of Hindu Law)* was posthumously published in 1794 and was reprinted several times in London and Calcutta. Jones primarily considered himself as a legislator and he intended the translation of Manu to be his most important work. This work was a prominent landmark in the legal administration of British India. It made it clear to the West that Indians did have a code of law, which to some extent gave the lie to the absolutist theories of Oriental Despotism then being circulated. However, the work was not used as much as Jones had hoped and most practical significance it might have had was soon swept away in the rising tide of Anglicization.

The effect of the *Shakuntala* was much more dramatic. Schwab refers to a 'Shakuntala era' (1984: 37) in the whole of Europe, especially in Germany following Georg Forster's immensely popular translation of Jones' work. It is interesting to note that (unlike Hastings in his preface to Wilkins's *Geetha*[2] Jones does not indulge in any special pleading for Indian literature. He admits in his Preface that his judgment was based on personal taste; but refers to Kalidasa as the "Shakespeare" of India and feels that the play can stand up to a judgment based on individual and intrinsic merit (1976: XII 369). Jones obviously appreciated the literary merit of the *Shakuntala* but also commended its "decorum" which he sees as the result of a highly complex and well-developed civilization:

> Whatever the age when drama was first introduced in India, it was carried to great perfection in the first century before Christ when Vikramaditya gave his encouragement to poets, philosophers and mathematicians at a time when Britons were unlettered and unpolished as the army of Hanumant. [sic] (1976: XII 368)

As has been noted earlier, this concept of a highly civilized India flourishing in its Golden Age when Britain was "yet in the woods" was introduced to great effect by Burke also. Schwab refers to the "double effect" of *Shakuntala,* whereby "Europe, thirsty for a golden age could fabricate the notion of a primitive India" and at the same time "the eighteenth century, with its fantastic taste for taste" could be sufficiently reassured by the classical graces of the *Shakuntala* (1984: 59-60).

The other works of Jones, which deserve mention from an Indian perspective, include his early poems "The Palace of Fortune" (the framework of which is clearly reflected in Shelley's *Queen Mab)* which is set in Tibet and has references to India. Jones also translated an *Upanishad* (the *Isavasyam*), Kalidasa's descriptive poem *Ritusamhara* (translated as "The Seasons") and wrote a story poem "The Enchanted Fruit" based on an episode from the *Mahabharata*.

Also significant are Jones' "Charges to the Grand Jury of Calcutta" (6 in all) in his professional capacity as a Judge. In these, Jones usually expresses the idea that the Indians were to be ruled by their own laws; administered of course by British officials. "The British subjects should be governed by British laws and the natives indulged in their own prejudices," (1976: VIII 19) he says, and later on states that Britain is obliged to give the natives "personal security and every reasonable indulgence to their harmless prejudices, conciliate their affection and promote their industry so as to render our dominion over them a national benefit" (1976: VII 21).

Finally, special mention needs to be made of Jones' *Hindu Hymns* addressed to several Hindu deities, which make use of Indian terms, settings, myths and even philosophy. According to John Drew, it was a concern not just with Indian imagery, but also with the mystical philosophy, which pervades that imagery which encouraged Jones to write his Hymns to the Indian deities (Drew 1987: 55). It is possible that Jones did not finally regard himself as a poet and would be critical of attempts to regard his poetical output as among his significant contribution to Indology. His biographer, Lord Teigmnouth, testifies to this when he quotes Jones to the effect: "The Hymns on the Hindu mythology, the translated poems and even the highly influential *Shakuntala* were considered as the lighter productions, elegant amusements of his leisure hours, of which it would be unbecoming to speak in a style of importance which he himself did not attach to them" (Jones 1976: x). However, as Schwab points out, Jones was as famous in England for his original poetry as for his introduction of India" (Schwab 1976: 195). Contemporary poets read him both as a poet and an Orientalist as is revealed by the commentaries and footnotes to the works of Shelley, Southey and to a lesser extent, Byron. From this perspective we are justified in considering the *Hymns* as worthy of examination.

Jones had a notion (rather misplaced as it turned out) that Indian imagery and specifically Hindu terms would serve to revitalize the arsenal of English poetic imagery. In the "Argument" prefixed to the "Hymn to Camadeo" Jones proudly claims: "He has at least twenty-three names, most of which are introduced in the Hymn" (1976: XIII 236). It is not only the names of Hindu Gods but of the local flora also that Jones employs in this Hymn to create an exotic ambience:

> Strong 'Champa' rich in od'rous gold
> Warm 'Amer' mus'd in heavenly mould
> Dry "Nagkeser" in silver smiling
> Hot 'kiticum' our sense beguiling
> And last to kindle fierce the scorching flame
> Loveshaft, which the Gods 'Bela' name. (1976: XIII 238-39)

In the long argument prefixed to the "Two Hymns to Prakriti" Jones undertakes a study of the poetic art in India till Kalidasa, summarizes the *Kumara Sambhava* on which these Hymns are based and explains at length the concept of the female divinity as martial power and fecundity in Hindu mythology (1976: XIII 242-49). The "Hymn to Indra" and the "Hymn to Lakshmi" incorporate many legends from the Bhagavata—those of Goverdhan, Sudama and Kaliya for instance. Indian terms are heavily scattered throughout these poems. Quite probably this had an effect entirely opposite to that intended by the author. At any rate, the trend of using Indian words was not adopted to any great extent by later poets, not even by those who acknowledge a deep debt to Jones for their Indian material.

Indeed, John Drew bestows lavish praise on the "Hymn to Narayena" which he calls the "most successful of the Hymns" (1987: 58). It is interesting to note that Jones' greatest success in communicating Indian philosophy through verse comes in the concluding lines of this one poem in which he divests himself as much as possible of external, exotic, "Indian" trappings, and sticks to general concepts:

> Hence! Vanish from my sight:
> Delusive pictures! Unsubstantial shows!
> My soul absorb'd one only being knows
> Of all perceptions one abundant source
> Whence every object every moment flows
> Suns hence derive their force
> Hence planets learn their course;
> But Suns and fading worlds I view no more
> God only I perceive, God only I adore. (1976: XIII 308-9)

Obviously, any study of Indology cannot afford to neglect William Jones. We also have his own testimony that his time in India was time well spent—in terms of benefits both for himself and for the natives:

> Having nothing to fear from India and much to enjoy in it, I shall make a sacrifice whenever I leave it. . . . I have twice as much money as I want and am conscious of doing very great and extensive good to many millions of native Indians who look up to me not as their judge only, but as their legislator. (Qtd. Mukherjee 1987: I 1)

Also, despite his firm conviction that the Mosaic Code was the standard by which all History should be judged, Jones did demonstrate, more than most contemporaries, an ability to appreciate Indian mythology, at least as literature and on those (very few) occasions where he did feel that the Christian theology could be bettered he expresses his view clearly:

> I am not a Hindu, but I hold the doctrine of the Hindus concerning a future state to be incomparably more rational, more pious and more likely to deter men from vice than horrid opinions inculcated by the Christians on punishment without end. (*Ibid.* 172)

Keeping in mind his undoubted erudition, painstaking nature and avowedly benign intentions, it is quite easy to conclude from the information so far considered that Jones' discourse with regard to India was one of unfragmented scholarship. That, however, would not be a conclusion that gives a clear picture. It remains to be seen in the light of certain other aspects of Jones' work, whether his discourse was well put together or carried the seeds of its own disintegration.

A suitable starting point for this examination would be a letter dated February 27, 1786, that Jones wrote to Macpherson which almost reveals two distinct personalities—the *man* with a racial phobia as opposed to the scholarly *Indologist:*

> I was unable to pay my Munshi and my physician and was forced to borrow (for the first time in my life) and what was worse, I was forced to *borrow from a black man* and it was like *touching a snake* or the South American eel. (1976: H 79, my italics)

One does not expect such a crude statement from someone who had composed voluminous paeans to Indian culture; but the statement exists in black and white. In a way, this contradiction illustrates the rigidity of the mental barrier most Indologists exerted between the glories of "ancient India" and the contemporary India they actually had to live in.

S.N. Mukherjee comments that Jones exhibited the typical British dilemma of reconciling privately held liberal views with the public role of upholding the authoritarian British regime in India (1987: 4). After the earlier quoted comment, in a letter obviously originally intended to be private, a few doubts do arise about even "privately held liberal views." However, considering both liberalism and imperialism in the *political* sphere, Mukherjee's statement is of significance. After circulating an extremely controversial pamphlet upholding "liberty" in England, Jones wrote to Lord Ashburton on April 2, 1783:

> As to the doctrines in that tract, I shall certainly not preach them to the Indians who must and will be governed by absolute power. (Qtd. Mukherjee 1987: 7)

In yet another letter addressed to "a friend at the Bar," Jones writes:

> Millions in India are so wedded to their inveterate prejudices and habits that if liberty could be forced on them by Britain, it would make them as miserable as the cruellest despotism. (*Ibid.* 8)

Such attitudes are to be found not only in letters, but also in his "public" works. In his "Tenth Anniversary Discourse"—"On Asiatic History: Civil and Natural," Jones writes:

> In these Indian territories which providence has thrown into the arms of Great Britain, for their protection and welfare, the religion, manners and laws of the natives preclude even the *idea of political freedom*. (*AR*: IV xiii, my italics)

The notion of Empire being providentially decreed for Britain, Britain's paternalistic responsibility and the natives' own situation "naturally" co-operating with imperialism—all these concepts are neatly integrated into the above statement. The implication of course, is that Britain would be only too willing to "give" liberty if possible, but since that option is *precluded,* she may as well derive what benefit she can from existing conditions.

Ancient India may have been glorious and cultured, as Jones himself has emphasized. But, he also asserts in unequivocal terms that "Oriental Despotism" had rendered the least progress totally impossible.

> He [any European observer] could not but remark the constant effect of despotism in benumbing and debasing all those faculties which distinguish men from the herd that grazes, and to that cause, impute the decided inferiority of most Asiatic nations to those in Europe, who are blest with happier governments. (*AR*: IV xx)

The stereotype of "Oriental Despotism" is employed here, not as a mere theoretical statement, but as a practical aid and acceptable justification for British profit. Immediately after commenting on the "fact" of Oriental Despotism, and the obstacle it poses to liberty, Jones adds:

> Our country derives essential benefit from the diligence of a placid and submissive people who multiply with such rapidity even after the ravages of famine. (*AR*: IV xxi)

One gets the feeling that certain zoological specimens are under discussion rather than human beings. The "placidity" and the patient nature of the Indian, their unchecked (and in this instance, *useful)* fecundity are the Orientalist stereotypes present in strength. They contribute to the clear statement that Empire can, should and would continue.

"Taste" is distributed on a geographical basis as can be seen in Jones' remark that "we may decide on the whole that reason and taste are the general prerogatives of European minds, while the Asiatics have soared to greater heights in the sphere of imagination" (1976: III 16-17). And if this appears merely a neutral statement of perceived fact, it would be as well to bear in mind the association of rationality with scientific progress and taste with correctness. Imagination, despite the 'Romantic' praise showered on it, was not reckoned as a very helpful attribute in politics or government which decided the trends of imperialism. Political freedom precluded in India, rationality and taste both European prerogatives—it is possible that at an idea level Jones was indulging in the "geographical morality" Burke accused Hastings of practising. At any rate, despite his undoubted scholarship and liberal orientation in British politics, Jones is not in any doubt about which emerges the victor in any comparison of primary value between Asia and Europe:

> Whoever travels in Asia especially if he be conversant with the literature of the countries through which he passes, must *naturally remark the superiority of European talents*. (*AR*: I 336, my italics)

Rationality and taste have already been granted in superior measure to Europe. Now that literature—the one field where imagination could count as prominent—has also been placed there, India is left with very little indeed.

Jones frequently asserts that his only concern, even in religious matters is with the "truth." So, it is very convenient indeed, that the "truth" which all his research invariably uncovers tends to confirm Christian Revelation. In the "Tenth Anniversary Discourse" Jones roundly declares:

> We cannot surely deem it an inconsiderable advantage that all our historical researches have confirmed the Mosaic accounts of the primitive world, and our testimony on that subject ought to have the greater weight, because, if the result of our observations had been totally different, we should nevertheless have published them,

> not indeed with equal pleasure, but with equal confidence, for truth is mighty and whatever be its consequences, must always prevail. (*AR*: IV xiii)

This eloquent avowal presupposes an evenhanded method of investigating which unfortunately has proved to be a chimera. The claims of Christian Revelation are reiterated, while the opposing system is subjected to analysis, mensuration, querying and speculation. The very possibility of the supernatural or even of the extraordinary is ruled out, in the discussion of the Indian system while it is accepted in relation to Christian accounts.

> If we remove the difficulty by admitting miracles, we must cease to reason and may as well believe at once whatever the Brahmins choose to tell us. (*AR*: II 93)

Attempts to disprove the accuracy of Hindu chronology occupy a great deal of Jones' attention. A major part of an essay on chronology is devoted to mathematical *speculation* (as any pronouncement on pre-historical periods must necessarily be) to show that the "Cal-Yug" could not have started as early as the Brahmins said it did. The underlying purpose is clearly to make Hindu myths conform—in some way, through some procrustean process if necessary—to Old Testament accounts. In the same breath as it were, Jones asserts that "myths are absurd in civil history" and supports as "fact" the Biblical account of the flood.

Yet another concern of Jones, which practically amounts to an obsession, is to draw parallels between Indian and European "pagan" cultures as well as with Biblical entities. Parallels drawn between Bali/Babel and Hiranyakashyap/Nimrod exemplify the latter tendency, while analogies between Rama/Dionysous and Hanuman's army/Satyrs illustrate the former. Adi Manu (Adim) is supposed to be derived from Adam (and Manu himself from Noah) while the reverse possibility is never even taken into consideration.

In the "Third Anniversary Discourse" Jones insists that "we now live among the adorers of those Gods, those very deities who were worshipped under different names in Old Greece and Italy and among the professors of those philosophical tenets which the Ionic and Attican writers had illustrated with all the beauties of their melodious tongue" (*AR*: I 350). We can observe an Aryanization/ Europeanization of India going on beneath this discourse. The intention is by no means a simple universalism; since *contemporary* India is excluded from the discussion. The discourse self-contradictorily stresses both the unbroken and unchanging tradition of India and the vast gulf between "the degenerate and abased" contemporary Hindus and their ancestors who flourished in some distant golden age (*AR*: I 347).

The attempt was to incorporate Indian culture also into British heritage, by tracing it back to a Greek original, and also by finding Biblical roots for the myths. This would naturally serve as a meta-justification of imperialism since Britain would only be reclaiming a part of her own heritage. As Romila Thapar remarks, ancient Indian civilization was perceived less as the Asiatic roots of a modern European civilization than "almost as a lost ring of European culture" (1968: 319). This enabled ancient India to function as a sort of Utopia, which through Jones himself would help to invigorate European culture.

In addition, the exclusion of contemporary India from the discourse enabled the Indologists to present as *their* "gift"—the gift of history—the knowledge of India's greatness to Indians themselves. Imperialism was doubly justified, because in the first instance, the imperialists were only reclaiming their own past and in the second, the natives had lost touch with their own roots which could be bestowed on them only by the European researcher/ administrator. Drawing a veil over the history of India between the Vedic Age and the Age of Imperialism, the Indologists propagated "a teleology that sought to erase History" (Tharu and Lalitha 1991: I 45). As Jenny Sharpe remarks, "In the Historical example of India, sympathy and identity are equally constitutive of Orientalist discourse as hostility and alterity" (1993: 38). The East does not have to be the Other to be subjugated; *exaggerated* attempts to make it the Same can be equally responsible for colonialism and imperial aggression.

Jones indeed makes no secret of the fact that he was primarily an administrator employed by the Company and that he expected his researches to benefit his employers and his country in clear economic terms. In the Second Anniversary Discourse, he urges the study of Indian history and resources because

> We have a near interest in knowing all former modes of ruling these inestimable provinces on the prosperity of which so much of our national welfare and individual benefit seems to depend . . . the natural productions of these territories, especially in the vegetable and mineral systems are momentous objects of research to not only an imperial but which is a character of equal dignity, a commercial people. (*AR*: I 337)

The same concept is urged in the preface to the translation of the *Manusmriti.* Tolerance for Indian laws is urged; not because they possess any intrinsic merit, but because they enable the best form of peaceful government, which could contribute most to the political and economic profit of Britain:

> Whatever opinion may be formed of Manu and his laws in a country happily enlightened by sound philosophy and the only true revelation, it must be remembered that these laws are actually revered as the word of the Most High by nations of the greatest importance to the political and commercial interests of Europe and particularly by many millions of Hindu subjects, whose well directed industry *would add largely to the wealth of Britain.* (1976: VIII 89-90, my italics)

This motif of "being *useful* to Britain" is not restricted to legal or historical study alone but even to mythology, fable and poetry; as can be seen in the preface to the "Hymn to Lakshmi."

> We may be inclined perhaps to think that the wild fables of idolaters are not worth knowing and that we may be satisfied with misspending our time in learning the Pagan theology of Old Greece and Rome, but we must consider, that the allegories contained in the "Hymn to Lakshmi" constitute, at this moment the prevailing religion of a most extensive and celebrated Empire and are devoutly believed by many millions whose industry adds to the lustre of Great Britain and whose manners are so interwoven with their religious opinions, who nearly affect all Europeans who reside among them. (1976: XIII 290)

On the whole, Jones' scholarship contributed immensely and evidently intention to letting Britain "know" more about India, *ostensibly* so that her rule could be rendered "better"—actually in effect stronger and securer.

The concept of furthering Empire, to Britain's undoubted profit, but avowedly to the greater benefit of the natives themselves is seen even in Jones' original poetic compositions, the *Hindu Hymns.* The "Hymn to Surya" contains a very self-assured portrait of the poet as the western scholar who retrieves and purifies the linguistic and ethical treasures of Ancient India, which the degenerate contemporary natives had "lost." Jones, in this Hymn requests the Sun to answer those who enquire about the poet's identity:

> Say "From the bosom of yon silver isle
> Where skies more softly smile
> He came, and lisping our celestial tongue
> Though not from Brahma sprung
> Draws Orient knowledge from its foundations pure
> Through Caves obstructed long and paths too long obscure."
> (1976: XIII. 286)

The "Hymn to Lakshmi" contains an obtruding reference to the glory and benevolence of the Empire:

> Oh! Bid the patient Hindu rise and live.
> Now stretch'd o'er ocean's vast from happier isles
> He sees the wand of Empire, not the rod.
> So shall their victors; mild with virtuous pride
> To many a cherish'd, grateful race endear'd
> With tempered love be feared. (1976: XIII 98-99)

This idea is carried even further in yet another Hymn where the argument describes it as "feigned to have been the work of a Brahmin in an early antiquity, who by a prophetic spirit, discerns the toleration, and equity of the British Government, and concludes with a prayer for its peaceful duration under good laws well administered" (1976: XIII 322). The Hymn concludes:

> Nor frown; dread Goddess on a peerless race
> With liberal heart and martial rage

Wafted from colder isles remote
As they preserve our laws and bid our terror cease,
So be their darling laws preserved in wealth,
in joy, in peace. (1976: XIII 333, my italics)

By this anachronistic masterstroke, a representative of ancient India itself is brought on stage to declare the glory of Empire to his own descendents. It is the Indian's own law which the British administer, but it is the British administrator who puts an end to Indian "terror." Even in Jones' more "literary" productions therefore, we can see an articulation of a theory of establishment and preservation of Empire—and moreover one where the interests of the natives were made to appear identical with those of the imperialists. As Edward Said remarks in *Orientalism,* Jones closed down large vistas "clarifying, tabulating, comparing" (1978: 77). There is no attempt here to detract from Jones' scholarly achievements or from his contributions to "knowledge" about India, but the more that knowledge increased, the more domesticated and more governable did India become. Knowledge in this imperial context functioned as a tool of Government. Indologist scholarship exemplified by Jones "not only described India as something that was in need of good government, but also restructured it as something that was *governable*" (Tharu and Lalitha 1991: 50, my italics).

At this point, some attention must be paid to works of a few other prominent Indologist scholars to illustrate their similarities or otherwise in connection with the analysis conducted here on Jones' works. It has to be kept in mind that many like Wilkins, Colebrooke and Hayman, who followed Jones' legacy of scholarship—and the group exemplified by William Ward, Carey and Marshman who openly used whatever their research unearthed to launch polemics against India, *both* figure under the title of "Indologists."

William Ward was shocked by the "idolatry and heathenish" practices he saw in India and devoted his two volume *History* to combating and decrying these practices. One of his blatant chapter headings speaks for itself—"Brahminical Fraud Detected"—and this is a good example of the general tenor of his works.

Scholars like Colebrooke questioned Ward's scholarship; but his picture of an India in desperate need of reform, which necessitated Empire, was as much a part of Indological research/ discourse as the more scholarly works of Jones or Wilkins. Also, while the clergyman Ward is immensely worried about the souls of the Hindus and keen on their "mental and moral improvement," he does not forget to repeat Jones' argument that such steps would be greatly to Britain's interest:

> But let Hindosthan receive that higher civilization she needs, that cultivation of which she is capable; let European literature be transfused into all her languages, and then the ocean from the parts of Britain to India will be covered by our merchant vessels. (1817: II 73)

Charles Wilkins' contributions to the *Asiatic Researches* are mainly translations; his major achievement of course, was the translation of the *Bhagavat Geetha.* Wilkins, in fact, seems to make considerable efforts to keep his pieces "descriptive" and in a similar way, Colebrooke attempts to "set forth without comment" (1976: 76) his descriptions of the ceremonies, philosophies and literature of the Hindus. However, it needs to be emphasized, that given its immense evocative and creative power, description can no longer be considered a value neutral activity.[2] Even in his elaborate accounts, very often commendatory of Hindu philosophy, Colebrooke reinforces the stereotypes of the apathetic" and "secretive" Hindus (1976: 258). Classifications such as "absurd exaggerations," "Fanatical work," "unmeaning work" and "indecent practices" are scattered through the body of his essays. Colebrooke also follows Jones' path in trying to identify the sources of Indian and Greek philosophy; a proceeding also seen in Horace Hayman Wilson's *Hindu Fiction,* which represents Hindu stories as "being derived from the spurious Gospels" (1979: 76).

The works of Wilson and Colebrooke also indicate the tendency pointed out by Said in *Orientalism* where "the Orientalist is required to *present* the Orient by a series of representative fragments, fragments republished, explicated, annotated and surrounded by still more fragments" (1978: 128). The focus is on the "anthology, the chrestomathy, the tableau, the survey of general principles" (Said 1978: 125), which textualize the orient and offer it up to Western scholars and the administrators. The Indologists stood *between* India and the West, but their role was effaced and what they presented was accepted *as* India. When the *presentation* encouraged imperialism, the interpretation was that *India* encouraged, in fact, demanded imperialism.

Only at one point does William Jones fleetingly consider the possibility that Empire need not be an unmixed blessing. Interestingly, even this is from Britain's perspective (India's welfare being inextricably linked with Empire) and is an expression of what Nigel Leask has called an "Anxiety of Empire." In his formal "Charge to the Grand Jury" delivered on June 9, 1792, Jones worries about British officials returning to Britain with a contempt for British institutions, inculcated by Indian conceptions. He remarks:

> If Asia corrupts Britons to not care for British laws; later ages may comment with cause: "It had been happy for us if our dominion had never been established in Asia." (1976: VII 71)

The Conservative discourse on India, and the Indological discourse closely connected to it were avowedly "pro-Indian." At least that was the major criticism levelled against them by Utilitarians, Reformers and Evangelists. However, I have attempted to demonstrate that these discourses could not be tied down under any clear "pro" or "anti" labels. They contributed in no small measure to the rhetoric of Empire and thereby stand self-exposed as fragmented entities, which cannot claim any distinction of being either monolithic or seamless. Burke was the defender of India against abuses; Jones was the archetypal Indological scholar. Yet, despite their concern for India, Empire had to continue. So, India had to be presented as *needing* British rule. Any aspersions cast on India for this purpose, could be taken as altruistic and objective, since after all people concerned about India voiced them. In this fashion the fragmented rhetoric made existence possible with a reasonably clear conscience.

The next chapter attempts an analysis of the Utilitarian discourse on India (represented by James Mill) with the intention of seeing if that rhetoric of domination stands the test of logical coherence any better than the Conservative or Indological texts.

NOTES

1. I do not think that any man sent out to India is sent with an ill purpose or goes out with bad intentions. No, I think the young men who go there are fair and faithful representations of the people of the same age—not corrupted, but corruptible from their age as we all are" (Burke 1963: 413-14). Said points out that even this youth was not a matter of chance, but involved a policy decision that the rulers should be constantly seen as "vigorous, rational, ever youthful and alert" (1978: 42).
2. Hastings wishes to "prescribe bounds for the latitude of criticism" and in estimating an Indian text excludes all rules drawn from European sources. He wants the allowance of "obscurity, absurdity, barbarous habits and perverted morality." (qtd. Gauri Viswanathan 1989: 121).
3. This is clearly brought out by Aijaz Ahmed when he explains the ideological strategies located behind so-called objective description. "Description is never cognitively or ideologically neutral . . . description has been central in the colonizing discourses . . . and through a monstrous machinery of description, these discourses were able to classify and also to ideologically master colonial subjects" (1994: 99).

Chapter IV

A Strident Nervousness: Utilitarianism and the Rhetoric of Reform

The wild fictions of the Hindus seem rather the playsome whimsies of monkeys in human shapes than the serious observations of a being who dignifies himself with the name of "rational."

James Mill

Utilitarian philosophy with its 'unsentimental' "discourse of improvement" (Niranjana 1992: 26) has been traditionally regarded as the chief oppositional philosophy to the tenets advocated by Conservatism and Indological study with regard to the administration of British India. Indeed, with James Mill's blanket denunciation of all that either ancient or contemporary India had to offer (in his *History of British India*), we are very far away from any notion of a Golden age in India when Britain was "yet in the woods," suggested by both Jones and Burke. In his *Imagining India*, Ronald Inden describes Mill's *History* as "the oldest hegemonic account of India" (1990: 45). Mill's account was intended not only to disprove the Indological claims for Indian culture, but also to establish a foundation for the employment of Utilitarian principles in India. It can be shown that this double motivation was precisely the rock on which the *History* foundered, the reason why despite the powerful rhetoric it constructed through a "discourse of repetition" (Niranjana 1992: 22) it could not finally emerge as "a confident body of doctrine" (Majeed 1990: 212).

However, at this initial stage of analysis, emphasis is laid not on Utilitarian principles or their effects, but on the way in which India was represented to gain acceptance for those principles. Mill's *History* stands as his contribution to nothing less than an entire worldview regarding India. It may be a matter of opinion whether or not to agree with Max Mueller's opinion in "India, What Can It Teach Us?" that "Mill's *History* was responsible for some of the greatest misfortunes that had happened to India" (Qtd. J.P. Guha, "Introduction" to Mill's *History* 1978: xii). However when we consider the immense contemporary significance bestowed on Mill's work—to the extent that the *History* was, by 1830, required reading for students at Haileybury, the East India Company's training college—the importance to be attached to his description of India becomes evident.

Mill can be credited with steadiness of purpose at least as far as his representation of India in degrading terms is concerned. His confidence here is immense; far from any diffidence on account of his entire lack of personal knowledge of India, he argues that the severity and firmness of his judgments was all the more assured due to that reason. Indeed, Mill puts forward one of the most strident defences possible of "armchair Orientalism" (Mill 1978: I 5-11).

A large part of the early volumes of the *History* is devoted to examining the state of India under Hindu rule, before the Mohammedan conquest. Mill had planned his strategy very carefully indeed. Most of the Indologist claims were based on ancient Hindu culture and it is therefore for this period that Mill reserves most of his vituperation. The Mohammedan culture is by contrast presented as comparatively preferable, a step upward on the ladder of progress. The next comparison is between Mohammedan rule and the benefits that could be conferred by Britain, which in turn is presented as infinitely preferable to the status quo. The composition of British rule is thereby presented with an air of inevitability as the next required and natural stage of evolution/progress for India. The whole structure is based on the "teleological view of world history" (Niranjana 1992: 23) with progress as inevitable and Britain as its historical agent.

The section on Hindu India is meticulously divided into chapters on Chronology and Ancient History, classification of the people, the form of government, the laws, the taxes, religion, manners, arts and literature. The Mohammedan culture is analyzed in just three chapters altogether; Mill concludes this account with a comparison between the two systems. The rest of the copious work is devoted to the account of Indian affairs since the arrival of Britain on the scene.

William Jones and other Indologists had themselves encountered difficulties with Hindu chronology and its incompatibility with Old Testament accounts—one of the "solutions" they adopted was to look for "inner" meanings in Hindu concepts. Mill refuses any truck with such tactics and bluntly condemns such attempts as fruitless:

> The wildness and inconsistency of the Hindu statements evidently place them beyond the sober limits of truth and History. Yet, it has been imagined . . . that they at least contain a poetical or figurative delineation of real events. . . . The laborious ingenuity bestowed upon this enquiry has not been attended with an adequate reward. The Hindu legends still present a maze of unnatural fictions in which a series of real events can by no artifice be traced. (1978: I 28)

The attempts of the Indologists are stigmatized and dismissed as "artifice" and unsuccessful artifice to boot. The antiquity claimed for Indian records, is accounted for, as a result of the propensity of "rude nations to derive a peculiar gratification from pretensions to a remote antiquity. As a boastful and turgid vanity distinguishes remarkably the Oriental nations, they have in most instances carried their claims extravagantly high" (Mill 1978: I 24). Even among these "rude" nations, the Indians were the worst: "The Brahmans are the most audacious and perhaps the most unskilful fabricators of whom the annals of fable have yet made us aware" (I 28).

Every single circumstance is used by Mill to indicate that the Hindu state of civilization was primitive and rude. The fact that the Brahmins and the Kshatriyas were high in the social hierarchy is attributed to the reason, that the ruder a society is, the higher the regard for the priesthood and the warriors. The Brahmins especially are described as "a people in whom the love of repose exerts the greatest sway and in whose character, aversion to danger forms a principal ingredient" (I 75). It has to be kept in mind that no proofs are adduced to any of these remarks, as if the author had intended them to carry conviction through sheer force of assertion.

The Hindu legal system is condemned as "rude and defective" in a chapter which confesses that it cannot undertake the "detail or even analysis of the Hindu code" (Mill 1978: I 60-61). The reader is obviously expected to take Mill on trust, a favour that he is simultaneously interdicted from extending to the Indological scholars. The *Manu Smriti* is described as "all vagueness and darkness, incoherence, inconsistency and confusion" (I 163), favourite words of Mill, as they are later repeated almost verbatim to describe Hindu religion. Mill postulates "completeness and exactness" as the two essential qualifications of a satisfactory digest of law. He regards the deviation of the Indian code from these principles to be so self-evident that no explanations or elaborations are necessary:

> To show in what degree the Hindu law recedes from the standard of completeness would require a more extensive survey of the field of law than can consist with the plan of this work. That it departs from exactness in every one of the particulars in which exactness consists is abundantly clear. (Mill 1978: 109-10)

It is necessary to emphasize yet again that Mill seems to consider proof as a total waste of time. He had adopted a point of view so totally and firmly centred in nineteenth century rational Utilitarianism that other value systems are not permitted to even exist on the periphery. He expects his audience to accept his comments as self-evident truths, precisely because the scale of excellence—which Mill and his readers were supposed to share in common—was held to be inherently the only valid one.[1] This assumption naturally gave Mill an edge over the Indologists, who first had to convince themselves of the validity and authenticity of their observations and only then circulate a new perspective among the public.

Mill's comments on the section of punishments for adultery in the *Manu Smriti* are extremely revealing:

> In the Hindu language, adultery includes every unlawful species of sexual indulgence, from the least to the most injurious or offensive.

> If their laws are any proof of the manners of a people, this article affords indication of one the most depraved states of the sexual appetite. Almost all of the abuses and all the crimes it is possible to commit are there depicted with curious exactness, and penalties are devised and assigned for every minute diversity as for acts the most frequent and familiar. There are even titles of sections in the code which cannot be transcribed with decency and which depict crimes unknown to European laws. (Mill 1978: I 102)

The same concept is articulated with regard to what Mill calls the "obscene symbols of Hindu religion,"[2] the grossness and depravity of the people being deduced in the first instance from the law and then from religion. The Indologists had presented a concept of the fecundity of India, which was extremely threatening to Mill's ordered rationalism. The very imagination, in which Jones had awarded primacy to the Asiatics, appears for Mill as a "threatening Eros," (Majeed 1990: 221) a Dionysian eruption into the Apollonian perfection Utilitarianism sought to maintain. These aspects of India—her fecundity, apparent lack of restraint and depravity—are therefore singled out for repeated condemnation.

Indologists had remarked that the mild taxation found in Ancient India was an instance of good government. For Mill, this only proves that agriculture was in its earliest stage. Though it paid little, it could afford to pay no more. "We may assume it as a principle, *in which there is no room for mistake* that a government constituted and circumstanced as that of the Hindus had only one limit to its exactions, that of the non-existence of anything further to take" (Mill 1978: I 44, my italics).

This is by no means the only instance where Mill takes away with one hand what he barely concedes with the other. His cautious, grudging acceptance of the fact that Hindus excelled in the art of weaving and a reluctant admission that their irrigation systems were well advanced are immediately followed by dismissive comments which take away all semblance of merit or achievement.[3]

A statement that Indians accomplish skilful work with scanty equipment provides Mill with yet another opportunity to employ his favourite adjective "rude": "a dexterity in the use of its own imperfect tools is a common attribute of a rude society" (1978: I 335). The very praise meted out to wise judges or kings who improved public systems is deployed as an indication to the effect that such phenomena were very rare indeed! The "gentleness" of the Hindu character is mentioned, but is immediately followed by a declaration of the impossibility of this being a positive attribute:

> Much attention has been attracted to the gentleness of manners in this people. . . . One of the circumstances which distinguish the state of a commencing civilization is that it is compatible with great violence as well as with great gentleness of manners. Nothing is more common than examples of both. Mildness of address is not always separated from even the rudest condition of human life. (Mill 1978: I 288)

There is practically nothing therefore, no sphere in which Mill is willing to concede that the early Indians had progressed to any great extent. Even their actual achievements appear as conclusive proof of their lack of civilization.

Another area where the Indologists had bestowed praise on Ancient India was that of philosophical and theological speculation. Mill summarily dismisses Indian cosmography in harsh terms:

> No people however rude and ignorant whatsoever have . . . ever drawn a more gross and disgusting picture of the universe than what is presented in the writings of the Hindus. In the conception of it, no coherence, wisdom or beauty ever appears; all is disorder, caprice, passion, contest, portents, prodigies, violence and deformity. (Mill 1978: I 187)

The Hindus are granted "lofty expression" in theology and subtlety in metaphysical speculation. However, Mill manages to reconcile these attributes with their primitive and "rude" condition. As far as lofty expressions conveying an elevated apprehension of Deity are concerned, Mill has this to say:

> To form a true estimate of the religion of these people, it is necessary by reflection to ascertain what those lofty expressions really

> mean in the mouth of a Brahmin. . . . It is well ascertained that nations who have the lowest and meanest ideas of the divine Being yet may apply to him the most sounding epithets by which perfection can be expressed. (Mill 1978: I 165-66)

The case of metaphysical speculation is treated even more drastically, to the extent that abstract speculation *as such* is condemned as barbarous:

> It is an error to suppose, that for the origin of unprofitable speculations respecting the nature and properties of thought, great progress in civilization is required—The highest abstractions are not the last results of mental culture and intellectual strength. . . . *The propensity to abstract speculation is the natural result of the state of the human mind in a rude and ignorant state.* (Mill 1978: I 376-78, my italics)

An excellent example of Mill's abrupt condemnation of speculative philosophy is his contemptuous dismissal of the doctrine of "Maya" on which the Indologists had expended considerable explicatory energy. All Mill has to say about "Maya" which he simplistically terms "denial" is that it is "lunacy" (1978: I 378). In Mill's dismissal of philosophy and later of poetry, one can see as a "unifying thread, his distrust of the imagination" (Majeed 1990: 214). The general Utilitarian attitude towards the imagination can be seen in Jeremy Bentham's phrase "the pestilential breath of fiction" (Qtd. Majeed 1990: 215). And this was the period when the Romantic cult of the Imagination was gaining ground! The Coleridgean Imagination, which if sufficiently employed, could assist the Indologists in defining cultural and natural identities, and could overturn his assimilationist tendencies was one of Mill's worst theoretical adversaries. It was on the basis of the products of the Imagination and speculation that the best cases for India were framed and therefore Mill had to deny these, not merely by showing India's inferiority, but by discrediting the criteria themselves.

Poetry, therefore is stigmatized as the rudest form of literature and Indian literature explicitly denigrated precisely because it consists mainly of poetry:

> The first literature is poetry. Poetry is the language of the passions and men feel before they speculate. The earliest poetry is the expression of feelings, by which the minds of rude men are the most powerfully actuated. . . . At this first stage, the literature of the Hindus has always remained. (Mill 1978: I 365)

As if it was not bad enough that literature was in this primitive stage, it is further argued that even among this type, Hindu literature exhibits the worst specimens. Of the *Ramayana* and the *Mahabharata,* Mill has this to say:

> They are excessively prolix and insipid. They are often, through long passages, trifling and childish . . . inflations, metaphors perpetual and these the most violent and strained; obscurity, tautology, repetition, verbosity, confusion, incoherence distinguish the *Mahabharata* and the *Ramayana.* (1978: I 367)

Mill's utter ignorance of any Indian language has to be kept in mind at this juncture. Even when he condescends to grant that there are a few tolerable passages in the Indian epics, these are mainly dismissed as a matter of mere chance.[4]

Mill demonstrates a great faculty for teasing out those exact parts of the Indian system; criticism of which would carry most weight with his audience. He also has the capacity to casually dismiss any record that may prove detrimental to his argument. One of his greatest charges against the Hindu religion was that it stressed only ceremonial observance and ignored moral duties. Since he certainly had access to Jones' translation of the *Manu Smriti* Mill is forced to at least acknowledge the existence of a passage that states the exact opposite of what he claims:

> A wise man shall constantly perform all the moral duties though he perform not completely the ceremonies of religion, since he falls low, if while he performs ceremonial acts only, he discharge not his moral duties. (Qtd. Mill 1978: I 204-5)

This passage is no sooner quoted than Mill dismisses it as of "little value since it was an insignificant and isolated exception" (1978: I 205).

Tejaswini Niranjana has pointed out the selective use Mill makes of Indian accounts: "Mill trashes the *Puranas* (mythological tales) as false history, but is willing to accept evidence from the play *Shakuntala* regarding the political arrangements and laws of the age. History is dismissed as fiction, but fiction—translated—is admissible as History" (1992: 24-25).

Judged as literature, Mills' verdict is that there are a few beautiful passages, but "beyond these few passages, there is nothing in the *Shakuntala* which either accords with the understanding or can gratify the fancy of any instructed people" (1978: I 370). (Goethe's enthusiastic praise of *Shakuntala,* quoted earlier, indicates the strong Oriental edifice Mill was trying to demolish.) Mill accepts the work as a good specimen of the pastoral, but stipulates that the pastoral itself is the production of a "simple and unpolished age" (1978: I 372).

This, however, does not prevent him from making liberal use of the text as social History when it suits his purposes to do so. The rate of land revenue is deduced from the fact that in Kalidasa's poem, the "King is described," at a much earlier period, "as that man whose revenue arises from a sixth part of his people's income" (1978: I 133). This is by no means an isolated or single example: the moral laxity of the Indians,[5] the territorial divisions of the country,[6] corruption of the officials[7] and the seclusion of women[8] are all declared and supposedly proved by passages in *Shakuntala.* This is a proceeding that certainly seems self-serving in view of Mill's known low opinion of literature and his outright dismissal of those sources that the Indologists had regarded as historical records.

According to Mill, the condition of women can be regarded as an indication of the civilization of a people, since rude people degrade women and civilized people exalt them. The Hindus fail the test of civilization by this standard also. "A state of dependence, more strict and humiliating than that which is ordained for the weaker sex among the Hindus cannot easily be conceived. Nothing can exceed the habitual contempt which the Hindus entertain for their women" (1978: I 280-81).

As "proof" of this statement, Mill quotes the verse from the *Manusmriti,* which holds that women should be dependent on male relations. It may not be out of place here to quote Mill on female suffrage in his "Essay on Government": "one thing is pretty clear, that all those individuals, whose interests are indisputably included in those of other individuals may be struck off (the voters' list) without inconvenience. In this light women also may be regarded, the interests of almost all of whom is involved either in that of their fathers or in that of their husbands" (1978a: 79). We have an ideal instance here of how conceptual contradictions are accommodated on the basis of geographic settings.

The language of the Hindus (which Jones had singled out for special praise) is also condemned by Mill. The main reason is that it has many names for the same objects, and "redundancy is a defect in language, not less than a deficiency" (1978: I 384).

Military tactics and medicinal systems are described as "scarcely having been even known to the Hindus" (1978: I 481). Colebrooke had published an entire volume on the art of war and medicine among the Hindus, which, if Mill had read, he did not feel inclined to acknowledge. In short, anything in the accounts that had reached Britain, which was in favour of early Indian civilization, is dismissed by Mill as pure fantasy and speculation. He roundly asserts, "everything we *know* of the ancient state of Hindustan conspires to prove that it was rude" (1978: I 461).

An effective summing up of Mills' condemnation can be found in an essentialized description where he includes the Chinese also (and by implication, the whole of rude, uncivilized Asia):

> Both nations are to nearly an equal degree tainted with the vices of insincerity, dissembling, treacherous, mendacious to an excess that surpasses even the usual measure of uncivilized society. Both are disposed to extreme exaggeration with regard to everything relating to themselves. Both are cowardly and unfeeling. Both are in the highest degree conceited of themselves and full of affected contempt for others. Both are, in the physical sense, disgustingly unclean in their persons and houses. (Mill 1978: 1 486)

The comparatively shorter analysis of India after the Mohammedan conquest is more "factual" in the sense that Mill is more willing to accept the available records as historical. The main concern here is with a comparison between Muslim and Hindu cultures, "for the purpose of ascertaining whether the civilization of the Hindus received advancement or depression from the ascendancy over them which the Mohammedans acquired" (1978: I 697). In every single field, the Mohammedan civilization is stated to be superior, with hardly any proof or even discussion, only subjective opinion and arbitrary statements being adduced.

With respect to religion, Mill remarks: "under this head, very few words are necessary, because the superiority of the Mohammedans in respect of religion is beyond all dispute" (1978: I 720). The statement with regard to literature is even more arbitrary: "In this important article, it will be impossible to show that the Hindus had the superiority in one single particular" (1978: I 723). Of course, Mill wastes no time in trying to prove what he has already declared to be "impossible." The conclusion of his comparative analysis is: "it will not admit of any long dispute that human nature in India gained and gained very considerably by passing from a Hindu to a Mohammedan government" (1978: I 700).

However, Mill was no admirer of India even after the Mohammedan conquest. The motives behind his Hindu/Muslim comparisons are clearly spelt out:

> The question is whether . . . the Hindu population lost or gained. For the aversion to a government, because in the hands of *foreigners*, that is, of men who are called by one rather than some other name, without regard to the *qualities of government* whether better or worse, *is a prejudice which reason disclaims*. (1978: 1 700, my italics)

Mill obviously did not share in the liberal opinion of his day that good government was no substitute for self-government. Once he had established that "foreign" governments were not in themselves to be resented, and that to so resent them, was in fact irrational, he could easily proceed to show that British rule was the next logical step in India's progress. Eric Stokes points out, that in his evidence before the Commons Committee of 1831, Mill argued: "the great concern of the people of India was that the business of government should be well and cheaply conducted, but it was of little or no consequence who were the people who performed it" (Stokes 1959: 64).

It appears that there was an ongoing conflict between Mill and the Indologists. Indeed, Mill considers Jones as a prime adversary. He refers to Jones as "prepossessed and credulous" (1978: I 379). His comment on Jones' codification of Indian law is quite uncompromisingly dismissive. The work is harshly described as:

> A disorderly compilation of loose, vague, stupid or unintelligible quotations and maxims, selected arbitrarily from books of law, books of devotion and books of poetry, attended with a commentary which only adds to the mass of absurdity and darkness; a barrage, by which nothing is defined and nothing established. (1978: III 398)

The intention is clear enough; Mill is positioning himself against the Indologists and the revitalized Conservatism they encouraged. As Javed Majeed points out, Mill sees in the Indological practice the features of the "*Ancient Regime*" which he hated: "respect for the uniqueness of cultures, their distinct ways of evolving, degrees of rank, ways of life, respect for the past and its importance for the present" (Majeed 1990: 211) In attacking the Indological framework Mill situates himself as an adversary to the past itself, which is the edifice he had to pull down before he could erect his new rational Utilitarian structure.

But, was Mill really so different from the Indologists or the Conservatives he sought to denigrate? Did he have no common ground, share no assumptions with them? In the first place, though Mill's technique of quoting the Orientalists against themselves was rhetorically successful, it does not follow that he was "catching them out" in self-contradiction. In other words, except for perhaps one occasion,[9] where he twists Halhed's words out of context to get the required effect, Mill is only reflecting the actual ambiguity, which his supposed adversaries themselves had towards India. He does not seem to realize that their attitude was not one of unqualified praise, to an extent which could question Britain's presence in India. On many issues, the Indologists themselves cherished no very complimentary views of India, though their language may be more restrained and subtle than Mill's. When Mill quotes Jones to the effect that "the cruel mutilations practised by the native powers are shocking to humanity," (1998: I 95) or that the punishments in the *Manusmriti* are "partial and fanciful, for some crimes dreadfully cruel and for others reprehensibly slight" (1978: I 100) he is not, as he fancies, *trapping* Jones. As has been seen, the Indologists and the Conservatives had their own problems with India, and if their articulation of these problems was somewhat subdued, it was in the name of "honouring" tradition as a general principle rather than out of admiration for India. Where Mill errs is in sharing the general assumption that the Indologists' works consisted—with only some unguarded slips—solely of paeans to India.

It can also be seen that certain presuppositions in Mill were shared by his adversaries in full measure. For instance, Mill firmly adheres to the thesis that the Hindus were an "unchanging" people; with the effect that his criticism of ancient India can apply equally well to contemporary society, thereby justifying a discourse of improvement. Some slight changes, he admits, may have been made after the Mohammedan conquest, but the majority of Indians were still in their depraved ancient situation and even the Mohammedan set-up by no means precluded an immense scope for improvement.

Mill insists that "the conclusion has been drawn, that the Hindus at the time of Alexander's invasion, were in a state of society, manners and knowledge, exactly the same with that in which they were discovered by the nations of modern Europe, nor is there any reason for differing widely from this opinion." (I 28) To preclude any discussion he adds: "their annals from that era till the period of the Mohammedan conquest are a blank" (1978: I 29). As a primary proof for this unchanging nature (stagnating, in Utilitarian terms) Mill puts forward the concept of "Oriental Despotism." The government among the Hindus is described as "absolute monarchy, according to the Asiatic model" (1978: I 66) and is stigmatized as being responsible for all society's ills, including "the absence of motives for labor among the

Hindus" which lead to their languid and slothful habits." (1978: I 294)

We have already seen that these concepts figured prominently in the discourses of both Burke and Jones. Mill and his adversaries function within the category Edward Said has called "vision" as opposed to "narrative." The 'Vision' represents the Orient as an "unconditional and ontological category, synonymous with stability and unchanging eternality: 'Whole' History and the narrative by which History is represented argue—that this does not do justice to the potential of reality for change" (Said 1978: 240). Mill has no monopoly over the triumph of vision over narrative in his depiction of India; the Indologists and the Conservatives are equally implicated.

To further elucidate the interconnections between Mill's attitudes and the ones he sought to attack, it is useful to look briefly at some other contemporary Histories of India. Though none of them attained the monumental status of Mill's work, Robert Orme's *A History of the British Military Transactions in India* (1763) and *Historical Fragments* (1782), Alexander Dow's *History of Hindustan* and William Robertson's *A Historical Disquisition Concerning Ancient India* (1818) were immensely influential works of their time. Both Orme and Robertson were regarded as Conservative historians and even Dow, despite Burke's dismissal of his work,[10] did not display an overtly antagonistic attitude to Hindu religion or traditions. It is interesting to observe certain judgments and comments of these historians in the light of Mill's already analyzed positions.

All three historians firmly believed that British imperialism was generally beneficial to the Indians themselves. The same pens, which lose themselves for pages in discussing "the wonder that was India," end up offering justifications for Empire in Appendixes, Notes and Prefaces. We can trace the existence of two conflicting pictures of India emerging through the fine mesh of supposedly "objective" narratology adopted in these Histories.

Orme affixes to his *Fragments* a separate essay blatantly titled "The Effeminacy of the Inhabitants of Indostan." The "fact" that Indians are effeminate is here presented as almost a scientific inevitability.[11] The contours of the masculine imperialist and the effeminate Indian are already spelt out in this work:

> The European sailor no sooner lands on the coast, than nature dictates to him the full result of a physical comparison with the natives; he brandishes his stick and puts fifty Indians to flight in a moment. Confirmed in his contempt of pusillanimity and incapacity of resistance suggested to him by their form and physiognomy, it is well if he reflects that the poor Indian is still a man. (Orme 1982: 299)

The idea of "Oriental Despotism" is also emphasized by Orme in *Fragments*: "If the subjects of a despotic power are everywhere miserable, the miseries of the people of Indostan are multiplied by the incapacity of the power to control the vast extent of its dominions" (Orme 1982: 25). Orme also uses Mill's practice of converting even accepted virtues into vices, when he asserts that Muslim "decorum" in India is the result of "subordination—joined to the deepest disguise and dissimulation" and that even the "charity" of the Hindus is the "influence of superstition" (Orme 1982: 278).

Dow's *History of Hindustan* is mainly a translated compilation of Persian writers. So, it is in the long Preface that we should search for the author's own assumptions. Dow accuses contemporary travellers of "prejudicing Europe—and by a very unfair account, throwing disgrace upon a system of religion and philosophy, which they have by no means investigated" (Dow 1973: xx). However, it is very doubtful if his practice lived up to the standards indicated here. His comment on Indian literature sounds like a direct quote from Mill: "Their poetry, it must be confessed is too turgid and full of conceits to please and the diction of their histories is too diffuse, verbose and redundant." (1973: ii)

Oriental despotism is of course emphasized and is also linked to a portrayal of the lethargy of the Indians:

> The history, now given to the public presents us with a striking picture of the deplorable condition of a people subjected to arbitrary sway. The people permit themselves to be transferred from

> one tyrant to another without murmuring and individuals look with unconcern on the miseries of others, if they are able to secure themselves from the general misfortune. (Dow 1973: xii)

The main body of Robertson's work is confined to describing trade relations between India and the West, from Roman days till the advent of the East India Company. This does not deter him from commenting on other aspects of life in India in an Appendix, which occupies a full quarter part of the book. Unlike Mill, Robertson admits that his lack of personal knowledge of India was a considerable disadvantage (1981: xi) and stresses the image of India as the lost Eden (1981: 1). At the same time, the permanency of Indian institutions is emphasized as follows: "the manners, customs and even the dress of the people are as permanent and as invariable as the face of Nature itself" (15). Robertson asserts: "whatever is now in India always was there and is still likely to continue." (114)

While discussing the *Shakuntala* Robertson cautions his readers that they should not apply to it rules of criticism drawn from Greek theatre or British propriety, which were unknown to the Indians. He insists that allowance should be made for modes of life and composition quite different from those of Europe. (123). But when analyzing the *Bhagavat Geetha* Robertson forgets his own strictures and applies a standard of the integrated work, connected to eighteenth century British taste:

> Two powerful armies are drawn up in battle array, eager for the fight, a young hero and his instructor are described as standing in a chariot of war between them. That surely was not the moment for teaching him the principles of philosophy and delivering eighteen lectures on theology and metaphysics. (Robertson 1981: 124)

Comparative cultural analysis does not figure here and no alternative set of standards are acknowledged. In keeping with Mill's own style, Robertson accuses the work of a "total lack of art and taste." (124)

When we attempt to reconstruct the impressions given by these three historians to the public consciousness, we may conclude that the generalizations and essentializations included in the narrative structures were the elements most likely to penetrate into general public awareness, precisely because those sections did not deal in 'dry' facts or statistics. The concepts of Oriental Despotism, effeminacy, fecundity and also the inevitability of imperial rule could be easily bolstered by fragments taken from these works. Ironically, the avowed intention of these writers was to bridge the chasm between the rulers and the ruled,[12] but their works contained material capable of producing exactly the opposite effect.

It is evident that Mill shared many of his basic assumptions with the Indologists and the Conservatives and with other Historians of his time. Does Mill fit in neatly then into the category of spokesman for Empire? We have seen that the Indological discourse through its fragmentations upheld the notion of continued imperialism. It remains to be seen whether Mill's stand was simply a variation on that position; if his Utilitarian discourse was functioning as an unconditional foundation for Empire.

Whatever Mill's position was on Empire as such, we can see that he certainly did not hold that the East India Company was doing a good job of it. He is quite scathing in his condemnation of the Company's policies and principles, including even their "attempted reforms." The Company's monopoly of trade itself was severely criticized (Mill 1978: II 137). Even with regard to the notorious Black Hole tragedy, Mill remarks, "the English had only themselves and their own practice to blame" (II 227). The Company is also accused of misleading the nation by their "absurd estimates of the pecuniary value of the Indian dominion" (II 279). They are also condemned for making unjust war, their doctrine sarcastically summed up as:

> Do you wish a good reason for effecting anybody's destruction? First, do him an injury sufficiently great, and then, if you destroy him, you have in the law of self-defence an ample justification. (II 645)

The Company had, according to Mill, sufficient *military* strength to "exterminate all the inhabitants with the utmost ease" but its civil weakness was so great that "the villain was more powerful to intimidate than the Government to protect" (Mill 1978: III 385). The argument of the Governor-General that rendering Indian princes dependent on British support was actually beneficial to them is dismissed as "neither more nor less than another of the pretexts under which the weak are always exposed to become the prey of the strong" (III 711).

It is interesting at this point to note that in his evidence before the 1832 Parliamentary Committee, Mill had adopted a most aggressive attitude towards the Indian states. He argues that the most obvious policy was "to make war on those states and subdue them" and that the period when they were allowed to survive independently "ought to be as short as you can conveniently make it" (qtd. Stokes 1959: 250).

We will see that these conflicting positions in Mill's attitude to aggression were mainly a result of his ambivalent view of Empire, produced by his Utilitarian doctrines.

Even while arguing for a doctrine of reform, Mill was not at all clear as to whether Anglicization was the solution to India's problems. Of education itself, which was the grand liberal panacea to all Oriental ills, Mill was considerably sceptical:

> Most of the Indian judges point to education as the only process from the operation of which a favourable change can be expected in the moral character of the people. . . . These views are superficial. Ignorance is the natural concomitant of poverty . . . and poverty is the effect of bad laws and bad government. . . . Before education can operate to any great result the poverty of the people should be redressed, their laws and government should operate beneficially. (Mill 1978: III 418)

Apart from this general distrust of formal education, in his Parliamentary Evidence, Mill specifically rejects *English* education as a means of progress, claiming that he failed to see how knowledge of English would in anyway benefit the natives.[13]

The attempts of the British at legal reform are also stigmatized. Lord Cornwallis' attempt at codifying the laws are criticized for relying on the "*Shastras* and the *Koran* which were just about as well calculated for defining the rights of the people of India, as the Bible would be for defining those of the people of

England" (Mill 1978: I 339). Nor are we to assume that Mill advocated the implementation of a Universal code based on the British system in India. His contempt for the English legal system in its existing form is immense. Indeed, the procedural format of justice is the one area where he proclaims that the Mohammedan system and even the system of the benighted Hindus had a definite advantage over the British system (1978: I 112, 710). The establishment, in India of a Supreme Court in 1773, supposed to act on British principles is condemned unequivocally; its proceedings described as "a black and portentous cloud, from which every terrific and destructive form might at each moment be expected to descend on the native" (II 780). Neither the English legal system, nor English education, the usual accompaniments to the rhetoric of Empire, was advocated by Mill.

As Nigel Leask suggests, Mill's "paranoiac prose and exaggerated denunciations" suggest his cultural anxieties related to Empire (Leask 1993: 90). Mill expresses this fear when he condemns the union between "Indian influence and parliamentary influence" and the corruption which was sure to ensure "the moment a proper channel of communication was opened between them" (1978: III 18). Unlike Burke, Mill does not fear that the Indian influences will inject corruption into an uncorrupted British system, for him the status quo is already corrupt. Nevertheless, the anxiety is precisely because it would bolster up the *ancient regime* which the Conservatives eulogized and which Mill wanted to dismantle. As Javed Majeed has pointed out, Mill employed his criticism partly because he saw that Empire propped up traditionally powerful groups in England: "colonies sustained the power of the aristocracy, who encouraged the myth of economic riches of India to justify Britain's role as an imperial nation" (Majeed 1990: 213).

Was Mill then a true spokesman for the Empire? The answer to a certain extent at least will have to be in the negative. In his "Essay on Colonies" Mill indicts colonies as merely sources of power and patronage for the ruling elite to perpetuate their position. And in his pamphlet on *Elements of Political Economy* (1807) Mill argues that as increased production would create domestic markets, foreign commerce was not useful in any strict sense (qtd. Majeed 1990: 213). In the *History* itself Mill argues that the Empire should be judged from a purely economic perspective:

> As regards the British nation, it is in these (financial) results that the good or evil of its operations in India is to be found. If India affords a surplus revenue, which can be sent to England, thus far is India beneficial to England. If the revenue of India is not equal to the expense of governing India, then is India a burthen and a drain to England. (1978: III 843)

Judged by these criteria, Mill finds the Empire in India to be an unprofitable and therefore not advisable procedure. He regards the arguments for the prosperity to be gained from India as mere fabrications. He bluntly states, "though nobody should believe it, India, like other countries in which the industrious arts are in their infancy and in which law is too imperfect to render property secure has always been poor" (1978: II 420). He accuses his countrymen of downright hypocrisy or incredible naiveté in crediting stories of Indian opulence:

> The cupidity natural to mankind and the credulity with which they believe what flatters their desires made the English embrace without deduction the exaggerations of Oriental rhetoric on the riches of India and believe that a country, which they saw was one of the poorest, was nevertheless, the most opulent upon the surface of the globe. (1978: I 323)

Poverty-stricken India could not meet her own needs, let alone contribute to the profit of Britain. Mill's final word on the economic folly of the Empire is backed up with impeccable statistics: "During that interval (1797-98) England sent to India and China, value more than it received from them to the amount of 5,691,689 pounds" (1978: I 849). Judged by Mill's own criteria then, Empire as an institution has failed in this context. But, at this point, Mill shies away from such an assertion. In Majeed's phrase, Mill suffers from a "loss of nerve in assessing the role of the British in India" (Majeed 1990: 213). The "Conclusion" of the *History* is symptomatic of this; it is no conclusion at all. Mill merely states:

> With regard to subsequent events, the official papers and other sources of information are not sufficiently at command. Here, therefore, it is necessary for the present that this history should close. (1978: III 849)

This is the very next sentence after Mill's statistical *expose* of the financial failure of the Empire. That argument is not carried on to any logical conclusion, there is no analysis, no interpretation, merely an abrupt "conclusion." Obviously, Mill could not explicitly pronounce that Britain would be well advised to withdraw from India.

Leask and Majeed have both indicated that this was due to the confusion inherent in Utilitarianism itself between a negative view of the Empire as such and a positive view where the Empire could help Utilitarianism to create a better society in the colonies more easily and quickly than in Britain itself (Majeed 1990: 213; Leask 1993: 88). The paternal streak in Utilitarianism triumphed over the liberal streak when it came to India. As Eric Stokes points out, Mill, though an ardent advocate of representative institutions had to claim that they were quite out of the question in India (Stokes 1959: 178). The past *had* to be wiped out so that a *Tabula Rasa* would remain for Utilitarian proceedings. This could be obtained with the help of the Empire in India, and could be obtained with less domestic opposition than if the experiment was to be tried in Britain itself. Obviously, representative institutions in India would foil this purpose.

The unstated assumption therefore was that the Empire was a necessary evil, which was to serve as a forerunner to clear the ground for a grand Utilitarian experiment. The problem was that by Utilitarian standards themselves, of free trade and economic calculation, the Empire was indefensible. This contradiction was not unnoticed by contemporaries, as Eric Stokes points out. The Utilitarians were accused of being "Demagogues at home and despots abroad, of judging Indian questions by rules and standards the very opposite of those they employ to decide all other questions whatever" (Stokes 1959: 60).

The issue is further complicated by the fact that such distinctions made on the basis of local and cultural differences went against the entire universalist and assimilationist foundations of Utilitarianism. The rational principles, which were to ensure "the greatest happiness of the greatest number" had to function across cultures and locales if they were to be valid. As Javed Majeed has stressed, "It is very difficult to make a distinction between colonial and domestic when questions of ideology in this period are being considered. Indeed, it was crucial to the emergence of Utilitarianism as a rhetoric of reform to ignore any such distinctions" (Majeed 1990: 222-23).

However, the distinctions had to be made, if the space was to be cleared for the experiment. Utilitarianism could not justify Empire and yet could not abandon its only practical ally in enforcing its reforms. This ambiguity pervades Mill's conclusions, indeed, leads him to be inconclusive in an attempt not to contradict himself too blatantly. The stridency of Utilitarianism does not imply complete self-confidence and logical coherence. The fragmentations are there, clearly to be seen if only the discourse is surveyed as a whole and in relation to the other discourses it defined itself against.

Conservatism and Indological scholarship, despite their many "positive" pronouncements on India, contribute to pro-imperialist rhetoric; Utilitarianism with its incessant condemnations cannot reconcile its inherent contradictions with regard to Empire. The point is not whether the "pros" outweigh the "cons" in any particular discourse, but that the contradictions exist, preventing discourses of domination, *theoretically* speaking, from being absolute. These rhetorical stances did support the Empire, both by what they said as by what they left unsaid. They were indeed forceful, but their forcefulness does not reduce their fragility as *coherent rhetorical positions.*

NOTES

1. "As Mill painstakingly interrogated the history, the laws, the manners and the arts of India, to tell his three volume story of the civilization, he drew quite unselfconsciously and in great detail on the assumptions and logic of his times. Mill invoked commonsense (which we must remember also grounded liberal utilitarian notions of human nature and civilized behaviour) in a tone that indicated that he regarded its soundness as obvious and its authority as rational and indisputable" (Tharu and Lalitha 1990: 48).
2. It may be a matter of controversy to what extent the indecent objects employed in the Hindu worship imply depravity of manners; but a religion which subjects to the eyes of its votaries the grossest images of sensual pleasure, and renders even the emblems of generation objects of worship; which ascribes to the Supreme God an immense train of obscene acts, which has these engraved on the sacred cars, portrayed in the temples and presented to the people as objects of adoration, which pays worship to the Yoni and the Lingam cannot be regarded as favourable to chastity. Nor can it be supposed that when to all circumstances is added the institution of a number of girls, attached to the temples, whose sole business is dancing and prostitution that this is a virtue encouraged by the religion of the Hindus" (Mill 1978: I 205-6).
3. "Weaving is a sedentary occupation and thus in harmony with his [Hindu's] predominant inclination. It requires patience, of which he has an inexhaustible fund; it requires little bodily exertion of which he is exceedingly sparing, and the finer the production the more slender the force which he is called upon to apply" (Mill 1978: I 329).
4. "That amidst numberless effusions, which a wild imagination throws forth, there should now and then be something of taste is so far from surprising, that it would be truly surprising if there were not. A happy description, or here and there the vivid conception of a striking circumstance are not sufficient; the exact observation of nature and the symmetry of the whole are necessary to designate the poetry of a cultivated people." (Mill 1978: I 367)
5. The marriage between Dushyanta and Shakuntala is described as "so precipitate a conclusion, irreconcilable as it is with the notions of a refined people, which is one of the numerous marriages legal among the Hindus" (Mill 1978: I 367).

6. "In the dramatic poem *Shakuntala* the daughter of the hermit asks the royal stranger who had visited their consecrated grove 'what imperial family is embellished by our noble guest?' The question undoubtedly implied that there were more royal families than one to which he might belong and these at no remarkable distance" (Mill 1978: I 470).
7. The fisherman who finds the King's ring in *Shakuntala* is obliged to give half his reward to the policemen 'to escape' it is said 'the effects of their displeasure.'" (Mill 1978: I 473-74)
8. "The monarch who forms the hero in the drama entitled Shakuntala had many wives and they are represented as residing in the secret apartments of the palace." (Mill 1978: 1 285).
9. Halhed's argument that laws should be studied from a perspective which does acknowledge cultural differences is used by Mill to deduce that "Hindu morals are certainly as gross as the Hindu laws, that the latter grossness is in fact the result of the former" (Mill 1978: I 124-25).
10. Burke refers to "the slander of Dow's History, a book of no authority, a book that no *man* values in any respect or degree" and also remarks that the "Dows and Hastings . . . trample with pride and indignity upon the first names and characters in India." (Burke 1987: I 107-8)
11. "Breathing in the softest of climates, having few real wants and receiving even the luxuries of other nations from the fertility of their own soil, the Indian must become the most effeminate inhabitant of the globe and this is the very point at which we now see them" (Orme 1982: 306).
12. Robertson expresses the hope that his work "would contribute in some small degree to rendering the character of Indians more respectable and their condition more happy" in which case he "would not have lived or written in vain" (Robertson 1981: 138).
13. "I [Mill] do not see, for example, how, for the administration of justice to his countrymen as a moonsiff, a native would be better qualified by knowing the English language. The other great branch of the local administration is collecting the revenue, acting under the English collector in dealing with the natives, fixing their assessments and realizing the demand. In this, also, it does not appear to me that there would be any peculiar advantage to the native in knowing the English language, provided only the Englishman knows the language of the native" (qtd. Viswanathan 1989: 91).

Chapter 5

Travellers' Tales: 'Personal Records'?

I beheld through the door the natives' terrific countenances and heard them incessantly calling "ao, ao."

Eliza Fay

Mrs. Fay is here describing how Hyder Ali's soldiers were waiting to conduct her to a place of confinement. I use the imagery to indicate how India itself has been pictured as calling "ao"—'come'—through the ages, a call to which numerous travellers from abroad, both men and women, have responded. This chapter deals with the travel literature produced by British travellers in India between 1757 and 1857. The texts are surveyed from a dual perspective, as works belonging to the genre of travel literature and as documents inscribed within a colonial context.

The O.E.D definition of travel is relevant in this context. After the simple initial definition of "go from one place to another" the elaborated meanings include *"pass in a deliberate or systematic manner from point to point."* This is a suitable way to describe the voyages of our colonial travellers—*deliberate and systematic* even in the most apparently impulsive wanderings. Constantly observing and narrating, the colonial traveller especially figures as "a kind of collective, moving eye which registers the sights/sites presented in a descriptive sequence" (Pratt 1985: 123).

Indeed, to a large extent, the individual element would seem to be strongest in travel accounts, centred as they are around the I/Eye concepts, around the fact of actually having "been there" and the process of eyewitnessing. Stephen Greenblatt refers to "the primal act of witnessing around which the entire discourse of travel is constructed" (1991: 22). The statements gain their power from the fact of the author's *personal presence*, the stamp of the individual existence on his utterances. From this perspective, these texts may seem to meet the criteria of "personal statement" that Edward Said suggests as a corrective to "Orientalism":

> Contributions to the library of Orientalism and to its consolidation depend on how experience and testimony get converted from a purely personal document into the enabling codes of Orientalist science. Within a text, there has to take place a metamorphosis from personal to official statement; the record of Oriental residence and experience by a European must shed or at least minimize its purely autobiographical and indulgent descriptions on which Orientalism in general . . . can draw, build and base further scientific observation and description. (1978: 157)

"Personal statements" are here presented as comparatively less "Orientalist." The travel documents considered in this chapter, except perhaps Burton's works (which were sidelined due to their unorthodox nature) and Sleeman's productions in his official capacity rarely underwent conversions to official status. This is especially true of the texts produced by women travellers whose works were certainly not even considered "serious" let alone required reading unlike the productions of the Indologists or James Mill. To a large extent, therefore, these texts remain at the level of personal articulation.

Meeting the requirements to be regarded as "personal statement" however, does *not* implicate these texts any less in the colonial process. Each text here considered is individual and different from other texts, but "these differences occur within larger discursive frameworks" (Mills 1993: 197). Travel writing despite its intensely personal characteristics was part of the colonial paradigm and it is essential to keep that discourse at the back of any analysis. As Foucault points out, eighteenth century travel writers had "schema" for collecting their data (1980: 74). Their descriptions were articulated from a particular position, which had been constituted by colonial discourses, large-scale constructs, which determined what one "could know" or "see." We cannot argue that these travel texts were not implicated in the colonial paradigm. At the same time, it is unnecessary to insist that they lose their personal character so as to be fitted into the colonial framework. As an analysis of these texts will indicate, the personal *as* personal *could* co-exist with the Orientalist statement.

However, no simplistic explanation of these texts as racist or imperialist or even "Orientalist" in the Saidean sense will encompass the dichotomy seen within them. Dennis Porter in "Orientalism and its Problems" argues that the very nature of writing about another culture entails a discourse marked by gaps and inconsistencies, in addition to which travel writing itself is subject to such a wide range of motivations as to render it inevitably heterogeneous (Porter 1982). We cannot read travel writing merely as one more contribution to the colonial archives. Critics who consider travel writing as History adopt a path fraught with difficulties:

> These socio-historical studies face a methodological problem that renders their findings ambiguous at best and misleading at its worst. By ignoring the literary conventions that govern what an author says, they assume that these accounts display the immediate personal experience of travellers and that these travellers in turn reflect the taste of the century in general. (Batten 1978: 4)

The literary conventions that govern travel writing cannot be ignored, even though the genre has only recently been granted a respectable status. The texts under consideration are all cast in the form of letters, diaries, or at the most, reconstructions from journals. The assumption of an individualistic tone, the rambling form of narration, scattered quotations, numerous digressions—these are all aspects characteristic to the genre to which the individual writers generally conform. Interestingly the techniques are calculated to disarm the reader—for example—the confessions of lack of scholarship or literary ability on the title pages. But, as Percy Adams points out, these very features, like the digression for example, actually serve to authenticate the record. "What may be called digressions in some forms of literature are, for travel accounts, structurally inherent"[1] (Adams, 1983: 109). The travel texts considered here have a claim to objectivity, as they were supposedly dealing, at an individual level, with verifiable facts of Indian life, with no ulterior motives. Though the authors explicitly disavow claims to scholarship, the texts are not avowed fictionalizations either. In fact these travel records make an ideal transition point from the scholarly Indological texts and Histories discussed earlier to the study of more 'literary' forms like the epic or the novel. Despite the claims to first-hand authenticity, however, these texts reveal more about the *observers and their attitudes than about any monolithic India which they all observed.*

While considering the texts of colonial travel writing in India as belonging to a discursive pattern, we cannot afford to overlook the inconsistencies produced by gender and class distinctions within that discourse. Though all Englishmen and women definitely belonged to the ruling elite in India as compared with the 'natives,' English society in India was itself highly fragmented on class lines. Eliza Fay was an adventuress with no money and no connections or institutional backing in India. James Forbes also occupied an inferior position as a Company writer in his early tenure before being promoted to higher posts. Sleeman, Broughton and Williamson as army officials and Harriet Tytler as a captain's wife shared roughly the same status. Burton's official status was of course considerably elevated, but he was generally regarded as an eccentric outcast who did not conform to social codes. Isabella Fane, the daughter of the Commander-in-Chief, and Honoria Lawrence, whose husband Henry Lawrence was "the virtual ruler of the Punjab" occupy very high positions on the social ladder. Acland and Martyn were both clergymen though of different natures altogether—Acland being the archetypal jovial parson and Martyn a soul incessantly tortured by a sense of spiritual inadequacy. Heber as Bishop headed the ecclesiastical strata in India. With Emily Eden, sister of Lord Auckland, the Governor-General, we are at the topmost level of the social hierarchy.

These differences of social position are to be clearly seen in the works of these travellers. For instance, Eliza Fay adopts a tolerant, not very snobbish attitude to India when compared with Miss Fane in whose case, snobbery reaches such heights that she never even condescends to once mention India or Indians without a sneer. This attitude is elevated into good-humoured irritation and patriarchal patronage in Miss Eden's case; who generally does not feel that the natives are worth even the trouble of despising; the same tone is used for favourite lap dogs and for natives.

The society to which these writers belonged was also fragmented on gender lines. The involvement of women with imperialism has always been a vexed question. Sara Mills refers to the women writers' problematic status in a colonial situation; "caught between the conflicting demands of the discourse of femininity and that of imperialism" (1993: 21). The Memsahib in India was criticized as being responsible for the crystallization of racial attitudes; of driving a wedge between the natives and the white men. At the same time, in keeping with the discourses of femininity, women were seen as occupying a higher moral level than men; as more interested in philanthropy, sensitive and also sympathetic, in fact as "God's police" in Kay Schaffer's telling phrase (qtd. Mills 1993: 44). Their position as members *of the ruling race* and the sympathy they were *supposed to feel as women* produced a certain extra ambiguity in the texts produced by women. Isabella Fane tries to deal with this by identifying entirely with the colonial discourse, but Emily Eden's text clearly reveals a struggle between these concepts throughout. "Women's texts are, just as men's texts are, about the colonial situation, but their relation to the dominant discourse differs" (Mills 1993: 39).

On analyzing these texts we find to a certain extent a desire to conform, to confirm what has been said before. As Stephen Greenblatt remarks: "In a sense, then, the best voyage will be one in which one learns next to nothing; most of the signs will simply confirm what one already knows"[2] (1991: 88). Emily Eden writes: "In short, just what people say of India, you know it all, but it is pretty to see" (1930: 12). The suggestion is that despite her many pages, she really has not much to add; all that it is necessary to know is "already known."

The tendency of these travel writers to quote at length from earlier texts can be attributed to this desire to have their works bolstered by authority and to confirm what has already been said. "Most colonial writers portray members of the other nation through a conceptual and textual grid constituted by travel books. This close intertextual relation, with other accounts can be seen in the fact that travel writing has always appropriated other writing, sometimes explicitly, but often by plagiarizing" (Mills 1993: 74).

The Indian travel writers are in no way behind in this matter of appropriating other written accounts. Sleeman in his *Rambles and Recollections* devotes eight full chapters to a detailed historical account of the contest for empire between Shah Jahan's sons. This entire account is practically a literal translation of Bernier's history, a fact that is not acknowledged by the author, but is pointed out in an editorial footnote in the 1915 edition. Sleeman also quotes extensively from Sir Thomas Munro, to the effect that Indians were not totally uncivilized.[3] James Forbes' *Oriental Memoirs* abounds in lengthy quotations from many sources. So slight an occasion as a brief reference to the *"Madhavi"* creeper brings in an elaborate quote from Jones' translation of the *Shakuntala* (1988: I 31). Jones is quoted with regard to the *Manu Smriti*,[4] the Vedas and references to Indian deities evoke long passages from Southey's *Curse of Kehama.* Jones' entire "Hymn to Camdeo" is quoted and a long extract from his translation of the *Gita Govinda* is included. Lengthy extracts from poems by Charles Grant are also included with regard to Vedic beliefs, conversion and imperial responsibility.[5] These quotes form authenticating devices and enforce the writer's view while their inclusion simultaneously confirms their own validity.

However, we can see a tension in these texts between the pressure to confirm the known and to seek out and describe the exotic and the strange. Paul Fussel considers that the 'anomaly' is central for the travel book, that travel writing is in fact an "implicit quest for anomaly" (1980: 167), a search for something strange to describe:

> Like any genre, the travel book carries about it the marks of its origins and if the Wonders of Antiquity, the Middle Ages and the Renaissance have in the full bourgeois age attenuated to mere anomaly; these anomalies are still a necessary element in travel writing. (Fussel 1980: 166)

The search for the exotic is of primary importance in the colonial context, where the colony is to be established, partly at least as the Other, the natives as different from the white spectators. Even more than searching out strangeness, narrative techniques are employed to render whatever is actually seen as strange; in fact to invest it with the necessary criteria of becoming an anomaly.

Meticulous description, as if of some other world and species altogether is one of the defamiliarising techniques employed in these texts to make India appear as "different." Forbes for example, describes the coconut tree and the betel nut, in excruciating detail, as alien creations, which can exist only in an alien/exotic land (Forbes 1988: I 22-74). The animals, birds, fishes, even the wasps are described for pages at length, the emphasis being on their "strangeness." Miss Fane's description of an Indian bearer deserves to be quoted at full length as a prime example of the defamiliarising and distancing technique, by means of which she seems to be not discussing a human being at all:

> *There was a figure in the pit*, which afforded much amusement. It was *a character known here by the appellation of bearer*. . . . *These beauties* wear nothing in the shape of clothes but a piece of coarse cloth in which they envelop the whole of their person. . . . *A figure of this sort*, I suppose he must have had a musical turn, actually came into the pit, holding on to the skirts of a half-caste. Down he squatted himself upon one bench, with his chin resting on another and during the whole of the performance he never stirred, but appeared in a maze or pleasure or some indefinable feeling. (1989: 38, my italics)

Sara Mills remarks that a "further way of 'Othering' a people is not to describe them as full individuals; but as composed of separate parts of the body" (1993: 89-90). Such a description is at work in Honoria Lawrence's description of Indian boatmen:

> These men were very dark, nearly naked and very repulsive looking. Among them all, I did not see one countenance that had a decidedly human expression; all looked like mere animals. (Lawrence 1980: 33-34)

> The boatmen seemed to have the facility of articulating without shutting their mouths, for while they chattered, *there seemed no closing of those awful chasms*, a ring of black lips on the outside; a rim of white teeth and within this setting a tongue and throat dyed red by the stuff the natives constantly chew—called paan. (*Ibid.* 39, my italics)

India is characterized as "such a talkative nation" and the natives' conversation itself described as "quite unintelligible and an unearthly noise" (Fane 1989: 110). Other techniques of alienation such as presenting the natives as mere children who have to be humoured are also used frequently. The stereotypical reference to the "dirty" native is also present. [Here, Forbes strikes a different note. He actually refers to the cleanliness of the natives: "The Hindoo religion requires frequent ablution, which is a custom wisely introduced in a warm climate, where cleanliness is very conducive to health" (Forbes 1988: I 83)].

Sleeman refers to the fact that European women can travel alone in India, without any harm coming to them. But, then this is not due to any particular virtue on the part of the natives, in fact it is treated as a testimony to the virtues of British rule. "Would men trust their wives and daughters in this manner unprotected among a people that disliked them and their rule? . . . We know and feel that the people everywhere look up to and respect us in spite of all our faults" (Sleeman 1915: 3). Eliza Fay, who was unlucky enough to have come to India when the British had yet not attained paramount power, when she was captured along with her husband by Haider Ali's troops, exclaims incredulously and indignantly:

> It is true we were in the hands of the natives; but little did I imagine that any power on the continent, however independent would have dared to treat English subjects with such cruelty as we experienced from them. (Fay 1986: 119-20)

Indeed, the establishment of British rule is presented as the best thing which happened to India and the natives are shown as actually courting British rule. Forbes describes as a very favourable native trait the supposedly generally affectionate and grateful attachment, which rising above religious and caste prejudices they show to their English rulers. Anyone who deviated from this pattern is stigmatized as ungrateful (1988: III 47). Broughton also refers to the high esteem in which the natives supposedly held Englishmen. "They all expressed themselves in terms of the highest admiration of the prowess, humanity and justice of the British government" (1977: 6).[6] In the Punjab, the child Dhuleep Singh was only King in name and Henry Lawrence for all practical purposes was the ruler. In her *Journal,* Honoria Lawrence seriously hopes that "some time, perhaps little Dhuleep Singh may know how much better off he is, brought up safely under kind instruction, then if he had still been called a King, with a daily chance of being murdered" (Lawrence 1980: 200). Quite evidently there is a consensus of opinion that the British are doing the natives a favour by ruling them. Sleeman indeed is so confident about British rule that he can even advocate leaving the few remaining native states independent, because:

> First, it tends to relieve the minds of other native chiefs . . . and secondly because by leaving them as a contrast . . . we afford to the people of India the opportunity of observing the superior advantages of our rule. (Sleeman 1918: 186)[7]

Yet another effect of this confidence in colonial rule is that the writers' presence in the country is taken as perfectly natural and rarely questioned. The fact that the colonial situation enabled these travels is hardly ever remarked on nor is it supposed that the effect of such travel—its collective consequences—could be anything but highly positive. There is an exception to this trend to be found in Emily Eden's criticism of British globe-trotting and overly commercial mentality:

> In short, Delhi is a very suggestive moralizing place—such stupendous remains of power and wealth passed away and passing away and I somehow feel that we horrid English have just gone and done it, merchandised it and spoilt it all. I am not very fond of Englishmen out of their own country. (Eden 1930: 98)

The theme of evanescent glory, especially as exemplified by the fall of the Mughals leads to frequent emphasis on mutability as a particularly Indian theme. For example, Sleeman gives a vivid account of the present deprived state of the Delhi royal family as opposed to their earlier greatness and philosophizes on it.[8] Ironically, this theme co-exists with the notion of the unchanging traditional nature of India. Indian customs, especially the daily tasks indulged in by the women are described as being exactly identical to descriptions of the patriarchal age" (Forbes 1988: I 52).

Religion, of course, is a topic of primary interest in these texts. Among the clergymen considered here, Acland maintained a good-humoured tolerance towards native customs. He was actually rather impressed by the asceticism of the Hindu sages which he contrasted to the "unwillingness of Christians to do even a little to please the true God" (Acland 1879: 119). Bishop Heber also does not go into any frenzy against "heathenism,"—indeed he openly accuses many missionaries of "being too intolerant" (Heber 1985: III 446). He gives a generally favourable account of the people and adds: "If it should please God to make any considerable portion of them Christians, they would, I can well believe put the best of European Christians to shame" (1985: II 309). We also have accounts of the Bishop visiting temples and mosques and behaving in a perfectly respectful manner.

The case is very different with the Reverend Henry Martyn who seems to have taken the entire responsibility for converting the heathens on his own shoulders. His initial reflection on India is: "I looked towards India and remembered that they were heathens, perhaps ten times worse than anything I had seen" (Martyn 1837: I 192). The sight of a new temple fills him with horror and anger; tolerance is quite out of the question:

> As we walked through the dark wood, which everywhere covers the country, the cymbals and drums struck up and never did sounds go through my heart with such horror in my life. The pagoda was in a court surrounded by a wall and the way up to it was by a flight of steps on each side. . . . In the centre of the building was the idol—a little, ugly, black image, about two feet high, with a few lights burning around him. I shivered at being in the neighbourhood of hell; my heart was ready to burst at the dreadful state to which the devil had brought my fellow creatures. I would have given the world to have known the language to have preached to them. (1837: I 449-50)

It is by no means the clergymen alone who were interested in religious questions in India. The last chapter in Forbes' *Oriental Memoirs* is frankly apocalyptic in tone and ends with a vision of India as the Great Other, desperately in need of reclamation through conversion. "We see in Forbes almost a schizophrenic split between a romantic attraction towards India, and an Evangelical revulsion from Hinduism" (Dyson 1978: 31). The early volumes of Forbes' work reveal tolerant on-the-spot responses to India. But since the work was put together for publication a long time after it was actually written, the last part is added on with the express intention of justifying conversion. A positive bundle of comments by "impartial authors" are gathered together in this volume by Forbes to testify to Hindu depravity and aid the cause of Evangelism. Forbes defends himself against the charge inconsistency by claiming: "My sentiments changed progressively as I became more and more acquainted with the higher castes of Hindus. I first admired the Brahmins, but then was shocked" (Forbes 1988: IV 300). The allowed "sublimity" of the Vedas is counterbalanced in Forbes by their "acknowledged puerility" (1988: IV 57).

Miss Eden does not indulge in religious prejudices to any great extent. She does confess to an "instinctive recoil" when the native servants wish her a Merry Christmas (1930: 54). Isabella

Fane is far more amused than disgusted or distressed by Hindu customs. Her only remark on the issue of religion is to remark after watching the ceremony of swinging by hooks: "poor benighted creatures, what a pity it is that they can't understand that such tortures are quite needless" (Fane 1985: 74). There is not a single reference to conversion in Eliza Fay's work. She does refer to "our purer religion and claims to have been told that the Hindu idols [which she has never seen] are very ugly indeed" (1986: 204). But she also accepts that the Indians were very sincerely, attached to these idols and feels no moral compulsion to compel them on to salvation. Indeed, as a private citizen with no institutional backing Eliza Fay was too busy with the problems of survival to spend much time on either criticisms or "saving" the natives. Harriet Tytler on the other hand seems to have come to India with specific missionary aims already well formed in her mind:

> I said to myself, when I grow up to be a woman, I will save all the little starving children and bring them up as Christians, an aspiration which never left me until thirty-three years later, when God in his goodness permitted me to carry out my heart's desire. (Tytler 1986: 10)

The condition of women in India and especially the custom of Sati were topics, which evoked much interest and comment. Interestingly, this is also the area where the texts by women writers differ sharply from those by men. In colonial iconography, the Oriental woman occupied a much more complicated position than her male counterpart. We have a very powerful discourse which posits the image of the Oriental woman as the Archetypal Other, alluring and dangerous precisely because of her Otherness. At the same time the pervasive notion of the entire colonial enterprise as a civilizing mission rendered it imperative that the colonized women be also represented as an *oppressed and silenced group who looked towards the colonizers for rescue and help.* We also have to contend with the wholesale feminization of the Orient as such which created "*feminine men*" and rendered the real women's situation even more ambivalent.

In keeping with their need to posit colonization as a lofty, self-sacrificing mission, the male writers, even though they confessed (on occasion) to an attraction for native women, usually followed it up with a qualification or disclaimer. James Forbes' comment that the "Hindu women when young are delicate and beautiful, *so far as we can* reconcile *the idea of beauty* with *the olive complexion*" (Forbes 1988: 1 73, my italics) is a useful illustration of this trend. Soon after describing the "usefulness" of concubinage with native women, Burton remarks: "the women may be described as very fine large animals; we never saw a pretty one among them" (Burton 1851: 347). However, such covering up techniques are often very transparent. Indeed, the threat posed by the sexual attraction of the native woman is a constant irritant which is a major motivation behind certain white women's jocular or contemptuous dismissal of miscegenetic relationships. Isabella Fane's sneer at the Governor-General's sexual preferences is an example of this trend:

> Among the presents for the Governor-General there was a tiger, which had been nursed and brought up by a native woman. Woman and all are presented, I hear. As Sir C- has the reputation of not caring for colour in his little amours, she may prove a most acceptable present. (1985: 48)

Though he often speaks of the British duty of "liberating" Indian women, Forbes on occasion gets carried away by his version of docile and malleable femininity and argues in true patriarchal fashion that the seclusion of Indian women has many advantages which adequately compensate for the lack of liberty" (1988: I 103).[9] The implication is that precisely because of their secluded life and the docility which it engenders, Indian women are ideally "feminine" creations. Of course, this was not an *officially* acceptable view for a British official from a supposedly liberal culture. So the effect is underplayed with references to Indian women's intellectual inadequacies. However, in spite of this anticipatory bail, the undercurrent of attraction comes through loud and clear.

This seems to be the spur behind the nearly total tendency among the British women writers to ignore the physical appearance of Indian women or restrict it to some accidental mention in passing. Emily Eden refers to the extreme seclusion of Indian women only to remark that "this must have made them very dull companions indeed" (1930: 211). Isabella Fane is seriously worried that her nephew may turn out to be "very black" as he had a native wet nurse (1985: 67). Eliza Fay criticizes Indian women for using too much art and thereby spoiling "whatever little beauty they naturally have" (1986: 205). These women writers are fierce champions of the emancipation of Indian women, the abolition of Sati and similar causes. But the line is firmly drawn at accepting a physical or romantic relation between "their" men and Indian women.

The notion of emancipating the native women was fundamental to the discourse of colonialism as a civilizing mission. In fact, the "liberty and protection" accorded to women functioned as a graph for plotting the success or otherwise of this mission. In Gayatri Spivak's formulation, the constant theme was that of "White men saving brown women from brown men" (1988: 296). This formulation confers a very limited subjectivity on the native male as agent of oppression but freezes the native woman as object of both native oppression and the colonizer's rescue. In the Indian context the custom of Sati was the ideal example (in its prohibition) of the colonial succour of native women. Nearly all texts included at least one detailed reference to Sati, either an eyewitness account or one based on hearsay.

Forbes includes a long eyewitness account of Sati, where he finds himself compelled to admire the "heroism" of the Sati[10] and his only regret is that she did not have the "Christian morality to teach her the futility of such an act" (1988: II 326). The entire incident is described as a grand spectacle. Forbes also records another occasion where British officials were able to persuade a woman not to commit Sati. The incident is presented as a triumph for British enlightenment, but the note of admiration is definitely absent. The same pattern of awe and admiration for a successful Sati and a more sedate account of a prevented one is to be seen in Sleeman also. As Lata Mani points out:

> It is her [Indian woman's] apparent willingness to attempt immolation, not her courage in rescuing herself that is seen as heroic. Her escape is rewritten as rescue. The escape is described as being primarily by physical processes and not one that implies both mind and body. (Mani 1992: 394)

Emily Eden refers to the Sati committed by two of Ranjeet Singh's queens, whom she calls "those poor dear Ranees" and dubs their act as one arising out of "obstinate courage." She also remarks that "they would have given it up if they had been sure of kind treatment" (1930: 309-10). Eliza Fay argues with a feminist zeal that "this rite [Sati] is but a part of the schemes of men in most countries to invent a sufficient number of rules to render the women subservient to their authority" (1986: 202). At the same time, she also adds that the element of courage was overemphasized to describe what was mainly a "result of custom and usage" (1986: 203).[11] The colonizers as a whole stressed the need for abolishing Sati. But the British men were more susceptible to the heroic and romantic associations of the ritual than the women who generally regarded it indignantly and impatiently. It is possible that the implicit suggestion that within certain paradigms, even *British* men were willing to glorify Sati was a disconcerting thought which led the women writers take all possible chances for condemnation. Sati, for them, was not just an exotic and barbaric practice, it was a potential threat.

The issue of Sati though most prominent was not the only issue in the discourse of saving native women. The susceptibility of the Indian women to "holy men" (who are invariably presented as sex crazed impostors) the misery of a widow's life, the Devadasi system, the lack of education and the extreme seclusion of Indian women are also noted and criticized. However, there is also the suggestion that all these precautions still do not serve to uplift the depraved Indian morality. In a characteristic digression in his *Oriental Field Sports*, Williamson comments: "The world is egregiously duped by the opinion that seraglios are conducive to security. Experience proves what reason would suggest; that where we repose trust in locks and walls, we are most frequently disappointed; and that the most private places are the most suitable to intrigue. Hence we find that in the boasted zenanas of India, libidinous practices are most prevalent." (1810: 1 59-60)

Native men are generally accused of deliberately and systematically denying women the chance to grow and develop into rational companions. Emily Eden refers to the native desire to ensure that women remained silent as one of the most difficult stumbling blocks on their road to progress. A servant of Harriet Tytler complains that as a result of the Western rule, his wife had actually threatened to take him to court; for which reason he found such trends which might enable women to break their silence a malignant influence (Tytler 1986: 27).

The process by which Indian women were denied subjectivity and were restructured as objects by the colonial discourse has been noted. This process was applied to the entire colony by means of a general feminization. The colonizer's masculinity showed to the greatest advantage when counterpointed by the ascribed femininity of the colonized. Ashis Nandy points out: "colonization too was congruent with the existing Western stereotypes and the philosophy of life which they represented. It produced a cultural consensus, in which political and socio-economic dominance symbolized the dominance of men and masculinity over women and femininity" (1989: 4). Forbes describes Indian men in the following fashion:

> In India, a people present themselves to our eyes, clothed in linen garments and somewhat low descending, of a garb and gesture we may say maidenly and well nigh effeminate, of a countenance somewhat estranged yet smiling out a glazed and somewhat bashful familiarity. (1988: I 55)

Shy, bashful, maidenly and quite explicitly effeminate—we can easily trace the process and progress of feminization here. Rather ironically, the British women writers also often adopt such techniques, thereby reasserting the idea of inferiority associated with femininity. Eliza Fay refers to the lack of strength in Indian men, who approximate female status when compared to the masculine Englishmen. She quotes a Bengali servant who told her he could not do some heavy work as "Oh, I no English. I Bengalman. I no estrong like English; one two three Bengalmen cannot do like one Englishmen" (Fay 1986: 177-78). It is possible, of course, that the "Bengalman" was using his supposed weakness as a convenient excuse—an example of Homi Bhabha's "sly civility." However, the emphasis is to be laid not on what the Indian said but on the white woman's unquestioning acceptance of it. Obviously there is a consensus that "Bengalmen" actually could not do what Englishmen could.

In fact the white women seem to place themselves in commanding "Masculine" positions in relation to the subservient, docile and feminine positions allotted to the Indian men. Honoria Lawrence and Isabella Fane both refer to the Indian men's incapacity for open fights and accuse them of resorting to secret political intrigues which are represented as subterranean, more suited to women and yet (or perhaps therefore) peculiarly "Indian." Emily Eden juxtaposes an account of "over sentimental" Hindu women falling at her brother's feet and embarrassing him with a description of two dismissed Indian servant men falling at her feet to beg pardon. She finds them so very feminine/childish that she "could not deny them anything" (1930: 143).

The accounts which indicate the feminization of India should be seen as an ideologically well-structured project intended to make the colonial rule seem "natural"—as "natural" as male domination. This process obviously rendered the position of both native and white women ambivalent. The native women (those who came into contact with Western trends at least) were continuously confronted with supposedly "rational" discourses, which presented a constructed image of native men as feminine. They were not offered a choice of liberty or individual agency, but were constantly urged to opt for a change of masters. At the same time, the white women, as collaborators in the colonial enterprise were often forced to submerge their female identity and denounce the feminine as inferior. The feminizing of India implicit in these texts created problems for natives as well as for white women, but of course the complications were very different in nature and implication.

In keeping with the different discourses which govern the kinds of texts which men and women are supposed to produce, we see that there are more of domestic details in the women's texts. Eliza Fay dwells for a long letter on the trickery of Indian servants; though she seems to regard the entire process as a battle of wits in which she enjoys triumphing (1985: 179-87). Such domestic details are found in most of the other women's texts also, while they are practically absent from male-authored works.

On the other hand, specific statements or discussions on political affairs are hardly to be found in the women's texts. Miss Eden's laconic statement that "Another man has been set on the Khelat throne; so that business is finished" is an indication of the trend. Much more obvious and detailed statements are to be found in the male writers. Forbes and Sleeman both discuss administrative affairs in detail, often revealing both complacence and anxiety in turns. For instance, Forbes worries over whether Anglicization could result in a bid for freedom and then consoles himself that internal squabbles would prevent any such attempt (1988: II 266). Sleeman argues that the natives themselves are not even keen on having Oriental systems followed and are perfectly happy with British methods if justly implemented (1915: 65-66). Burton gives us a hint of the political situation at "Home" also when he talks of Sind "as an Eastern Ireland on a larger scale"[12] and of the inhabitants as "Hibernian like" (1851: II 125). Broughton advocates English rule on the ground that native governments are made up of measures as much distinguished by weakness and rapacity as they are deficient in justice, honour and good faith" (1977: 145).

These descriptions, whether they be of practical politics or domesticities both contribute to a large picture of "India" and "the natives." As Edward Said points out, generalized statements are one of the most effective techniques of "Othering." The writer in a colonial situation "tends to speak in vast generalities, seeks to contain each aspect of Oriental or Occidental life into an unmediated sign of one or the other geographic half" (Said 1978: 246-47). Mary Louise Pratt substantiates this view when she says that the task of the writer within colonial discourse is to "incorporate a particular reality into a series of interlocking information orders . . . to make this information seem natural . . . rather than as *products/producers* of European knowledges or disciplines" (1985: 125, my italics).

There are no shortages of generalized statements in the travel texts discussed here. Not only the physical appearance (as seen earlier) but also character and behaviour of the natives are described in generalized/essentialized terms. According to Forbes, the Muslims (as a whole) are "robust and hardy when compared to the disciples of Brahma." The Hindus are "avaricious, indolent and effeminate" and "if to the two former vices we add ambitious valour and jealousy we have the Muslim character" (Forbes 1988: I 94). The virtues of the natives are no less essentialized than their vices. Burton, describing the affection of a Hindu mother for her child essentializes and over-emphasizes to such an extent that the effect is absurd: "The Hindoo mother sees her child as everything. From the hour of his birth she *never* leaves him . . . nor does this cease when the child ceases to be a toy" (Burton 1851: I 248).

The description of the landscape in these texts is also significant. The system of alienating by overly minute description is extended to the scenery also. Of course, the tone varies from each individual text to another. For Honoria Lawrence, the landscape is disappointing and threatening with "nothing to give the idea of a home where the heart could live" (1980: 33). The initial description given by Forbes is in striking contrast: "The town of Cochin is pleasantly situated near the road, with woody hills and majestic mountains forming a noble boundary" (1988: I 13).

This difference of judgment based on difference in perspective is to be found in the meagre accounts we have of Indian art and literature.

It is only in Forbes and Sleeman that we find any references worth mentioning to Indian literature and even here, the main impression left is one of factual misinformation producing unintentional comedy.[13] As far as architecture is concerned, these travel texts illustrate Sara Mills' statement that there was a prestructuring of sites/sights, which governed what could actually be said. "Before the traveller had even arrived, the site was already categorized" (Mills 1993: 83-84). The Taj for instance is *always* praised, that too in identical terms, by everyone, including those like Miss Fane who had already made it quite clear that they detested all Indian art on principle. This tendency can be seen in historical accounts also—in every condemnatory tirade on Oriental despotism—an exception (with often no stated reason) is made for the "great Akbar."

There is a certain (minimal) amount of self-criticism in some of the texts. Emily Eden mocks the overconfidence of the British troops, who after they have been routed by Ranjit Singh's Sikhs in a display can only assert that "they are sure the Sikhs would run away in a real fight" (1930: 209). Sleeman argues that the notorious Indian "perjury" was a direct consequence of foisting alien British systems on them (1916: 388). Burton clearly states that in many parts of India, far from welcoming British rule, the Indians looked upon the white men as "horrors which had to be endured; endemic calamity" (1851: I 212). Emily Eden expresses herself as sincerely wondering "why the natives do not cut all our heads off and be done with it" (1930: 294).

The style in which these texts are written and certain linguistic choices are also interesting. Mary Pratt points out that the process of "Othering" is achieved through language structure also—with the people to be Othered "homogenized into a collective 'they,' distilled even further into an iconic 'he' and made the subject of verbs in a timeless present tense" (1985: 20). This trend can be seen over and over in the travel texts. There is no appeal against recurrent statements like "They are dirty" or mendacious or even positive qualities as the case may be. The statements are absolute and the tense is for all time—all natives for the past, present, and the future.

At the same time, as Greenblatt points out, "to be accused of lying is the travel writers' greatest fear" (1991: 147) and so the texts abound in authenticating devices. The authors have attempted to disavow literariness and subjectivity; as Percy Adams argues, "the more of personality they include, the more they approach the novel and seem to be lying" (1962: 97). A considerable effort has gone into making the works look effortless, but the literary conventions are still present below the surface.

Travel writing, given its ambiguous position on the borders of literature can be described (to adopt Sara Mills' definition) as "a form of writing whose contours both disclose the nature of the dominant discourses and constitute a critique from its margins" (1993: 23). Within the colonial discourse, the texts analyzed here do subscribe to the dominant paradigm. But there are moments of self-doubt, criticism and awareness. Also significant is the fact that even accommodation into the same paradigm is negotiated in widely differing ways by each text. We should not allow our notion of the colonialist structure to be so homogenous as to render it unproblematic. Only then can we see how the contradictions as well as the similarities in these texts moved towards destabilization, but at the same time sustained and enabled the edifice.

NOTES

1. Williamson in *Oriental Field Sports* openly asserts that digressions are essential since a certain pleasure is afforded only by the "admixture of the curious anecdote" (1810: II 239).
2. Greenblatt quotes Jonson's poem to William Roe:

   This is that good Aeneas, passed through fire
   Through Seas, storms, tempests, and embark'd for hell
   Came back untouched: This man hath traveled well.

   (1991: 179-80)
3. Munro says (qtd. Sleeman) that he "does not really know what is meant by civilizing the people of India" as he does not assume they are uncivilized to begin with (Sleeman 1995: 3).
4. Jones is initially quoted to praise the *Manu Smriti,* but later when Forbes' evangelism takes over, he is used to authenticate the entirely opposite argument.
5. One of Grant's poems quoted by Forbes begins:

Britain, thy voice can bid the light descend
On thee alone the eyes of Asia bend.

6. In the much later 'Introduction' to Broughton's letters, Grant Duff indicates his impatience with "ungrateful natives" who should be exposed to the horrors Broughton describes in pre-colonial India so that they would appreciate British rule (Broughton 1977: xxv-xxix).
7. Sleeman reiterates the same idea when he comments that the mis-rule of native kings has its uses—seeing it, "the people are fair dis-posed to estimate the advantages of living under our rules" (1915: 519).
8. "Here are crowded together twelve hundred *kings and queens,* lit-erally eating each other up!" (Sleeman 1915: 519).
9. Forbes argues that seclusion keeps women from "many delusions and temptations" which leave the mind free from later "regrets and remorse" (1988: II 103).
10. Forbes' eyewitness account of the Sati describes the woman as "rushing onto the bower and embracing her husband" (1988, III 225).
11. Eliza Fay argues that if Sati had been the custom in Britain and linked to a woman's fame, many Englishwomen who had never loved their husbands would still "mount the funeral pyre with all imaginable decency and die with a heroic display of fortitude" (1986: 203).
12. It will be seen in a later chapter that parallels between India and Ireland are drawn by Wordsworth and Byron also. This should en-able us to consider political/racial problematics as not entirely trapped between a black/white binary opposition.
13. Forbes confuses the honorary epithet Veda Vyasa (meaning com-piler of the Vedas) bestowed on the saint Vyasa as referring to two distinct persons he calls Vedom and Vyasa. He calls these two "friends of the Pandavas" and adds that "some of the most respect-able Hindus of the present day still believe that the rock inscrip-tions in India are messages for the Pandavas left by Vedom and Vyasa" (1988: II 448).

Chapter 6

A Fancied Fear: Gothicism and Exoticism

Who has not heard of the vale of Cashmere?

Lalla Rookh

This chapter undertakes an analysis of three "Indian" works by authors who were considerably popular in their own day. The term "Indian" in this context refers specifically to those works in which the setting, theme, characters and atmosphere are, ostensibly at least, Indian. The texts considered are two narrative poems-Robert Southey's *The Curse of Kehama,* Thomas Moore's *Lalla Rookh* and a historical novel by Walter Scott—*The Surgeon's Daughter.* The focus is on the creation of an image of India in these works as well as on general views with regard to the imperial enterprise. Southey and Moore quite unabashedly essentialize India and distil exotic imagery from all possible sources. Scott does try to deal in "real" historical characters, if not events—but it is evident that the history followed, in itself highly conditioned by political compulsions, is further subordinated to the demands of contemporary market trends and conceptions of Orientalist aesthetics. The India which emerges from these texts is an embodiment of the colonial discourse to which they contributed and in which they partook.

In his Indian epic, *The Curse of Kehama,* published in 1810 (and dedicated to Landor; himself a writer of Oriental poetry) Southey makes elaborate use of Hindu mythology, but refers to it his preface as "monstrous." Indeed, the poet takes considerable trouble in the Preface to exculpate himself from any accusation of sympathy with "heathenism." Southey was especially careful on this point because he had earlier been accused of misrepresenting Islam and presenting it in a flattering light in his *Thalaba.* In the original Preface of 1810, Southey refers to the Hindu religion as "of all false religions, the most monstrous in its fables and the most fatal in its effects." He adds:

> No figures can be imagined more anti-picturesque and less poetical than the mythological personages of the Brahmins. However startling the fictions may appear, they might almost be called credible when compared with the genuine tales of Hindu mythology. (1873: 548)

In the later Preface to the Collected Edition, Southey claims: "the spirit of the poem was Indian, but there was nothing Oriental in the style." He had adopted a "high strain of poetry":

> Here, neither the tone of morals nor the strain of poetry could be pitched too high; nothing but moral sublimity could compensate for the extravagance of the fictions and all the skill I might possess in the art of poetry was required to counterbalance the disadvantage of a mythology . . . which would appear monstrous if its deformities were not kept out of sight. (1873: xv)

It is not even as if the mythological personages in the poem are presented in such an appealing fashion so as to render a disavowal in the Preface necessary to prevent Oriental corruption/ seduction. In fact, the poem to a great extent concentrates on the horrific, repellent portrayal of Indian practices. The negative stereotypical images of Sati, "Juggernaut's" procession and temple prostitution are painted in detail. It is quite significant that despite such a portrayal, the author is still eager to express his disapprobation of his material in the Preface. While pandering to the contemporary craze for Oriental works, Southey also manages to position himself outside the poem and indicate to the reader also that an external perspective would be the ideal one.

The "hero" of Southey's poem, the peasant Ladurlad, kills Arvalan, the son of the evil Rajah Kehama, to protect his daughter Kailyal's honour. Kehama, who through sacrifices and penances has attained sufficient power to be feared as the "Almighty

Man"; pronounces a terrible curse on Ladurlad in revenge. Ladurlad is sentenced to an eternity of torment, which the elements or death itself cannot terminate. Kailyal is also pursued by agents of Kehama's wrath, but she is temporarily saved by a "Glendoveer"[1] named Eerenia with whom she shares a highly spiritualized love. However Eerinia's powers are not enough to oppose Kehama and he has to seek help from the 'Highest God"—Shiva. Kehama in the meantime completes his penance and lays claim to omnipotence. Descending to the abode of Yama, he drains the "Amreeta cup."

Southey manipulates mythology for his convenience, as his "Amreeta" is supposed to have positive or negative effects, depending on the nature of the person who partakes of it. Kehama does attain immortality, but is transformed into a living statue, destined to hold up Yama's throne forever. Kailyal too attains immortality and is united with Eerenia. Ladurlad is released from the torments of the curse and all is well that ends well.

However, the poem does not follow a technique of straightforward narration. Indeed, the narrative framework is extremely convoluted, so as to accommodate the numerous descriptions and exotic incidents Southey wished to include. For instance, in an incident which has no necessary connection with the main plot, Kailyal is once kidnapped by the priests of "Juggernaut."

To facilitate this episode, Ladurlad who by virtue of the curse of eternal torment, has been rendered indestructible—who is invulnerable to elemental forces and even death itself, who overcomes huge monsters in single combat—is presented unconvincingly as helpless before the priests who abduct Kailyal. The episode, of course is necessary for Southey to include his extremely Gothic description of Juggernaut's procession:

> On Jaga-Naut they call
> The ponderous car rolls on and crushes all
> Through flesh and bones it ploughs its dreadful path
> Groans rise unheard, the dying cry,
> And death and agony
> Are trodden underfoot by yon mad throng
> Who follow close, and thrust the deadly wheels along. (1963: 598)

In keeping with the extremely diffuse narrative route, several Indian mythological personages—Casyapa, Bali, Camadeva, Indra, Pollear and Martially for example—as well as locales—Mount Calsay (Kailas), Padalon (the Netherworld) Swerga (Heaven) and the city of Bali are introduced. The heroine and her father are plunged into episodic adventure after adventure, so that these representations can be indulged in. Southey is obviously determined to pack in as many mythological images—though from a "monstrous" mythology—as he can into this poem.

On the terrestrial level also, Southey provides numerous word pictures. The objects selected for description are those which could be regarded as typically Indian, like the Banyan tree, the elephant and the man-eating tiger. The cumulative effect of these descriptions is to create an "Oriental" ambience, with stress being laid on India's "difference," geographical as well as mythographical from what the western readers would be accustomed to at "Home." The vision of the locales created is that of an area where the "monstrous fictions" referred to can credibly originate.

Nigel Leask points out that the prolific use of Indian motifs and imagery was in fact an "appropriation of those emblems into the imperial heraldry" (1993: 8). A contemporary reviewer, John Foster, while pronouncing a generally harsh verdict on Southey's poem, commended its success in using Indian mythology "for the augmentation of our national splendour" (qtd. Leask 1993: 9). Obviously, Oriental poems, even when ostensibly presented as quite apolitical had their imperial affiliations.

The images, the motifs, the works themselves—all contributed to the "Imperial Archive"[2] maintained by the Empire. Southey's statement in the Preface that "the spirit of the poem is Indian" merits discussion. With his prejudice against the entire schema he is dealing with, Southey is quite unable to handle his machinery with either insight or sympathy. Only on one occasion, perhaps, does Southey seem to concede and depict a certain level of conceptual sublimity in Indian thought in the description of Shiva as the indestructible Almighty power:

For all around is light,
Primal, essential, all pervading light!
Heart cannot think, nor tongue declare,
Nor eyes of Angel bear
That glory unimaginably bright,
The sun himself had seem'd
A speck of darkness there
Amid that Light of Light! (1873: 612)

John Drew refers to the "limitations imposed on Southey by his Christianity" (as opposed to the atheist Shelley) and points out this epiphanic description as an exemplary occasion of how he overcomes them. However, one instance among a plethora of representations should not be overstressed. For the major part, Southey in his poem is advancing European ideals in Indian garb.

The supposedly "Indian" peasant, Ladurlad is unmistakably a European philosophical revolutionary whose principles are encapsulated in his declaration: "The virtuous heart and resolute mind are free" (Southey 1873: 609). His characteristic traits, like those of Shelley's Prometheus, are: "Stern patience unsubduable by pain/And pride triumphant over Agony" (Southey 1873: 608). George Bearce comments that Ladurlad "was a symbol of the romantic faith in the genius of men to endure all suffering; to resist all the evils imposed by society; and with a return to the principles of natural religion and the natural order to restore mankind to its natural well being. Of course, the hero exhibited very few Indian characteristics, he has the Western urge to attain moral freedom, to throw off the shackles of ecclesiastical and civil despotism and usher in the dream of a Golden Age." (1961: 104)

In this context—that of Ladurlad's obviously European/British traits (his adversary Kehama is presented as thoroughly Oriental)—a suggestive "misreading" in Foster's review gains significance. Foster says: "It is impossible that such a person as Kehama should have been in India at that time, without coming into collision with General Clive, who would have saved Seeva the trouble of interfering to put him down" (qtd. Leask 1993: 97-98).

The whole point is that the Englishman (even in the absence of a single direct mention) is *not* absent, he is an absent presence in the figure of Ladurlad. As Robert Sencourt points out: "For whole books we remain far from the Hindu atmosphere and see a plot developing harmonious only to English morals. *The Curse of Kẹhama* is a better expression of the ideals and personality of a British poet than of the system and influence of Hinduism." (1990: 290)

Southey cherished a firm belief in the discourse of imperialism, as illustrated in his 'Ode on the Portrait of Bishop Heber.' Here, Britain's imperial responsibility is emphasized and she is accused of gross negligence in allowing Indian "malpractices" to continue:

Large, England is the debt
Thou owest to heathendom;
To India most of all, where Providence
Giving thee thy dominion interest
Rises against thee, from beneath the wheels
Of that seven headed idol's car accurst
Against thee, from the widow's funeral pile
The smoke of human sacrifice
Ascends even now to Heaven!
Thither our saintly Heber went
In promise and in pledge
That England from her guilty torpor raised
Should jealously and wisely undertake
Her awful task assigned. (1873: 207-8)

Obviously, Southey was in favour of both imperial "civilization" and conversion of the heathen. His portrayal of India fits into the genre of "imperial gothic" (Leask 1993: 51) which underlined the necessity of the civilizing mission. Nor did the poem miss its mark; as Sencourt notes: "it aroused little sympathy to India and much repugnance and it is not surprising that its publication was followed by a great new effort of the missionaries and the appointment of an Anglican Bishop to Calcutta" (1990: 302).

Given Southey's (somewhat muted) early claim to radicalism, he does not in *Kehama* directly introduce a British presence to bring about the overthrow of 'Oriental Despotism" (unlike Jones whose Hymns are filled with anachronistic indications of the British presence). But, in the first place, as Leask points out, the very fact of representation on British terms is "itself the talisman of authority" (1993: 97). Secondly, though Southey makes use of the Indologists' works to a great extent, he manages to put across the Anglicist and assimilationist viewpoint at the same time, by making his hero an epitome of the desired product of such an assimilation. "The ambivalence of *Kehama* indicates that Orientalist and assimilationist positions are at moments mutually supportive than antagonistic" (Leask 1993: 96). Sir Walter Scott's review of the poem approved of it because of the exposure of "the abyss of outrageous and monstrous fictions" in Indian religion (qtd. Bearce 1961: 106). This seems to have been the dominant reading, which encouraged missionary and civilizing activity. Bearce comments that Southey offered an "allegoric quest for the Indian man" (1961: 105). What he does not note however is that the allegory is based on the Indian *becoming* man, attaining manhood through Europeanization.

At the end of the quest, we have a product of successful imperial assimilation. Bearce's suggestion that the attacks on Indian religion and superstitions were not directly intended for conversion; as at an allegorical level, "Christianity is *not* the antagonist in the struggle" is somewhat misplaced (1961: 106). The dark side of the struggle is Oriental superstition and tyranny personified in Kehama. If his adversary Ladurlad is not specifically Christianized, we yet have to insist on the fact that he is prototypically a Europeanized Indian. Also, in contrast to Kailyal's eager protestations of faith, we have not a single such testimony from Ladurlad, who often doubts the powers of the Hindu divinities. He is as far removed from an actual participation in Hindu doctrine as possible without being a declared Christian (in which case the story would have been chronologically impossible).

Setting his revolution against tyranny in distant India also enables Southey to avoid unpleasant charges of a desire to disturb the status quo at Home. Among the three statues already supporting Yama's throne (Kehama makes the fourth one) one represents avarice, one religious falsehood and the third is being punished because:

> I o'er my Brethren of mankind the first
> Usurping power, set up a throne sublime
> A King and conqueror: therefore thus accurst
> Forever in vain I repent the crime. (1873: 624)

Shelley in a letter records that "Southey says he designs his three statues in *Kehama* to be contemplated with the republican feelings, but not in this age" (Shelley 1964: I 154-55). To this, Leask correctly adds: "and not in *this* country" (1993: 96).

The numerous notes which Southey appends to his text so as to authenticate his Indian material serves to enforce this "not here, not now," conception of a republican revolution. Southey quotes at length from Jones' *Works*; from the *Asiatic Researches;* Williamson's *Oriental Field Sports,* Moor's *Hindu Pantheon,* the works of British and other European travellers in India and translations of the *Manu Smriti, Bhagavat Gita, Ramayana, Mahabharata, Shakuntalam* and *Nala Damayanti.* These lengthy quotes (one is nearly ten pages long!) do not only function as authenticating devices, they also establish the scene firmly in India, an exotic locale at a safe distance away from the British metropolis.

Leask points out that Shelley, unlike Southey, Moore or Byron does not give copious footnotes to his Oriental works, so that he could disavow the Oriental setting at a theoretical level and project his revolutions as "universal" (1993: 74). By the same token, Southey's copious footnotes indicate his need to avow and endorse the Oriental setting as the very restricted and *only* locale where he advocates revolution. Significantly, the revolutionary republicanism here is ushered in through an *assimilation by European values*; itself one of the projected desires of imperial domination.

B

In *Lalla Rookh,* Thomas Moore lets his imagination run riot in the realms of exotic fear and fantasy; after providing the readers with a barely plausible frame tale. The work consists of a series of Oriental stories; each complete in itself. The connecting thread is the journey of the young Mughal princess, Lalla Rookh (supposedly, the daughter of Aurengzebe) who is travelling from Delhi to Kashmir to be married there to the king of Bucharia.

The tedium of the journey is mitigated by the verse tales narrated by a young poet, Feramoz, with whom the princess falls in love. Fortunately, the poet turns out to be the bridegroom King in disguise and matters end on a happy note. The immense amount Moore received as payment for this work and the numerous editions it went into testify to its popularity in contemporary England. Raymond Schwab points out that apart from popularity at home, "Moore's widely famous *Lalla Rookh* written in 1817, gave him an international reputation. It was translated into French in 1820 and also adapted for the opera" (1984: 197). The prevalent discourse of exotic Orientalism contributed much to this grand success:

> The circumstances and timing of its production gave [Lalla Rookh] an importance quite apart from its intrinsic worth, i.e., it is a valuable document of English interest in Orientai things. The popularity it enjoyed gauges the extent of that interest in the first place, and secondly, the poem itself decided to a great extent the form in which the cultivated world of England pictured India. (Sencourt 1990: 303-4)

Actually, only a very minor part of *Lalla Rookh* explicitly deals with India. Among the tales narrated by Feramoz, the first one, the "Veiled Prophet of Khorassan" deals with the false prophet Mokanna, who starts a cult to fight against the Muslim Emperor. Mokanna is presented as cruel, deceitful and sensual. The hero Azim joins him only through a mistaken *Greek* ideal of liberty. Mokanna traps, ravishes and corrupts Azim's love Zelica and the lovers are united only after death. The false prophet's attempt at world domination fails and he commits suicide after murdering those who remain of his beguiled band of followers. The second story relates how a Peri gains entrance to Paradise by conveying there, in succession a drop of a patriotic hero's blood, the sigh of a maiden who dies for her lover and a tear from a repentant sinner. The third narrative deals with the rebellion of the ancient Fire Worshippers' of Persia against the invading Mohammedan Sultan and the love of the Persian leader and the Sultan's daughter whereby both perish. Only the last tale, which tells of a love quarrel between Jehangir and Nur Jehan and their reconciliation is actually even located in India; specifically in the valley of Kashmir.

India, however is an informing presence throughout the work. There are many scenic descriptions in prose, concerning the progress of Lalla Rookh, interwoven with the verse narratives. Not only is the landscape referred to, but the customs, manners and traditions are also described. Unlike Southey, who chose to concentrate on the Gothic aspects of India, Moore prefers to give idealized, exotic pictures. Also, a few references to India are to be found even in those verse stories which are not actually set there. Feramoz is described as "graceful as that idol of women; Crishna [sic], such as he appears to their young imaginations, heroic, beautiful, breathing music from his very ears, and exalting the religion of his worshippers into love (Moore 1986: 7). We also have references to Brahma (15) Hanuman (39) Ghazni's invasion (29) and to Indian "despotism" (5) apart from idealized landscape descriptions.

A good example of Moore's exoticizing of the Indian locale[3] can be found in these (still quoted) lines from the last tale:

Who has not heard of the vale of Cashmere?
With its roses the brightest that earth ever gave
Its temples and grottos and fountains as clear
As the love lighted eyes that hang o'er the wave! . . .
If woman can make the worst wilderness dear,
Think, think what a heaven she must make of Cashmere.

(1987: 256-57)

Nurjahan's song in this story has the refrain, "If there be an Elysium on earth/It is this, it is this!" (283) referring to Kashmir. In the second tale, India is described as a "Peri's paradise" (126) and there are also many prose passages which extol the beauty of the landscape.

Sencourt lists in detail the "mistakes" Moore makes in describing the locale and records many instances of the poet's lapses from authenticity or geographical exactitude. (Sencourt 1990: 308-9) This is to miss the point that exoticism, the most important factor in this context, was not dependent on authenticity. The *Edinburgh Review* laid stress on precisely this aspect of the poem:

> The land of the Sun has never shone out so brightly on the children of the North—nor the sweets of Asia been poured forth nor her gorgeousness displayed so profusely to the delighted senses of Europe. (qtd. Bearce 1961: 108)

This idealized exoticization of India, with all its lack of authenticity was as much a part of the essentialization and appropriation of Indian motifs into imperial heraldry as Southey's "imperial gothic."

It has been pointed out that the essentially contradictory but supportive motifs of an attractively exotic and frighteningly bizarre orient are presented symbolically in *Lalla Rookh:*

> Moore's romance contained the stock details of what the East was supposedly like: doe eyed women in abundance, languishing with love and expiring of desire, wicked men who kept them in captivity, rich banquets, gorgeous brocades and cashmeres, jewels, perfumes, music, dance, and poetry. But this lyrical rhapsody was not free from the traditional Western hostility to Islam. Moore did not at all distinguish between history and legend—there reappear in his text medieval motifs of Muhammed as imposter, magician and sensualist. (Kabbani: 1986: 34, my italics)

Apart from a few isolated references to Hindu customs, Moore's "India" is as completely Islamic as the generalized "East" in which the first three tales of *Lalla Rookh* are set.

Through this tactic of simultaneous exoticizing and alienating, Moore manages to have his cake and eat it too. He indulges himself, and his readers to the utmost limit in exotic Orientalism, through luxurious and voluptuous descriptions. At the same time, an undercurrent of morality articulated by the "heroes" serves to underline the "Western virtues" of abstinence and rectitude, clearly here identified as unIslamic/non-oriental.

Moore may be said to have made use of the triadic structure of Othering described by John Barrell—consisting of "This, That and the Other" (Barrell 1991: 9). The actual Other is progressively distanced by absorbing aspects of it into the "This," making it merely a "That" and not really "Other." Moore's Azim is motivated by explicitly "Greek" ideals, his Hafed is an ardent opponent of Islam and a supporter of a Europeanized version of Fire Worship; Feramoz himself, the poet hero, is "modern and progressive" as opposed to the Chamberlain Fadladeen who is a typical representative of amusingly decadent Islam. These *reclaimed* Oriental characters are absorbed into the Occidental self, retaining only a minimal amount of difference. They *are* Oriental, but only Oriental enough to be able to carry out the work of self-civilization on European terms. The actual other of the threatening Orient is left outside, moved further away by its distancing from even these ostensibly *Oriental* heroes themselves.

Francis Jeffrey's 1817 review of *Lalla Rookh* gains importance from this perspective. He remarks that the poem is:

> The poetry of rational, honourable, considerate and humane Europe, filtered off from the childishness, cruelty and profligacy of Asia. So far as we have yet seen there is no sound sense, firmness of purpose or principled goodness, *except among the natives of Europe and their descendants*. (qtd. Bearce 1993: 22, my italics)

There is no real need for such a statement of value judgments in a supposedly literary review, unless the sub-text of the imperial civilizing mission was kept well to the forefront. As we have seen in the case of Southey also, the literal absence of a representative of English power does not indicate that their presence is written out of the text. The Orientals, who *themselves* overthrow Oriental despotism and representation have internalized the European virtues and function as proxy Englishmen/ Europeans.

Leask and Bearce both note the importance of the Irish context in interpreting Moore's stand against Islam. There is an identification between Zoroastrianism/Catholicism and Protestantism/ Islam and the Fire Worshippers under the Islamic yoke can be seen as standing in for the Irish predicament under British domination (Leask 1993: 103). From a different perspective Bearce argues that the attacks on Indian religion could be interpreted as self-criticism; equally applicable to Roman Catholicism (Bearce 1961: 109). Both these interpretations are valid in their own right, but they must not be allowed to overshadow the fact that no matter whatever else Moore's Islam/Orient is, it is also, quite simply, Islam/Orient. The Fire Worshippers, at one level, are but convenient mouthpieces to criticize the self-consciously distanced Islamic Orient. And if in the "Veiled Prophet" Islam seems to triumph over the prophet's policy of destruction, it must be remembered that the victory is in many ways presented as the personal triumph of the *"Greek"* Azim.

It remains to be noted, as Leask points out, that the revolutions in Moore, whether the negative one of the prophet or the positive one of the Fire Worshippers are "failed revolutions" (Leask 1993: 58). At one level, there is a warning against supposedly republican revolution, based on the principles of Jacobinism. The final unveiling of the prophet can be seen as the unmasking of the deluding Jacobin ideology:

> Not the long promised lights,
> The brow whose beaming
> Was to come forth, all conquering all-rendering
> But features horrible than hell ever
> Traced on its own blood. (Moore 1986: 110)

Leask identifies this as a warning to fellow Irishmen about pernicious Jacobin principles, which are not acceptable, even in a figuratively distanced Indian locale (1993: 113). At the same time, it has to be noted that on another level, rebellion when aimed against Oriental tyranny itself (instead of colonial aggression) as in the case of the Fire Worshippers is desirable and its failure is to be regretted. If even the civilizing mission pales into insignificance beside the need to suppress Jacobinism represented by Mokanna, it has to judged mainly as a question of priority.

A revolution based on French principles is not desirable, at home or abroad, the status quo in any shape is preferable to such a process. But the civilization of India/East through justifiable revolution based on British/Greek principles is desirable and necessary. If, as in *Lalla Rookh,* the ambivalence of the colonial presence could be masked through the representation of European values in assimilated Orientals themselves, that would be the ideal situation.

C

Scott's novel *The Surgeon's Daughter* is different from the two epic/narrative poems examined in this chapter in as much as it does have an avowed British presence and that the British characters play the role of moving spirits in the action. Scott stresses the exotic and fabulously wealthy aspects of India, but he does so to give increased credence to the concept of India as a land of European/British adventure. For Scott's Anglo-Indian characters, the East/India is, as Disraeli comments in *Tancred* "a career." Though this aspect is dismantled later by a revelation of the Gothic and corrupting aspects of India, it nevertheless functions as a motif of extreme significance throughout the text.

In the fictional introduction to the novel, a friend, Mr. Fairscribe advises the author to "send his Muse of fiction . . . as many an honest man does with his own sons. . . . Send her to India [where] the most wonderful deeds [were] done by the least possible means" (Scott 1920: 16-17). This suggestion kindles the author's imagination and he launches into a rhapsody on India as the land of adventures and infinite possibility:

> The non-commissioned officers and privates . . . are like Homer's demi-Gods among the warring mortals. Men like Clive and Caillard influenced great events like Jove himself. Inferior officers like Mars or Neptune and the sergeants and corporals may well pass for demi-Gods. (17)

After such an ardent account, one would expect Scott to plunge right into his story. But he does register one small caveat: "The only objection is that I have never been there [India], and know nothing at all about them" (17). This, of course, is hardly a great objection when we consider the flourishing number of contemporary metropolitan "armchair" Orientalists. Indeed, as we have seen, James Mill actually considered a lack of personal contact with India as a positive advantage in writing about the country.

In any case, what any British novelist could say about India, was to a large extent circumscribed, by the discursive framework of imperialism. Edward Said observes:

> Even the most imaginative writers of an age, men like Flaubert, Nerval or Scott were constrained in what they could either experience of or say about the Orient. For Orientalism was ultimately a political vision of reality, whose structure promoted the difference between the familiar and the strange. . . . Orientals lived in their world, "we" lived in ours. (Said 1978: 43-44)

Quite in keeping with this argument, Scott presents a stereotypical version of the 'Other' in India, where the Europeans are adventurers in a world which is not and cannot be the 'Same' for them.

The surgeon's daughter of the title is Menie Gray, who is loved by two young suitors—Richard Middlemass and Adam Hartley. She loves Middlemass, an orphan who grew up under her father's care. The rejected Hartley goes to India where his upright character enables him to make good. But the fickle Middlemass is soon seduced by stories of India's wealth and proceeds to India, leaving Menie behind. His career is a series of disasters which end in his leaving the British camp altogether and taking up with Begum Montreville, a European adventuress in league with "Tippoo Sultan." Jealous of what she hears about Menie, the Begum entices her to India and plans to offer her to Tippoo's harem, a plot in which the reluctant Middlemass is compelled to share. Menie applies to Hartley for help and through the good offices of a Fakeer (actually Hyder Ali's spy) he manages to bring the situation to Hyder Ali's notice. There is a dramatic climax where Hyder arrives in disguise and foils the Begum's plans. Richard Middlemass is brutally killed and Menie is allowed to return to England.

The image of India as the land of fame and wealth is reiterated throughout the novel. Upon hearing that Hartley is leaving for India, Middlemass exclaims: "Happy dog, to India! Oh Delhi! Oh Golkonda! . . . India where gold is won by steel, where a brave man cannot pitch his desire of fame and wealth too high, but that he may realize it if he have fortune for his friend" (118). Obviously, Delhi, Golkonda—indeed India itself—all these are vague phrases which connote fabulous possibilities. This general conception among the youth of the time is fully exploited by the member of the Company press gang who lures Middlemass to India with a glowing account of what was on offer:

> Not a stream did he mention but flowed over sands of gold and not a place that was inferior to that of the celebrated Fata Morgana. His descriptions seemed steeped in colours and his every phrase perfumed in attar of roses. (120)

Starting from the unscrupulous practices of the company in recruiting its soldiers, the actions of the British in India come in for sharp criticism. Scott bluntly states that "a back stair was the necessary appurtenance of every government in India" and describes the President of British Council as:

> An able and active but unconscientious man who neither in his own affairs nor in those of the Company was supposed to embarrass himself overmuch about the means he used to attain his objects. (140)

The comment of the Fakeer when Hartley refuses payment after having treated him is revealing in this context: "A Feringhi can then refuse gold! . . . I thought they took it, from every hand, whether as that of a Houri or leperous as Gehagi's" (131). This is a rare instance of the British being portrayed as the natives must often have seen them—as greedy and quite unscrupulous adventurers.

Nevertheless, such criticism is finally relegated to the past and Scott is careful not to advance anything against the better-regulated, reformed contemporary system. He takes an anticipatory bail against any charge of radicalism by remarking in a note: "Of course, such things should be deemed possible only in the earlier period of the English settlements when the check of the Directors was imperfect and that of the crown did not exist" (142). Bearce observes that Middlemass represented the violence and cupidity of early British adventurers in India and that a linear progress is traced to the stature of Hartley who "had a Burkean sense of responsibility and morality in India" (Bearce 1961: 112). Scott had no problem with British rule in India, so long as it was of the kind to be expected from men like Hartley.

Also, if the British authorities were criticized, their Indian agents were painted in positively demoniac terms. The President was supposed to carry on all business through his native steward or *Dubash*. The *Dubash* Paupiah is described as follows:

> The thin dusky form which stood before him wrapped in robes of muslin embroidered with gold was that of Paupiah, known as a master counsellor of dark projects, an oriental Machiavel, whose premature triumphs were the result of many an intrigue in which the existence of the poor, the happiness of the rich, the honour of men and the chastity of women had been sacrificed without scruple to gain some private or political advantage. (140-41)

The associations with Burke's portrayal of devious Indian Banyans during his impeachment speeches are obvious. Paupiah is shown as drawing Richard Middlemass even deeper into the web of Indian intrigues.

An extremely sensitive issue touched upon by Scott is the fear of miscegenation. Being included in Tippoo's Harem is evidently the worst fate that could befall a pure English girl like Menie. Begum Montreville's speech in which she "offers" Menie to Tippoo is suggestive in the extreme:

> I am so void of means that I can only pray your highness will deign to accept a lily from Frangistan to plant within the secret garden of

> thy pleasures. Let my lord's guards carry yon litter to the Zenana. (160)

The image of the lily is extremely evocative, conjuring up visions of the fair English woman being entrapped. The phrase "secret garden of thy pleasures" hints at unspeakable sexual practices, which were "unnatural" by Western mores, but were willingly projected on to the Orient.

Since the novel is set in a time when the native princes retained some degree of sovereign power, the exotic pomp of their rule is presented in some detail. The description of Tippoo's procession[4] attempts to encapsulate incredible splendour and gorgeousness. Sencourt remarks:

> Scott is the only great British novelist who drew on India for romantic material, who brought home to the general reader . . . an accurate idea of the strange terror and fascination of the jungle, of the blaze of the princely procession as it passed through the ancient bazaars of the native city. (Sencourt 1990: 323)

The claim of Scott to be the "*only* great novelist" in this context is open to debate; but the gorgeous effect created by his descriptions, especially by that of the procession has to be acknowledged:

> Long before the appointed hour, the rendezvous of Fakirs, beggars and idlers before the gate of the palace extended. . . . The noise increased as the procession traversed the outskirts of the place . . . shouting at the top pitch of their voices the titles and virtues of Tippoo. . . . In this manner, the procession advanced . . . the houses were ornamented with broadcloth, silk shawls and embroidered carpets . . . so that the whole street had a singularly rich and gorgeous appearance. (156-57)

However, it should not be assumed that such descriptions were intended to suggest anything more positive than a temporary attraction of the Fancy. The gorgeous descriptions are offset with accounts of the implications of the religious beggars, the desperate scramble for money, the hollowness of Oriental titles and the brutal way the commoners were whipped and pushed about. As Edward Said remarks, "European representation was always a way of controlling the redoubtable Orient" (Said 1978: 60). Scott's detailed descriptions help to domesticate the Orient through over-familiarization, to reduce its threatening qualities by the very process of representing them, to temper its exoticism, precisely by elaborate descriptive indulgence.

Hyder and Tippoo are presented as imposing figures and Hyder especially is shown as a just and fair ruler. His speech after the rescue of Menie is notable:

> Hakim [Hartley] . . . thou shalt return with the Feringhi woman and with gold to compensate her injuries wherein the Begum as is fitting shall contribute. Do thou say to thy nation, Hyder Ali acts Justly. (163)

The sense of justice here is obviously meant to be admired. But despite all his bravery, Tippoo in the final analysis is a sensualist; despite his justice, Hyder is a despot who indulges in tyrannical cruelty to the top of his bent; as is indicated by his having Middlemass trampled to death by an elephant. To quote Said:

> The general category in advance offers the specific instance a limited terrain in which to operate. No matter how deep the specific exception, no matter how much a single Oriental can escape the fences placed around him, he is *first* an Oriental, *second* a human being and *last* again an Oriental. (1978: 102)

Despite the occasional favourable portrayal or positive attribute bestowed on him, in the last instance Hyder is yet an Oriental tyrant whose defeat by "the better class of Englishmen" is definitely to be desired. Hyder swears to be a "destroying tempest in the Carnatic" and Scott comments: "It is well known how the Nawab kept this promise, and how he and his son afterwards fell back before the discipline and bravery of the Europeans" (163).

Despite all qualifications, the final European triumph is not only desirable, but also inevitable. Yet, even in the face of this conclusion, we have to assert, in order to escape from a constricting absolute binarism, that even in this stereotypical vision, the ambivalences—for whatever they are worth—did exist. The question of their existence however is not as important as the fact that these gaps were *needed* for the edifice to persist.

NOTES

1. Though Southey is somewhat doubtful about it in his footnotes, "Glendoveers" appear to be a corruption of the Orientalist "Gandharvas." The section on Wordsworth in this book refers to his similar use of the term.
2. The process of creating and maintaining the "Imperial Archive" has been examined in detail by Thomas Richards in his study *The Imperial Archive* (1993).
3. A similarly idealized/ ascription (not just of India; but of the East as such as a locale) is given by Byron in 'The Bride of Abydos' with the addition that "man is vile" there in contrast to the ideal landscape:

   Know ye the land where the cypress and myrtle
   Are emblems of deeds that are done in their clime?
   Where the rage of the vulture, the love of the turtle
   Now melt into sorrow, now madden to crime?
   Know ye the land of the cedar and the wine
   Where the flowers ever blossom, the heavens ever shine;
   Where the bright wings of Zephyr, oppressed with perfume
   Wax faint o'er the gardens of Gul in her bloom
   Where the citron and olive are fairest of fruit
   And the voice of the nightingale never is mute,
   With the tints of the earth and the hues of the sky
   In colour though varied in beauty may vie
   And the purple of ocean is deepest in dye,
   Where the virgins are soft as the roses they twine,
   And *all save the spirit of man* divine?
   It's the clime of the East, 'tis the land of the Sun.

   (Byron 1970: 264, my italics)

4. Southey of course pictures a very different procession in his account of "Jaga-Naut's" process. A similar description of a gorgeous procession, with decorations is presented by Moore in his account of Lalla Rookh's reception at Kashmir (Moore 1986: 291-92).

Chapter 7

Songs of Empire? The Major Romantic Poets and India

Rattling with clanking chains, the Universal Empire groans.

William Blake

We have already seen in the last chapter how certain full-length works of the Romantic period dealt with the theme of India. This chapter uses their specific references to India as a starting point from which to focus on the concept of Empire in general in the works of the canonical "major" Romantic poets—Blake, Wordsworth, Coleridge, Byron, Shelley and Keats. The quantitative aspect of the actual references to India varies from elaborate usage in Shelley and Coleridge to minimal symbolic presence in Blake. However, the focal point here is on India as an "Empire symbol" rather than as a concrete entity.

A considerable amount of textual interpretation with regard to individual poems is undertaken here. However, emphasis is also laid on these writers not just as poets, but also as individual actors/actants[1] in a particular social and political set up wherein Imperialism was a prime component of social structuring. From this perspective, prose works including political treatises, biographical/ autobiographical accounts, letters, journals and notebooks are taken up for study, with the concept of Empire as the connecting thread.

A

In the works of William Blake, it is North America which primarily illustrates the spatial concept of Empire. Still, India does figure in his corpus often enough to justify us in postulating a hypothesis of symbolic awareness at the very least.

The specific references to India/Hindostan in Blake are easily enumerated. In his "Milton" we come across the lines:

> And all nations wept in affliction, Family by Family
> Germany wept towards France, Italy, England wept and trembled
> Towards America, India rose up from his golden bed
> As one awakened in the night. (1912: 519)

It has to be indicated in passing that both "golden" bed and the suggestion of sleep are almost perfect objective correlatives for an "opulent and indolent" portrayal of India in contemporary parlance. However, at least the usual connotation of femininity is absent here, the possessive pronoun 'his' clearly shows India as masculine! In another poem "Jerusalem" Blake describes "Urizen's temple which spans the globe" as follows:

> Within is Asia and Greece, ornamented with exquisite art
> Persia and Medea are his halls, his inmost Hall is Great Tartary
> China and India and Siberia are his temples for entertainment
> (1912: 690)

The globalizing vision here blithely telescopes historical enmities and geographical hurdles into a total vision of integration. Greece, the archetypal Occident, and her pre-historical Oriental rival Persia are yoked together here. In the same poem however, we find India, China and Japan (along with Sodom and Gomorrah) figuring as the areas (major ones, though Greece and Italy are mentioned) where "the polypus of generation" spreads its tentacles. The disgust with which sexual generation is opposed to spiritual regeneration is a significant aspect in certain parts of Blake's thought. One is led to ponder on the possible associations of Oriental fecundity and uncurbed passion (which also characterized the Biblical "Cities of Sin") with the given description.

In Book I of "Milton" Hindostan is viewed as part of the mythical body of a symbolic Albion; which also includes Tartary, China, and "Great America" as well as Italy, Greece and Egypt. It is tempting to consider an assimilative tendency towards the East as operating in this context. However, two European countries are also included among the Asiatic names and in Blake's symbolic system Albion does stand for much more than just geographical England. It is very unlikely that Blake is suggesting that the countries mentioned were (or should be) integral parts of Britain, the suggestion is far more likely to be that these representatives of distant climes all participate in a global project of rejuvenation which is symbolized by a youthful and (largely) non-localized Albion. But (as we will have to insist on many occasions in this chapter) whatever *else* Albion may be symbolic of, it *is* also England—and contemporary England *was* Imperial.

In Book 11 of "Milton" we have a reference to "Euphrates & Hindu to the Nile" (575) where "Hindu" obviously indicates the "Indus." In *Jerusalem* Hindostan is one among the thirty-two privileged nations which are to dwell in a Utopian "Jerusalem's Gates" (712). Again, in the same poem, Hindostan figures as one of the nations to be "created" (born anew) by "the looms of Enitharmon and Los" (725). On the whole such references are mainly useful only to convey an idea of geographical inclusiveness and vastness. Yet, the importance of this very function should not be under-estimated. As Thomas Richards points out in *The Imperial Archive:*

> Romanticism contributed a great deal to imagining the Empire as a concordant whole. The impulse towards the universal in Shelley, the project of a complete knowledge of the world in Coleridge, *the ability of Blake's visions to span the globe,* the sense of a fully surveyed landscape in Wordsworth: these differing but exhaustive projects were carried forward in the literature of Empire. (1993: 7, my italics)

As Raymond Schwab has demonstrated, it was after the "Oriental Renaissance" that "the world became truly round, half the intellectual map no longer a blank" (Schwab 1984: 16). Even passing references to India/Hindostan/East have in this context a significance as indicators of a new world view which could now expand and aspire to inclusiveness.

Another reference to India in Blake occurs in "The Song of Los." Discussing the distribution of Philosophy, Law, Mathematics *et al* among the Nations, Blake writes: "Rintrah gave Abstract Philosophy to Brahma in the East" (1972: 245). There is an obvious echo here of the tradition which associated abstract metaphysical and theological speculation with ancient India.

A significant indication of both Blake's awareness of India and Indian affairs as well as the considerable contemporary vogue of the Indian motif is to be found in his "Descriptive Catalogue of Pictures" painted by him in watercolours. The "Index" indicates that picture X was titled "The Brahmins—A Drawing."[2] The elaboration in the body of the "Catalogue" reads:

> The subject is Mr. Wilkins translating the Geeta, an ideal design suggested by the first publication of that part of the Hindoo scriptures translated by Mr. Wilkins. I understand that my costume is incorrect, but in this I plead the authority of the ancients, who often deviated from the Habits to preserve the manners. (Blake 1972: 583)

John Drew draws attention to this item and also points out that John Flaxman, Blake's contemporary painter, friend and correspondent did "a monumental drawing of Jones collecting information from the Pandits for his digest of Hindu and Mohammedan laws" (1987: 78). Obviously the Indian themes were of sufficient contemporary significance both to inspire the artists and to enable them to hope for enough public interest to create the chances of a sale.

It is also possible (purely as a speculative exercise) to trace relations between Blake's thought and traditional Hindu philosophy, though not always relations of equivalence. Schwab remarks:

> With Blake, a solitary visionary, we again encounter affinities between occultism, Neo-Platonism, and pantheism, extending towards fellowship with animals and objects as well as towards the annihilation of the self. I have not seen any definite contacts with Hindu texts pointed out, yet the accumulation of coincidences among the intellectual fashions which promoted Boheme, Schelling and the Upanishads simultaneously is striking. (Drew 1984: 197)

Drew further points out that "Neo-Platonism is not only the philosophical scheme which has been used most frequently to explicate the nature of imaginative literature, it is also the philosophical scheme which has been used most frequently to explicate the nature of Indian culture" (14). The Neo-Platonic system has been described as:

> A combination of Greek Philosophy and Oriental religion; it is theistic in teaching a transcendent God, pantheistic in conceiving everything down to the lowest matter as an emanation of God. (Thilly 1993: 31)

To the extent of conceiving all existence as an emanation and representation of the One, Blake can indeed be said to partake of both Indian and Neo-Platonic thought.

(However, the synthesis of this concept in Blake with Boheme's[3] notion of contraries is too significant to be ignored. Blake, who declared, "Without contraries, there is no progression" can by no means be fitted into an Advaitist category, with all that implies philosophically and poetically.)

Apart from the concept of the fellowship of life and transcendence of the Self as pointed out by Schwab, the theory of Action (Karma) and the concept of the body as garment[4] are all areas where Blake displays affinities with Indian thought. In his "Annotations to Lavater" Blake remarks that "Active Evil is better than passive good" (1972: 77) and also that "Accident is the omission of the Act in self and the hindering of Act in another. This is vice, but all Act is virtue" (88). In his "Annotations to Bacon" Blake further elaborates the concept of Action with the remark, "Thought is Act" (400). Perhaps a simpler version of the action idea (*at least in a state of innocence)* can be seen in the closing lines of "The Chimney Sweeper" "so if all do their duty, they need not fear harm" (I 18).

In the "Ninth Night" of the *Four Zoas,* Blake emphasizes the non-significance of the body:

> Terrified at non-existence
> For such they deemed the death of the body. (357)

In "King Edward the Third," the body is referred to as "the prison house" the soul must escape from if it is to reach the bliss of heaven. In the epilogue to "The Gates of Paradise" the soul/body—essence/garment distinction is made:

> Truly, my Satan, thou art but a Dunce
> And dost not know the garment from the Man. (771)

Similarities of thought could of course occur independent of influence and this is even more so for differences. Still, one particular marked divergence in Blake from a cardinal Indian "method" has to be mentioned, mainly because the opposite trait in Shelley has been discussed in detail by Drew. The reference here is to "defining" God or the Supreme Force. The Indian scriptures often adopt the way of negatives, the "Neti Neti" strategy to "define" the indefinable and "name" what is unnamable. As Damrosch points out: "There is nothing in Blake of the via negativa, the detachment from all phenomena in search of an unnamable God of infinite negation" (1980: 47-48). Blake's God whether as Nobodaddy or Christ is eminently nameable and closely linked to concrete presence.

So, points of similarity as well as occasions where Blake's thought seems to define itself "against" Eastern/Indian thought can be traced. However, it is important to keep in mind that Blake's poems or correspondence do not indicate, unlike in the case of Coleridge or Shelley, any specific perusal of Indian sources.

With regard to the specific question of Blake's relation to Empire, the initial picture at least that emerges is one of a staunch anti-imperialist. "Empire is no more! And now the lion and wolf shall cease" (1972: 100) is the climactic cry with which Blake's "Song of Liberty" concludes. The line is later repeated verbatim in "America" where Blake equates Empire with slavery. David Erdman in *Blake: Prophet against Empire* has examined Blake's staunch opposition to a policy of imperial expansion. He points out that "from first to last, Blake set the Republic of Art above the Empire of the Sword and pits Joy against the pride of Kings" (Erdman 1977: 45) and that his prophecy of the disappearance of Empire is "applied retrospectively to America and prophetically to the Spanish and Papal empires, to the commercial importance of London's free trade and London's God Urizen" (192). Does India figure by implication? The question is debatable and any answer provocative.

It is possible to look at Blake's works, especially the Prophetic Books as an "endless monologue of fantasy about a Biblical hereafter" (Bronowski 1972: 10). To leave it at that, however, would amount to leaving a considerable and forceful part of Blake's conceptual range unconfronted. Blake had strong radical views on the historical actualities and social phenomena of his time. The revolutions were welcomed and tyranny condemned by Blake who, despite his pervasive use of esoteric symbols to mask the real force of his radicalism, remained a revolutionary by temperament till the end of his days, unlike Southey or Wordsworth who faced the charge of being political renegades.

Empire/Imperialism in Blake's works obviously meant more than just territorial expansion. All confining practices—political, commercial, religious or cultural—were viewed by Blake as being one with the imperialistic worldview and condemned accordingly. As Bronowski remarks: "This is the prophetic power of Blake, that he felt the coming disasters of War, Empire and Industry in his bloodstream long before politicians and economists shivered at their shadows." (1972: 16) It is possible to consider Imperialism in Blake as a collective term for all discursive systems which perpetuated hegemonic practices.

Edward Said in *Culture and Imperialism* quotes Blake to emphasize his own formulation of Empire:

> The process of Imperialism occurred beyond the level of economic laws and political decisions and—by predisposition, by the authoritatively recognizable cultural formations, by continuing consolidation within education, literature and the visual and musical arts—were manifested at another level, that of the national culture, which we have tended to sanitize as a realm of unchanging intellectual monuments free from worldly affiliations. William Blake is quite unrestrained on this point. "The foundation of Empire" he

> says in his Annotations to Reynolds's *Discourses* "is Art and Science. Remove them or Degrade them and the Empire is no more. Empire follows Art and not vice versa as Englishmen suppose" (Said 1993: 12-13)

In his "Public Address" Blake further remarks that "let it no more be said that Empire encourages Arts, for it is Arts that encourages Empires. Let us teach Buonoparte [sic] and, whomsoever else it may concern that it is not Arts that follow and attend upon Empire, but Empire that follows and attends upon the Arts" (1972: 597). Blake is evidently aware of the complex relationship between culture and imperialism and he does not regard the cultural/artistic realm as profiting as a result of this relation. If anything, the flow is in the opposite direction.

Francis Bacon, in his *Essays: Moral, Economical and Political* sets out the commercial justification for Empire:

> It is likely to be remembered that for as much as the increase of any estate must be on the foreigner—(for whatsoever is somewhere got is somewhere lost). (Qtd. Blake 1972: 402)

Blake annotates this as follows: "The increase of a state as of a Man is from Internal Improvement or Intellectual Acquirement. *States are not Improved at the expense of foreigners.*[5] Man is not improved by the hurt of another. Bacon has no notion of anything but Mammon" (Blake 1972: 402, my italics). This conception strikes right at the foundation of Empire. Again, in his annotations to Bishop Watson's *An Apology for the Bible,* Blake insists: "God never makes one man murder another nor one nation . . . to Extirpate a nation by means of another nation is as wicked as to destroy an individual by means of another individual which God considers as murder and commands that it shall not be done" (1972: 388).

In Erdman's words, "If military glory was one side of the false coin of Empire, the other side was the love of commercial prosperity" (1977: 329). Blake ridicules the latter as the worship of Mammon and on several occasions, debunks the romantically glorified conception of war and military glory. In his fragmented play *King Edward the Third* the war-mongering rhetoric of the

King and his nobles is presented with an overdose of bombast so that it ends up ridiculing itself. In the "Ninth Night' of *Vala or the Four Zoas* Blake refers to war as "Energy Enslav'd" and to the fighting man as the "slave in extremity" (1972: 362).[6] This image of slavery is further emphasized in *Jerusalem* where conscripted soldiers (whom we may imagine, had to fight for Empire as well) are allowed to speak for themselves:

> We were carried away in thousands from London and in tens
> Of thousands from Westminster and Marybone, in ships clos'd up
> Chain'd hand and foot, compell'd to fight under the iron whips
> Of our captains, fearing our officers more than the enemy.
>
> (1972: 700)

Even trade and commerce, on which Britain laid hold as the foundations of her prosperity, are fiercely indicted by Blake as being directly responsible for Empire and through it for corruption and slavery. Urizen in "Night the Seventh (b)" of *The Four Zoas* states in clear terms his intention to build up an oppressive Empire primarily through commerce:

> First Trades and Commerce ships and armed vessels he built laborious
> To swim the deep, and on the land children are sold to trades
> Of dire necessity, ...
> Rattling with clanking chains, the universal Empire groans
>
> (1972: 333)

Empire evidently is not an isolated phenomenon for Blake, but a pervasive malaise, a collective term for the aggregate of all oppressive practices. The sinister relation between trade and Empire (oppression) is expressed in a more complex fashion in "Night the Second" of the *Four Zoas,* where Blake accuses the daughters of Albion of stripping Jerusalem's curtains from mild demons of the hills" for their "needlework" and of "binding Jerusalem's children to Babylon" while they "go across Europe and Asia, to China and Japan like lightning" (1972: 281). In Erdman's effective paraphrase, "the British textile industry strips wool from sheep, binds children to factory labour and leads imperial armies as far as China in search of markets" (Erdman

1977: 332). Industrial tyranny and imperialism are seen by Blake as necessary concomitants of each other.

All *institutions* come under Blake's scourge for what he sees as their inherent hypocrisy. In the "Seventh Night" of the *Four Zoas* he presents the subtle way in which the so-called Righteousness and Morality (conversion and civilizing missions in the imperial context) exploit the public and expect to get thanked for doing so:

> when a man looks pale with labour and abstinence, say he looks healthy and happy; and when his children sicken, let them die, there are enough Born, even too many and our Earth will be over-run Without these arts. If you would make the poor live with temper, *With pomp give every crust of bread you give with gracious cunning, magnify, small gifts.*
>
> *REDUCE THE MAN TO WANT A*[7] *GIFT and then give with pomp.* (1972: 323, my italics)

Here, we have a clear exposure and furious indictment of the discriminatory and Malthusian practices of the ruling group—the rich or the imperialists, wherein the "breeding" of the poor or the natives alone seemed to constitute a threat of overrunning the Earth. Blake's argument can be aptly applied to a colonial context where the colony's past is sought to be forcibly excised, the natives' very biological and reproductive rights questioned and then gratitude expected for the new "culture" bestowed on them.

Imperial attempts to erase differences and impose homogeneity are also criticized by Blake. His "later imperialist"[8] Urizen attempts such a regimentation with

> One command, one joy, one desire
> One curse, one weight, one measure
> One King, one God, one Law (1972: 224)

and later admits the defeat of his project because "no flesh and blood could keep his iron laws one moment" (235). Politically motivated global reform movements initiated by imperialism inspired no trust in Blake and he rejected them in favour of reform from the inside. In a speech of the democratic Orleans in Blake's "The French Revolution" we find a warning for both conservative lawgivers and reformist theorists, asking them to doubt the infallibility of their projects:

> But go, merciless man! Enter into the infinite labyrinth
> of another's brain
> Of another's high, flaming, rich bosom and return unconsum'd
> and write laws.
> If thou canst not do this, doubt thy theories. (1972: 142-43)

The incapacity of forced "reform" to overcome inherent difference and the tyranny implicitly present in the attempt itself is emphasized here.

These parts of Blake's world view, where he examines the question of a universal Humanism versus a belief in the necessary presence of difference is significant in this context. He has asserted on occasion that human nature, despite different external trappings, is essentially the same. In "The Little Black Boy" both White and Black skin are pronounced to be clouds, equally opaque and cumbersome (1972: 125). At the same time, the only occasion when Blake bestows an "Excellent" on his despised rival Reynolds is when the latter writes: "If an European, when he has cut off his beard or bound up his own natural hair in regular hard knots as unlike nature as he can make it . . . meets a Cherokee Indian who has laid on with equal care and attention his yellow and red ochre . . . who ever of these two despises the other for this attention to the fashion of his country is the barbarian" (qtd. Blake 1972: 476). Blake's comment indicates his leaning towards cultural relativism and tolerance alongside and underlying his belief in an essential similarity.

The 'Other' for Blake is mainly the female. To quote Damrosch, "whatever Blake cannot reconcile himself to in the phenomenological world—bodies, matter, nature, physical space is symbolized as Female" (1980: 198). There is a constant fear of this female Other draining the power of the Self. However, "female" in this context is more of a symbol for divisive tendencies from the One than a biological category. Damrosch indeed goes so far as to assert that Blake desired a negation of the very category of the Other:

> If, in the end, Blake's myth is in some sense solipsistic it is also an act of faith that strives mightily to overcome the mode of thinking that accepts otherness as a fact of existence. (1980: 150)

In other words, the question of adjustment to the Other can be transcended by denying Otherness and solipsism is not just justified, but positively heroic since the Self then encompasses the All.[9]

This, however, is too sweeping a conceptualization, for Blake has clearly stated his belief in necessary diversity. In "The Marriage of Heaven and Hell," he remarks: "These two classes of men (the Prolific and the Devourers) are always upon earth and they should be enemies, whoever tries to reconcile them seeks to destroy existence" (1972: 155). To rephrase this in Blake's own terms: "Without contraries there is no progression" (1972: 149). In the imperial context we could say that Blake does believe in a universal humanist concept where rich and poor, colonizer and colonized can meet as one, but this, as he accepts, is an Edenic vision. In the world as it is, he accepts that the incessant dialectical struggle-synthesis-struggle process between contraries has to continue so as to ensure the continuance of existence itself.

It should also be noted that while much of Blake's radicalism developed out of a genuine love of liberty, a certain part was also produced from what Nigel Leask has termed the "Anxiety of Empire." We can trace a continual fear in Blake of the oppressive forces employed by the imperial power boomeranging/ rebounding upon itself in a worsened form from the colonies. Women drain the powers of ruling men; plague and pestilence as well as corruption flows back from the sites of oppression with an increased vitality. Blake's favourite formulation for this process, often repeated, but first seen in *The Four Zoas* is:

> Terrified at the shapes enslav'd humanity put on, he became what he beheld
> He became what he was doing, *he was himself transformed*
> (1972: 300, my italics)

The fear that the Self would be debased and transformed, that it could not oppress and tyrannize over the Other without degrading itself prominently underlies Blake's bitter aversion to tyranny at home and Empire abroad. Ironically, the voices of Burke and Blake, the arch-Conservative and the Radical, merge at this point. For Burke the corrupted Orient may spread its roots, for Blake debased practices essential to Empire may rebound. But though the phrasing may vary, the fear is the same—that of the Self being overrun and losing its Selfhood.

Given the fact that we cannot deny Blake's passionate hatred of the concept of Empire and the symbols of oppression he attaches to it, it is worthwhile to consider why Britain's Indian Empire itself is not very often referred to, let alone explicitly condemned, in Blake's works. Leask's argument in relation to Shelley, that liberal writers of the period did not specifically place their radical polemics in India because they *could* not (Leask 1993: 75) is relevant in this context. The Indian Empire was too close to home for comfort even for a radical like Shelley, general condemnations could not afford to be locale specific. As a harsh indictment in Coleridge, of his own and his compatriots' conspicuous consumption of Empire-produced goods indicates, no one was fit to throw the first stone.

This argument may be stretched to incorporate Blake to a certain extent. It could be concluded that the very 'inclusive' nature of Empire in Blake's corpus indicates that even as *more* than territorial expansion was involved, it was also *less,* since the actual fact of the geographical terrain involved was not directly confronted.

But the issue merits a pause at this point to consider the compulsions which may have applied to Shelley and not to Blake. As will be elaborated in the discussion on Shelley, his commitment to reform was in itself a compulsion to accept the only too clearly despotic implications of imperialism. One needed a site and subjects (an incredibly appropriate word in both its senses) if one was to experiment with reform. So, in the light of the greater good, uneasy silence had to be maintained with regard to the basic premises of imperialism—despotic control and denial of liberty.

We cannot trace such handicapping tendencies towards compulsive reform in Blake. His suggestions are both immediate and total—there has to be total change in all systems everywhere if there is to be progress. If not, piecemeal, oppressive, cross-culture reform schemes with their mechanized regularity are best left alone. It does not seem therefore that India being too close is the main reason for Blake's seeming silence. The 'inclusivity' we see in Blake has certain parallels with what (for want of a better term) I call a 'naiveté' in Keats (to be discussed later in this chapter). Though coming from two very opposite directions these qualities make the attitudes of these two—the earliest and the youngest of the canonical Romantics *comparatively* more "open-ended" towards the question of Empire than Shelley's radicalism, Coleridge's philosophy, Byron's "fellowship" or Wordsworth's benevolent paternalism. Empire, for Blake, is more than Britain in India. Maybe he is open to the charge of evading the specific issue. But at least his condemnation of *his personal of concept* Empire is consistent and he does not end up unwittingly making excuses for imperialism, a trap into which Shelley, for example, was too prone to fall into.

B

Samuel Taylor Coleridge, who is primarily remembered today as a poet and literary critic, exerted a seminal influence on the ideological currents of his age. His writings encompassed poetry, philosophy, religion, politics and science. J.S. Mill has paid tribute to Coleridge as being "one of the two seminal minds of the England of their age," the other being Jeremy Bentham (qtd. Reardon, 1971: 60). Even more than in the other Romantics, we have to look beyond poetry to judge any dimension of Coleridge's thought, including the Indian element.

A comparison with Burke made by D.P. Calleo, in *Coleridge and the Idea of the Modern State* is noteworthy in the context of Coleridge's positions[10] on India:

> Coleridge's later political philosophy is an important moment in the creation of a dynamic conservative tradition in English political thought. For it is Coleridge even more than Burke who is the true philosopher of that tradition. (qtd. Cooke 1979: 153)

This argument is borne out to a large extent by the evident Conservatism of the later Coleridge. However, it would appear that he had never managed to quite comfortably discard all of his earlier radical opinions. This, on occasion leads to an impasse in Coleridge's opinions on many sensitive subjects, including those of colonialism and imperialism.

We see in the early writings of Coleridge, a considerable respect for Indian philosophy which later jostles with his role as a committed Christian apologist. Several vehement pronouncements against hegemony and slavery in the abstract co-exist with comparatively scanty reference to actual political events. (In any case, West Indian slavery is far more often directly referred to than East Indian affairs.) When forced to comment directly on imperial affairs, Coleridge's Conservatism manifests itself as a gentlemanly pragmatism which deplores the many flaws in the status quo but is not going to consider any reform more radical than an increasingly benevolent paternalism. Certain anxieties regarding the morally and mentally weakening effects colonial/ Oriental contacts (concepts which Leask has examined in detail with regard to Byron and Shelley) could have on the British psyche make their presence felt in Coleridge's writings also.

The specifically Indian dimension in Coleridge includes certain imaginative concepts in his poems. These images lead directly enough to India. However, the importance of these at best scattered references to India should not be over-estimated, except to insist on their gesturing towards India as a usable and available signifier. John Drew in *India and the Romantic Imagination* undertakes a rather fanciful exercise in which an "Indian reading" of "Kubla Khan" is presented on the basis of an imaginative congruence between Coleridge's conceptions and the actual figures in Indian mythology. An Indian reading of "Kubla Khan" is indeed possible and as relevant as any other reading. But we should not carry this trend so far that we reach a stage where, to quote Coleridge himself on the writer of an article in an Encyclopedia, "India-India-India—the writer can see nothing but India from Arctic to Antarctic, from Chile to China" (Coleridge 1971: 191). Drew refers more to an "ideal image of India" (Drew 1987: ix) than to the political, social or even geographical entity called India which was under British rule. This analysis takes the philosophical dimensions into account, but also depends on specific references to India and to imperialism in general.

Coleridge, more often than not, was regarded, at least during his youth, as a traitor to the glorious cause of Britain by many of his countrymen. A review by Alexander Hamilton (Sanskrit scholar and East India Company army officer) in the *British Critic* June 1799 is representative in its concerns. He quotes the following lines from Coleridge's "Fears in Solitude":

> From East to West
> A groan of accusation pierces heaven
> The wretched plead against us, multitudes
> Countless and vehement.

Hamilton then proceeds to comment:

> We, by no means deny this writer the praise of sensibility and poetic taste and on this account we the more sincerely lament his absurd and preposterous prejudices against his country. We would seriously ask Mr. Coleridge where Englishmen have been so tyrannous as to justify his exclamation which we deny. (qtd. Jackson 1970: 48)

Most of Coleridge's statements on liberty and abolition of slavery were vehement enough to justify Hamilton's anxiety in any context including an East Indian one. However, they were mainly more specifically related to the West Indian slave trade and to his early opinions on the French Revolution.

In Coleridge's poetic corpus, India figures most prominently as the identifiable source of one repeated image—that of the God asleep on the lotus leaf. Apart from this, Coleridge in a Notebook entry (dated 1974) refers to the finding out of a desert city in Asia as a subject for a Romance, and to the mythical conquest of India by Bacchus as source (dated 7-9 November 1803) for a poem to be composed in Hexameters. [The Notebooks are unpaginated.] These schemes, as we know, did not materialize. We also have a brief reference to "Golconda's jewels" in a poem composed during 1834 entitled "Honour" (1970 1: 272).

A piece of "evidence" linking "Kubla Khan" to India is to be found in an entry Coleridge in the *Gutch Memorandum Notebook* (undated):

> In a cave in the mountains of Cashimere [sic], an image of ice which makes its appearance thus two days before the new moon; there appears a bubble of Ice which increases in size everyday till the fifteenth day at which it is an ell or more in height then as the moon decreases, the image does also till it vanishes. Read the whole 107 page [sic] of Maurice's Indostan.

The Collected Poetical Works edited by E.H. Coleridge includes this entry in its notes to "Kubla Khan." Coleridge also wrote in a Notebook (dated November 1802): "Kubla Khan ordered letters to be invented for his people" a sentence taken verbatim from William Jones' "Essay on the Tartars." John Drew has also traced similarities between Jones' landscape descriptions (content and style) in this essay and the imaginary landscape described by Coleridge in "Kubla Khan" (Drew 1987: 197-98). These are the basic (and maybe the only ones outside of pure speculation) foundations on which an Indian reading of "Kubla Khan" can be constructed.

Another poem, titled "A Lover's Complaint to his Mistress" is subtitled "who deserted him in quest of a more wealthy husband in the East Indies" (perhaps a quite common incident during the period!). At any rate, Coleridge does not seem to have too good an opinion of the famed British explorers and travellers, as these lines from 'The Delinquent Travellers' indicate:

> Of all the children of John Bull
> With empty heads and bellies full
> Who ramble East, West, North and South
> With leaky purse and open mouth
> In search of varieties exotic. (1970: 447)

An elaborate description of the Banyan tree can be found in Coleridge's *Poetical Fragments* dated 1806-7. Now, the Banyan tree has been described by many English poets including Milton and Southey. But Coleridge's work here is notable for the way it combines description with a religious horror of idolatry, typical of his later philosophy:

> As some vast tropic tree, itself a wood
> That crests its head with clouds beneath the flood
> Feeds its deep roots and with the bulging flank
> Of its wide base controls the fronting bank
> [By the slant current's pressure scoop'd away
> The fronting bank becomes a foam-filled bay]
> High in the fork the uncouth idol knits
> His channeled brow, low murmurs stir by fits
> And dark below, the horrid Faquir sits
> And horror from its broad head's branching wreaths
> Broods o'er the rude idolatry beneath. (1970: 1498)

This picture subscribes neatly to the Orientalist stereotypes of a benighted, superstition-ridden India, which aroused Christian horror. A similar, contemporary image of the Upas tree, poisonous and destructive is also to be found in a notebook entry dated 7-9 November 1803.

The image of the God asleep on the lotus leaf deserves greater elaboration because of its recurring nature (in the letters as well). In the "Night Scene" (a dramatic fragment published in 1813, salvaged from an incomplete play *The Triumph of Loyalty*), we find the image being introduced in a conversation:

> Earl Henry: "Oh there is joy above the name of pleasure
> Deep self possession, an intense repose."
> Sandoval: (with a sarcastic smile): "No other than as eastern sages paint
> The God who floats on a lotus leaf
> Dreams for a thousand ages; then awakening
> Creates a world and smiling at the
> Bubble; Relapses into bliss."
> Earl Henry: "Ah! Was that bliss
> Feared as alien and too

Vast for man?" (1970: 422)

In the existing first draft of the *Triumph of Loyalty* (1801) the entire speech is attributed to Earl Henry, without Sandoval's intervention. By 1813, obviously, Coleridge entertained no comparably favourable attitude to the image, which may explain why it was rendered vulnerable to Sandoval's sarcasm. The effects produced by the two presentations are quite different in nature.

An earlier version of this image can be found in a letter from Coleridge to Thelwall dated October 14, 1797:

> It is but seldom that I raise and spiritualize my intellect to this height. At other times, I adopt the Brahman Creed and say—it is better to sit than stand, it is better to lie than sit, it is better to sleep than to wake—but Death is the best of all. I should much wish like the Indian Vishna [sic] to float along an infinite ocean cradled in the flower of the lotus and wake once in a million years for a few minutes—just to know that I was going to sleep for a million years more. (1971: 143)

John Drew's remark on this letter bears repetition: "Coleridge regrets that by contrast to the spiritualized state of intellect, he more frequently falls into a state of lassitude, where the more supine the posture and the more insensate the consciousness, the better. At such times, he says, he has become a Brahmin in his attitude. *This is of course, a travesty of traditional yogic teaching*" (Drew 1987: 189, my italics).

A similar travesty can be seen in a variation of this image found in a speech of the Moorish woman Alhadra in Coleridge's successful play *Remorse.* Though the play was finally enacted in 1813, the primary draft entitled *Osorio* was complete in 1797. Alhadra is musing on the strangely softening powers of solitary communion with nature which renders her temporarily incapable of taking revenge on her husband's murderers:

> I need the sympathy of human faces
> To beat away this deep contempt for all things
> Which quenches my revenge.
> Oh! Would to Alla
> The raven and the sea mew were appointed

To bring me food or rather that my soul
Could drink in life from the universal air!
It were a lot divine in some small skiff
Along some ocean's boundless solitude
To float for ever with a careless course
And think myself the only being alive (1970: 11 323)

Alhadra has to break free from this apparently soporific image to prosecute her justified revenge. The association of the Indian image with a lassitude and torpor which precluded action could well be a (unconscious, perhaps) contribution to the troping of India as feminine and indolent. It is interesting to note here that Leigh Hunt in *The Examiner* (1821) refers to Coleridge himself as "a kind of *unascetic* Brahmin among us, one who is always looking inwardly and making experiments on the nature and power of his soul" (qtd. Jackson 1970: 474, my italics). A concept of Brahmanism as peaceful and contemplative could easily modulate into one of inaction and torpor with all "asceticism" elided out of notice.

Coleridge admits to an early fascination with the religion and philosophy of India. But his later reaction against them is vehement. Passages from his "Opus Maximum" manuscript (Muirhead 1930: Appendix III 283-84) indicate the extent of his later eager efforts to discredit any ideal image of India as a model source of philosophy. The Vedic philosophers and their religious writings are uniformly stigmatized as "childish intellects living among gigantic objects, of mean thoughts and huge things, living Lilliputs among inanimate Brobdignags." The concept of "oneness" in the Indian scriptures is dismissed as "the natural result of an imbecile understanding producing indistinction half from indolence and half intentionally by a partial closure of the eyelids, and when all hues and outlines melt into a garish mist, deeming it unity." The *Bhagavat Gita* is criticized for "passing off bigness for greatness." Orientalists like Jones and Wilkins are condescendingly excused for their "mistake" in judging the merit of Indian works; as they had circumstantial excuses, "which more than acquits the judges, though cannot prevent the reversal of their decision."

Coleridge admits in the same passage that he too had paid "this debt of homage" to the Indian texts when he first perused them. Later, however, he sought to use the antidote of common sense, took a second look and asked himself:

> And what then have I seen?
> What are
> These Potentates of inmost Ind?

The answer to these questions did not provide a verdict favourable to India. The whole Brahmin Theosophy was characterized as being "without growth, without production."[11] Coleridge then sums up his argument: "Abstract the enormous shapes and phantasms, the Himala, [sic] the Ganges of the fancy and what remains? A baby!" [All quotes from the 'Opus Maximum' fragment are taken from Muirhead (1930) (Appendix III)].

In *Biographia Literaria* India is mentioned as one of four countries (the others being Egypt, Greece and Palestine) where "the analysis of the mind had reached its noon and manhood while experimental research was still in its morning and infancy" (Coleridge 1971a: 43). In an issue of *The Friend* (No. 3, August 10, 1809) Coleridge refers to "the interesting *deformities* of ancient Greece and India" (1970a: XI 49, my italics). Papal and Brahminical superstition are equated with each other in the same issue. Obviously, by this time, not even philosophy was accepted as a successful domain for India. The concept of the "pariah" class and of the destructive procession of "Juggernaut" are employed as similarly evocative symbols:

> As if literature formed a caste like that of the Pariahs in Hindostan, who however, maltreated must not dare to dream themselves wronged.[12] (1971a: 112)

Coleridge found himself "bound in conscience to throw the whole force of my intellect in the way of their triumphal car on which the tutelary genius of modern idolatry is borne even at the risk of being crushed under the wheels" (1970a: IX 47). The reference to "Juggernaut" in this passage from *Aids to Reflection* is unmistakable. Again in the *Statesman's Manual* Coleridge refers to superstition on its "pilgrimages to Loretto, Mecca or the temple of Juggernaut, arm in arm with sensuality on one side and self torture on the other" (1953: 33).

In a significant Notebook entry (dated November 1810) Coleridge uses the image of "the naked savage and the gymnosophist" to indicate a meeting of extreme opposites. The reference to India is clear enough. Later, obviously the naked savage image comes to dominate over that of the gymnosophist. The later Coleridge had no qualms in asserting the superiority of Christianity even at the cost of factual accuracy. A May 1810 entry in the Notebooks refers to "the wild or the extravagant traditions which have gathered round the History of all other founders of Religions, except Christ—as Zoroaster, Odin, Brahma, Mahomet, Francis and all the Roman saints." Apart from the fact that there could very well be a dispute over the "non-extravagant" nature of traditions gathered around the figure of Christ, anyone acquainted with Indian mythology, as Coleridge certainly was, should at least have known that "Brahma" was in no way the "founder" of a religion like the other names mentioned.

In the fifth issue of *The Friend* (September 14, 1809) Coleridge remarks:

> It is highly worthy of observation that the inspired writings received by the Christians are distinguished from all other books pretending to inspiration from the scriptures of the Brahmins and even from the Koran in their strong and frequent recommendations of truth. (1970a: IX, 87)

The Christian scriptures are accepted as "revealed"; all other texts dismissed strongly as "pretenders to inspiration" with such conviction as to preclude all further discussion. An 1818 Notebook entry indicates quite clearly what Coleridge would have liked to put forward as his theory on comparative religious philosophy:

> And then I saw there is no other religion in the world that can stand in comparison with Christianity. Heathenism and Mahometanism are kept up by tyranny and bestial ignorance and blush to stand at the bar of reason.

Coleridge evidently quite heartily approved of the work of conversion though he deplored the nature of many individuals concerned. However, the East Indies furnish an exception even to this reservation. "I have long regretted the too general unfitness of the men chosen as missionaries, with some splendid exceptions in the East Indies," Coleridge writes in a letter to Joseph Hughes, 14th January 1831 (1971: 92). However, when on rare occasions they give some credit to the natives, Coleridge is not willing to accept the testimony of even the "splendid exceptions," witness a Notebook entry dated April-June 1809:

> A common error of religious persons—missionaries among the Hindostanee for instance is to wish that the true rational religionists possessed and showed the same zeal and fervour for the truth that these show for superstition and detestable idols—forgetting that thoughtlessness and Holiday Revelry are the causes and effects of this superstition and that it belongs to degraded man.

Since the objects of the natives' zeal are from the Christian apologist's perspective misplaced it is seen as an error to commend even the natives' zeal in itself. "Self Torture" among the natives, taken as an indication of zeal comes in for severe criticism in a Notebook entry, April-May 1809:

> O! if Folly were no easier than wisdom being so very much more painful and pleasureless, what might not a legislator have brought these men to? But alas, to swing with hooks through the back, to walk in shoes with nails of iron turned in upon the feet—all this is so much less difficult, tho' so much more painful, than to think.

Indeed the native's inability to "think" even though they can undergo great physical torture is further emphasized in another Notebook entry of the same period as almost a sign of essential racial difference. He records the comments of certain missionaries with full approval:

> Examine the journals of our humane and zealous missionaries in Hindostan. How often and how feelingly do they describe the difficulty of making the simplest chain of reasoning intelligible to the ordinary natives, the rapid exhaustion of their whole power of attention and with what pain and distressful effort it is exerted while

> it lasts. Yet it is among this class that the hideous practice of self-torture chiefly indeed almost exclusively prevails.

The "worst" (from the European perspective) of native practices are presented in focus and the stereotype of the unthinking (the emotion/ reason dichotomy) native is uncritically perpetuated.

Coleridge's interest in Indian affairs should not be viewed from the perspectives of religion or philosophy alone. He was perfectly well aware of the political and economic ground realities of the imperial relationship. A November 22, 1803, Notebook entry indicates a clear grasp of the commercial foundation of Empire: "The prodigious effect of the love of spices on the human race—the cause of the East Indian voyage—viz. of Columbus." A June-July 1810 entry in the Notebooks makes it very clear that Coleridge was not a visionary unaware of the often brutal imperatives of imperialism:

> The famous apostle of the Indies, Xavier, once said 'that missionaries without muskets did never make converts to any purpose.' At all events, I call upon the opponents to show any other way which has pleased Providence to appoint for the extended civilization of the human race. Can they mention any one savage country, Christianized even by the Apostles, even in the miraculous ages of the Church before the Roman Arms and colours had preceded them?

Imperialism is quite clearly presented here as a civilizing mission with Christianity as its necessary concomitant and even naked, brute military force as a means is perfectly justifiable since the end is the glorious one of "civilizing the human race."

In the sixth of his 1795 *Lectures on Politics and Religion* Coleridge discusses the economic underpinnings of the imperial enterprise and the moral dimension involved:

> If he be a commercial man, can he always be sincere? Let him look around his shop. Does nothing in it come from the desolate plains of Indostan? From what motives did Lord Clive murder his millions and justify it to all but his own conscience . . . it has been openly asserted that our commercial intercourse with the East Indies has been the occasion of the loss of 8 million lives, in return for which most foul and heart rending guilt, we receive gold, dia-

> monds, silks, muslins and calicoes for fine ladies and prostitutes. Not one thing necessary or even useful do we receive in return for the horrible guilt in which we have involved ourselves. (1970a: I 225-26)

There is a clearly articulated and undeniable concern here with the devastation of India. However, the sub-text which rises into prominence is *the guilt* incurred by the Britons, which is *not even adequately compensated for*. The confessional is uncomfortably abutting on the ledger here. The morally sapping nature of imperialism, it is regretted, is not made up for by the material benefits received. On balance, therefore, it is not absolutely certain whether the Empire is a good bargain or not. James Mill had the same doubts regarding finances, but at least he had a reform mission to urge. Coleridge's conscience does not seem to allow him either alternative.

The anxiety is manifested on occasion as a purely physical fear. In a letter to H.N. Coleridge, dated Tuesday 28 August 1832, cholera is referred to as "this travelling Nabob from the swamps and jungles of Hindustan" (1970a: V 923). This anxiety is further elaborated in a letter to J.H. Green, 25 April 1833: "In its long journey of the vast steppes, the enormous moonholes and Dead Seas of Tartary and Asia, the East wind has been freighted with contraband waves" (1970a: V 937).

This physical exposition is translated into more psychological terms in this extract from the "Opus Maximum" manuscript:

> Every epidemic disease, every epidemic or endemic should awaken us to the deep interest which every man and every country has in the well-being of all men and in the consequent humane progressive humanization of the surface and with it of the atmosphere of the planet itself. As man, so the world he inhabits. It is his business and duty to possess it and rule it and assimilate it to his own higher nature. If instead he allows himself to be possessed, ruled and assimilated by it, he becomes an animal like the African Negro or the South American savage and is a mischief to man even by the neglect of his function as a man. The neglected earth steams up vapours that *travel*.

The trope of progressive humanization indicates that before the imperial civilizing enterprise the natives were not really "human" at all. Anxiety—both of disease and of a loss of vitality—is here linked to the continuation of imperialism. If civilization is not spread, then the diseased vapours will "travel" and so it is almost self-defence to embark on an imperial mission to ensure that the vapours do not emanate. The exclusive definition of "man" together with the fear of noxious corruption/infection from the Other add up to a strong defence of imperialism.

An entry under "On the Power of Turkey" while justifying imperial aggression makes a hair-splitting distinction: "We seem to have forgotten that the Turks and their Asiatic neighbours are semi-Barbarians and not savages" (1970a: III 163). To this can be added Coleridge's approving quote from Crawford's *History of the Indian Archipelago:* "wherever agriculture is the principal pursuit, there it may certainly be reckoned, the people will be under an absolute government" (1970a: HI 578). Semi-barbarianism, mixed with absolute despotism serves to indicate that Asia was indeed ripe for the western civilizing mission. In an 1810 Notebook entry, Coleridge indulges in a spectacular piece of special pleading, to actually list reasons to prove that the good behaviour of colonists *has* to be in an inverse proportion[13] to the freedom and virtue of the Mother Country. Hence, the better Britain becomes, the worse her colonists' behaviour will necessarily become.

A very clear and concise formulation of Coleridge's attitude to the question of imperialism may be derived form the following Notebook entry: June-July 1810. Indeed, it has a ring of finality. Though the specific reference is not to India, the underlying assumptions can easily be adapted to fit the Indian issue:

> I do affirm that if it be an absurdity to affirm that 2 or 3 hundred naked savages[14] have not by the accident of preoccupation a fair right of property in the whole of that immense island continent, then it must likewise be absurd to observe that the colonists of a civilized nation have not the same right to serve themselves and the rightful objects of their colonization, thro' coercion of those savages or even compelling them into a form of civilization were

> necessary, provided that in truth of conscience, the moral good and personal happiness of the savages were part of the end and that the means be appropriate both *morally and prudentially*. If this be denied, I do not see how we can justify the coercion of children and lunatics. (my italics)

"Accident of preoccupation," savagery versus civilization, conscience as arbitrator, moral upliftment, a comparison of natives with children and lunatics—these arguments of a Romantic philosopher poet have a strangely contemporary ring. It is possible to speculate endlessly on the "ideal image" of India and its influence on the Romantic psyche. The 'ideal' as well as the 'romantic' are after all concepts which admit of great elaboration and interpretation. But when individual cases such as Coleridge are considered in the light of available evidence, a commitment (subtle or tenuous perhaps, but definitely *existent)* to the further expansion and consolidation of imperialism becomes evident under the Romantic imagery. The Indian images, however evocative, are mainly adaptable symbols in Coleridge's poetic corpus. The geographical reality of India was equally if not more significant for him as both source of anxiety and valued possession. The contradictions, which as we have seen, thus engendered between Romantic ideal and practical statement can be pointed out as the chinks, the exploitable gaps in his Romantic edifice. Or else, perhaps more realistically, they could be seen as the necessary constituents of the imperial edifice—a structure which thrives on contradictions.

C

There is a comparative scarcity of specific references to Eastern sources, or locales in Wordsworth's poetry, prose or even correspondence. Also, since Wordsworth's philosophy is mainly incorporated in the poetry, we have no stock of explicit comparative discussions of philosophical systems to draw upon as in the case of Coleridge. Indeed, apart from the meagre scattered Indian references in his poetry all we have to guide us in tracing any Indian dimension are a few cryptic clues. I have attempted to piece these together and also draw upon the somewhat more elaborate discussions of Empire as such to illuminate a probable attitude towards imperialism.

Wordsworth's correspondence almost never mentions any direct perusal of Indian philosophy or even "popular" Indian works (unlike almost all the other poets discussed here). It is most probable that the Eastern affinities in his thought were transmitted through classical intermediaries rather than through any first hand Oriental source. Speculations regarding the Indian influence on Wordsworth's philosophical pantheism have their own importance. Raymond Schwab in *The Oriental Renaissance* has examined this aspect (Schwab 1984: 196). More attention is paid, however, in my analysis, to piecing together the direct references to India and to Empire that we *do* have in Wordsworth and to constructing from these, a reasonably clear picture of Wordsworth and the Oriental Other in an Imperial context.

Wordsworth's personal life (like perhaps that of almost every Englishman/woman of the time) was at least indirectly connected to the Indian enterprise. His brother, John Wordsworth perished in discharge of his duty as Commander of the Honourable East India Company's vessel 'the Earl of Abergavenny' (Wordsworth 1936: 120). The intended recipient of his poem 'Liberty' "accompanied her husband Rev William Fletcher and died of cholera at the age of 32 or 33 on her way from Sholapur to Bombay, deeply lamented by all who knew her" (1936: 414). The trope of India as a land of "sudden death and strange regrets" must have prevailed alongside the concepts of exotic locale and source of philosophy.

Wordsworth's apparent lack of interest in the contemporary craze for Oriental themes and locales did not go unnoticed. In a letter dated 19 December 1828, Baron Field comments, "Bye the Bye, all your travellers 'step westward.'" The letter goes on to say: "you have no Oriental poem. I wish you would write me one as unlike *Lalla Rookh* as possible" (Wordsworth, 1937: III 695n). (Apparently, the feverish enthusiasm for *Lalla Rookh* was not universal.) Wordsworth himself had earlier dismissed *Lalla Rookh* as "Moore's ugly named poem" (1937: II 394). In reply to Field's letter, Wordsworth writes:

> I should like to write a *short* India piece, if you could furnish me with a story—Southey mentioned one to me in Forbes' travels in India . . . it is of a Hindoo girl who applied to a Brahmin to recover a faithless lover, an Englishman. The Brahmin furnished her with an ungent with which she was to anoint his chest while sleeping and the deserter would be won back—if you can find the passage—pray transcribe it for me and let me know whether you think anything can be made of it. (Wordsworth1937: III 695-96)

Obviously, nothing came of this idea since we find no hints of such Indian material in Wordsworth's poems. A pity since it would have been interesting to see what the philosopher poet made of this "magic" theme.

In a letter to Basil Montagu dated 20 March 1827, Wordsworth comes up with a rather ingenious explanation for the prevalence of the custom of Sati in India:

> Are you aware that the horrid practice of wife sacrifice in India is the result of the polygamous husband's schemes to guard his own life from the attacks of the malcontents among his numerous wives by making it a point of honour that such sacrifice should take place upon his decease? The natural dread of death gives the whole band an interest in prolonging his existence. (1937: 522)

The custom must have gripped popular imagination considerably when casual correspondence evidences attempts to rationalize it.

A reference in another letter to Sir Beaumont gains some significance because of its suggestions of Oriental "excess" and extravagance as opposed to a well-bred British stiff upper lip policy:

> The voice of the minister was accompanied and almost interrupted by the slender sobbing of a young person, an Indian by half blood, and by the father's side a niece of the deceased wife of the person we were interring. She hung over the coffin and continued this *Oriental lamentation till* the service was over. Everybody else except one faithful servant being apparently indifferent. (1937: 231, my italics)

The implication is that such indecorous lamentation could only be "Oriental" and if at all a British parallel could be found, it would be among servants.

The direct (and mainly casual) references to India in Wordsworth's poetry can be quickly enumerated. In "A Farewell" he refers to "an Indian shed" (1936: 84), we have an "Indian bower" in "Her eyes are wild" (I 15), an "Indian Conjurer/quick in feats of art" in "The Kitten and Falling Leaves" (175). In *Peter Bell* there is a reference to "temples like those among the Hindoos" and the Ganges figures in "Miscellaneous Sonnets" (200). In Sonnet XI, we have an "Indian Citadel" (203) and "Indian isles" in the "Blind Highland Boy" (240). In the "Sonnet to the River Duddon" there is a brief description of the Banyan tree (300) and in the "Ecclesiastical Sonnets" we find a commendatory reference to the Prester John legend in the mention of "Christian Indie" [sic] which held "sacred intercourse" with King Alfred. There are also references to "Indian mats" (670), "Indian deserts" (547), "Indian Cabins" (552), "lascars" (540) and the "Indian bird" (657). In *The Excursion,* the process of imagining the fount of human life is compared to "the Hindoos" drawing "their holy Ganges from a skyey fount" (617). These few references, scattered as they are over a vast poetic corpus do not function very usefully as aids to interpretation. Apart from an indication that India was present as a source of comparison when something "different" was to be suggested there is not much further scope for analysis here.

There are however, a few slightly more elaborate references remaining, which need to be examined—some of these serve to indicate the concept of the Orient/India as the scene of unimaginable luxury and voluptuousness. In Book X of the *Prelude* we have:

> They—who had come elate as eastern hunters
> Banded beneath the Great Mogul, when he
> Erewhile went forth from Agra or Lahore
> Rajahs and Omrahs in his train intent
> To drive their prey enclosed within a ring
> Wide as a province. (1936: 562)

Sonnet XLVI in "Poems dedicated to National Independence and Liberty" mentions:

. . . as the power of light
was inexhaustibly in precious gems
Fixed on the front of Eastern diadems
So shines our thankfulness for ever bright (263)

In "The Haunted Tree" we find:

That Eastern Sultan amid flowers enwrought
On silken tissues might diffuse his limbs
In languor (175)

Voluptuousness, ease, riches,[15] splendour, pre-planned languor even in the hunt, indicate that the exotic titles—though few in number, these references serve to indicate that the conception of the East/India as the land of *Lux et Volupte* was flourishing. Another reference in The *Prelude* to people who stand

With Indian awe and wonder, ignorance pleased
With its own struggles (533)

adds tinges of the dark night of superstitious slavish ignorance co-existing with the tempting false light of a voluptuous facade. Certain lines from the poem entitled "Suggested by a picture of the Bird of Paradise" need to be quoted at length as they indicate Wordsworth's only excursion into the realms of Indian mythology:

This, this the Bird of Paradise! Disclaim
The daring thought, forget the name;
This the sun's bird, whom Glendoveers might own
As no unworthy partner in their flight
Through seas of ether, where ripping sway
Of nether air's rude billows unknown
Whom sylphs, if e'er for casual pastime they
Through India's spicy regions wing their way
Might bow to their Lord. (184)

"Glendoveers" on the authority of Southey's *Curse of Kehama* seems to have been a general version for Indian "Gandharvas." Since Wordsworth leaves no record of direct Indian sources and does mention perusal of Southey's poem, it is reasonably safe to assume a debt to Southey here. The "Glendoveers" are native to

India and form a contrast to the more classical "sylphs" who may merely fly over India for "casual" pastime.

In the notes to "The Egyptian Maid or The Romance of the Water Lily" we read: "The lotos with the bust of the Goddess appearing to rise out of the full blown flower" (293). This, together with the reference in the poem to the "two mute swans" (293) who accompany the "lotos lady" seems, without laying too much emphasis on it to accord closely with the traditional Indian depiction of the Goddess Saraswati, a parallel which indicates some awareness of Indian iconography.

Wordsworth has not specifically referred to his approval or otherwise of Britain's colonial enterprise in India or in Africa. But he does indicate in a letter to Captain Paley that he did possess a very clear concept of "the White Man's Burden." Not only is colonization by Britain beneficial to the colonies, it is positively *undesirable* from Britain's own point of view.

> As far as concerns ourselves and our security, I do not think that so wide a space of conquered lands is desirable and (as a patriot,) I have no desire for it. If I desire it, it is not for ourselves directly, but for the benefit of those unhappy nations whom we should rescue and whose prosperity would be reflected back on ourselves. (1937: II 478)

Imperialism here is presented as a totally altruistic project, where Britain undertakes arduous conquests which do not even benefit her, for the sole purpose of rescuing unhappy nations. The moral dilemma is resolved quite comprehensively through a process which negates its existence—unstinted—altruism, especially if undertaken when undesirable from a selfish perspective *cannot* be morally suspect.

The same concept of Imperial benevolence is elaborated by Wordsworth in the Irish context.[16] As Vincent J. Cheng has amply demonstrated in *Joyce, Race and Empire,* England's actions in Ireland were more often than not blueprints for those in her far flung colonies. The "asset" of a shared white skin did not save the Irish who were referred to as "white Negroes" and "white Chimpanzees" (Cheng 1995: 19, 33). Chitra Panikkar in discussing Joyce's depiction of Ireland's problems refers to "Ireland's subjugated identity in the European world which keeps her for ever colonized/provincial. The portrayal of Ireland's history in Joyce is shown to "allow vast spaces for the histories of [other] subjugated national identities" (Panikkar 1996). References to Britain's policies in Ireland can to a great extent legitimately be read as statements on Imperial/Colonial activities in general.

From this perspective Wordsworth's elaborate comments in his letter of 11 June 1875 to Sir Robert Inglis are very revealing:

> The condition of Ireland is and long has been wretched; lamentable is it to acknowledge that the mass of her people are so grossly ignorant and from that cause subject to such delusions and passions that they would surely destroy each other were it not for the restraint exercised upon them by Britain. This restraint it is that protects their existence, in a state which otherwise the course of nature would provide a remedy for, by reducing their numbers through mutual destruction. So that English civilisation may fairly be said to be the shield of Irish barbarism. If then these swarms of degraded people could not exist but through us, how much does this add to the awfulness of responsibility of England. . . . English capital would flow into Ireland, with English persons to manage and apply it, English Arts, manners and aspirations—thus would the grovelling peasantry be raised; they would become discontented and ashamed of their nakedness and ruggedness, of their peat bogs—and their hovels and the destitution of household accommodation in which they *breathe* rather than live. (1937: III 361)

Britain's disinterested responsibility, the animal imagery, poverty ascribed to the people's own "natural" inferiority, mutual destruction but for Britain's presence, barbarism as opposed to English civilisation, upliftment of the natives—substitute India or Africa for Ireland and the texture of the argument holds together just as easily.

The early Wordsworth, it must be admitted, was sometimes critical of British imperial policies; sometimes (but very rarely) an echo of these criticisms can be traced in the later works also. In "Humanity" Wordsworth especially criticizes the legal double standards for home and abroad:

Shame that our laws at a distance still protect
Enormities which they at home reject! (1936: 393)

Book VIII of *The Excursion* indulges in considerable criticism of the state of England's domestic affairs. The lack of true liberty and the extremely inequitable distribution of material and intellectual property were the chief targets of attack. These often very bitter criticisms can justifiably give rise to the question: "How is an England who manages her own internal affairs so badly in any way qualified to rule and guide other countries?"

This question seems to have been anticipated and poetically answered by Wordsworth in his Sonnet XXI from "Poems dedicated to National Independence and Liberty." The argument here is that British rule may not be an unmixed blessing, but despite all her faults, she is *still* the best choice since her enemies are so much worse:

England! The time is come when thou shouldst wean
Thy heart from its *emasculating food*
The truth should now be better understood;
Old things have been unsettled, we have seen
Fair seed time, better harvest might have been
But for thy trespasses and at this day
If for Greece, Egypt, India and Africa
Aught good were destined, thou wouldst step between
England! All nations in this charge agree:
But worse, more ignorant in love and hate
Far, far more abject is thine enemy:
Therefore the wise pray for thee, though the freight
Of thy offences be a heavy weight.
Oh grief, that Earth's best hopes rest all with thee!

(1936: 245, my italics)

England's rule may even prevent good for Africa and India, but *still* she is shown as the best available hope. Imperialism's doublespeak or is the issue more complex?[17] British Control, bad as it is, is so much better than that of the other European powers could be that it is to be tolerated. Of course, Europe *has* to figure, India, Africa et al (and in Europe, poor outdated Greece) cannot be dreamt of as managing on their own. Wordsworth elsewhere refers to "the flood of British freedom" (1936: 2441) and of liberty as "a refreshing incense from the West" which is to be wafted across to Asia and Africa (260). Liberty and Justice are the generous gifts of the West (here England) to the Orient which is passively "willing" to receive them. Wordsworth did think that Britain herself could do with quite a lot of improvement, but he *still* insists that she so much outranks all her competitors in the Imperial sweepstakes to remain the odds on favourite for guiding towards the Light a benighted Orient which could not do without an Occidental mentor.

Finally, mention should be made of Wordsworth's poem entitled "Address to my Infant Daughter Dora." The poem begins: "Hadst thou been of Indian birth" and goes on to list in detail the hardships such a birth would have entailed, mainly due to the ravages of nature which civilisation had not tamed. Indian infants are "thy unblest coevals," the English child being fortunate enough to be "warm clad and warmly housed." Indian (Oriental or Amerindian) children suffer in every respect, with even maternal instinct "there" being visualized as a "joyless tie of naked instinct." The poem ends on a note of fervent thanksgiving: "Happier, far happier is thy lot and ours" (1936: 136-37).

This, in plain terms is a celebration of having been fortunate enough to be born in Britain and so avoid Indian birth. The Other is mostly an instinctual creature, shut out from the rarefied, rational pleasures which the British/European Self can claim as its birthright. It is doubly ironic that it is Wordsworth, the high priest of Nature, who is here considering a life supposedly shaped by natural influences to be so "unblest" in comparison with the more manmade ethos of Europe/England. This perhaps sums up a basic complexity with regard to the Other in an imperial context—despite fascination, temptation, unwilling admiration or fear, and even if it involves one in contradicting one's life-philosophy—the Self rejoices in its Selfhood and thanks its good fortune in not actually being the Other, which at best remains second best.

D

The 'East,' by Byron's own testimony was the most valuable source of his poetic inspiration. In a letter to Thomas Moore, dated 17 November 1816 he says: "It is my intention to remain at Venice throughout the winter, as it has always been (*next to the East*) the greenest island of my imagination (Byron 1804: 136; my italics). The same idea is repeated in a letter to Murray, dated November 25, 1815: "Venice pleases me much, as I expected and always haunted me the most—*after the East*" (my italics; 358). This scrupulous privileging of the East over even Venice is of considerable significance. An examination of Byron's poetic reference and prose statements with regard to the East do seem to force the admission that however much of an "Orientalist" he was, he cannot be clubbed with thorough going Orientalists such as Moore or Southey.

On the other hand, it would be Utopian to expect any individual to completely transcend the prejudices and stereotypes of his age, so as to come up with a totally "new" version. This paradoxical situation has led to considerably varied views on the Oriental dimension in Byron.

Apart from a few scattered references, the mention of Byron in Edward Said's *Orientalism* is restricted to a remark: "Romantic writers like Byron and Scott consequently had a political vision of the Near Orient and a very combative awareness of how relations between the Orient and Europe would have to be conducted" (1978: 192). In his *Colonial Transactions,* Harish Trivedi flatly negates Said's statement: "In this unsubstantiated assertion, Said's geography is vague, his chronology is shaky and he has got hold of the wrong man as well" (1993: 112). Both Trivedi and Leask argue that Byron cannot be fitted into the conventional Orientalist paradigm. According to Trivedi:

> Byron does not seem to have 'produced' the Orient in Edward Said's formulation. . . . Indeed, Byron does not seem even to have subscribed to the *ineradicable distinction*[18] between Western superiority and Eastern inferiority which is said by Said to be the essence of Orientalism. (1993: 116, my italics)

Trivedi concentrates on the "authenticity" of Byron's descriptions and the surprises, variations and complexities which attest his power to deconstruct stereotypes, even as he may seem superficially to be subscribing to them. From this perspective, Byron is practically exonerated from the charge of Saidean Orientalising.

Nigel Leask in *British Romantic Writers and the East: Anxieties of Empire* pursues a somewhat different argument to draw very much the same conclusion. According to Leask, Byron's Oriental poetry could be viewed from two distinct perspectives. In the first place, we see a business venture, a market aimed production strategy. From the second perspective Byron's sympathies were too liberated to allow him to rest content with 'mere Orientalism' and his *Eastern Tales* "finally chose a transgressive path which represented a peculiarly contorted escape from their ideological impasse" (Leask, 1993: 16).

Perhaps a statement to the effect that Byron *attempted* to transgress contemporary stereotypes would be the best compromise, since complete success in such an endeavour is too idealistic to expect. Also, the very fact that Byron was alienated from British society may have led to some amount of negation of the notion of British superiority over the Orient in his works.

Despite the British colonial presence in India, Byron's East was primarily the Near East of Turkey and Asia Minor. It is interesting to note that John Drew's *India and the Romantic Imagination* which studies Coleridge and Shelley in detail, does not have even an index reference to Byron. Leask also reserves the Indian dimension for exhaustive study in relation to Shelley and confines Byron to the Near East. However, as Trivedi has demonstrated, it is possible to pick up quite a few references to India in Byron's poetic corpus. [Trivedi's list is built upon and enlarged in my analysis.] But apart from exploring the Indian references, considerable importance is given to the Orient as such in Byron's works, so as to tackle questions of imperialism and the Other *per se*.

The one deliberate attempt at an "Indian" piece on Byron's part is entitled "Stanzas to a Hindoo Air"—a sentimental performance which has the refrain: "Oh! My lonely-lonely-lonely-pillow!" (Byron 1970: 111). It is hard to see in what specific way these lines were especially Indian, let alone "Hindoo." Trivedi's suggestion is that the poem was intended to be "a palpably exotic and un-English poetic production, so excessively tender so as to convey the impression that Byron sought fully in it to match the reputed sentimentalism and alliterative and iterative wordplay of the (so-called) Hindoo literature itself" (1993: 102). The stanzas, at any rate (in a fashion similar to Shelley's "Indian Serenade") give us a picture of the conventional expectations from an image of Indian literature during the time.

There are a few references to India to be found in Byron's correspondence. Sheridan's famous "Begum Speech" is mentioned as the best oration of the time and Alexander's conquest is referred to in a letter to John Murray (1984: 237, 239). We also learn that Byron's lack of personal contact with India was not due to any disinclination on his part. In a letter to his mother, dated November 2, 1808, Byron writes:

> I wish you would enquire of Major Watson (who is an East Indian) what things will be necessary to provide for my voyage. . . . I can easily get letters from Government to the Ambassadors, Consuls and also to the Governors at Calcutta and Madras. (1974: 1, 122-23)

Byron further elaborates his plans for a voyage to India in a letter to Hanson (18 November 1808):

> In the first place, I wish to study Indian and Asiatic policy and manners. I am determined to take in a wider field than is customary with travellers. . . . I have written to government for letters and permission to the (East India) Company, so you see I am serious. (1974 1: 175)

It is interesting to note at this point that both Shelley and Keats had also made attempts to visit India, which were, like Byron's, unsuccessful. Byron's request was turned down by the government and he had to content himself with the Near East. We can only speculate as to what effect the proposed Indian journey would have had on his poetry if it had materialized.

The casual references to India in Byron's poetry are scattered widely over his works. In 'The Blues' a writer's fame is conveyed through the image of his works "reaching to the Ganges" (1970: 154). Both the Ganges and the Indus (160) as well as a "nabob" (166) find place in 'A Vision of Judgment.' *The Giaour* features "the insect queen of eastern spring/ o'er emerald meadows of Kashmeer" (256). In a note to *Childe Harold's Pilgrimage,* Byron bluntly states: "I do not think the honour of England much advanced by plunder, whether of India or Attica" (878). In *Marino Falerio, Doge of Venice,* a precious necklace is tellingly referred to as "an India in itself" (424) and Venice is addressed as the city which had "opened India's wealth to Europe" (442). In the "Age of Bronze" we have a mention of Jews who 'waft a loan from Indus to the pole" (177).

"Brahmins" make an appearance in *The Island* as a simile for "gentle hearts" (3561). There are quite a few references to India in *Sardanapalus*—The Ganges figures twice (456, 457) in relation to Semiramis' expedition to India. Bacchus' mythical conquest of India is referred to (456) as well as a "mirror" from India (471). "Hindoos" figure among "Greeks, Romans and Yankee Doodles" (624) in *Beppo.* In Canto III of *Don Juan* we have "Indian mats and Persian Carpets" (693); a Cashimire [sic] shawl figures in Canto V (719) and a maid in Canto VI is described as "dusk as India" (735). There is a mention of Sanskrit in Canto VIII (760) and in Canto IX we find mention of Nadir Shah's invasion of India (773), "Cashimere breeches" (774) and an "East Indian sunrise" (776). Canto XII has a reference to "ships from Inde" (800) and Brahmins appear in Canto XIII (816).

Trivedi also points out that through Cuvier there is a reference to the Indian view of creation in which one world succeeds another (773) and also an allusion to an image in the *Bhagavat Geetha* in the "mildly ironical" exclamation:

What a curious way
The whole thing is of clothing souls in clay (798)

These references to a large extent may be referred to as "topical smattering" (Trivedi 1993: 104). They serve mainly to indicate the need for exotic images and the availability of India to fill that need. There are, however, a few more references which deserve to be looked at in slightly greater detail.

In the "Monody" on Sheridan's death, he is praised for having upheld the cause of India:

> When the loud cry of trampled Hindustan
> Arose to heaven in her appeal from man
> His was the thunder, his the avenging rod
> The wrath—the delegated voice of God! (Byron 1970: 96)

There is a suggestion here of sympathy with India and a condemnation of British oppression which justifies an "appeal to heaven." Again, in "The Curse of Minerva," Britain's despoiling of Greece is condemned and as retribution, a rebellion in India is predicted:

> Look to the East, where Ganges swarthy race
> Shall shake your tyrant empire to its base
> Lo! There rebellion rears her ghastly head
> And glares the nemesis of native dead
> Till Indus rolls a deep puerperal flood
> And claims his long arrears of northern blood
> So may ye perish! Pallas, when she gave
> Your free born rights, forbade ye to enslave (144)

The suggestion that India and Greece are both wronged and the parallel drawn is instructive. The idea of liberty is paramount here, transcending for the moment, distinctions of race and locale, of East and West.

The Indian word 'Avatar' is used in a peculiarly English sense in the title of a poem: 'the Irish Avatar' (109). A reference in *Don Juan* to "the glowing India of the soul" confers a metaphysical sense on India, as an ideal image apart from its material reality. In *Sardanapalus,* there is a mention of Sati. The Ionian slave Myrhha demands:

> And dost thou think
> A Greek girl dare not do for love that which

> An Indian widow braves for custom? (492)

The rite itself seems to be romanticized here, if undertaken freely out of love, the bad part being the role of "custom." Credit is denied to the Indian widow who is the slave of tradition, but the Greek girl's image is enhanced.

At this stage we need to undertake an examination of those statements which may be considered part of Byron's "policy statement" in the East, in conjunction with the tracing of Indian references. There is no doubt that his Oriental settings were part of a well-planned market strategy for Byron. He extends his advice on the poetic share market to Moore in a letter of 22 August 1813:

> Stick to the East—the oracle De Stael told me it was the only poetical policy. The North, South and West have all been exhausted, but from the East we have nothing but Southey's unsaleables, these he has contrived to spoil. . . . His personages don't interest, yours will. You have no competitor. . . . The little I have done in that way is merely a "voice in the wilderness" for you and if it has any success, that will also prove that *the public are Orientalising and* pave the way for you. (1974: III 101, my italics)

Byron obviously knew what he was talking about; as Moore's *Lalla Rookh* enjoyed a stupendous contemporary success and earned its author the unprecedentedly vast sum of three thousand guineas.

It is true that Byron later deprecated his contribution to the taste of the day and tried to shrug off his *Eastern Tales* as amateur productions. In an 1812 letter, he condemns his earlier productions as "exaggerated nonsense which has corrupted the public taste" (1974: 161). While criticizing those who put up contemporary productions against the classicism of Pope, Byron both inculpates and excuses himself in a simultaneous process:

> I shall be told that amongst those, I have been (or it may be, still am) conspicuous—true and I am ashamed of it. *I have* been amongst the builders of this Babel attended by a confusion of tongues, but *never* among the envious destroyers of the classic temple of our predecessors. (qtd. Leask 1993: 63)

Evidently, there is an effect of overkill in these strictures, but even then they should put us on our guard against assuming that Byron had "turned Turk" completely. The same idea, that composing Oriental verse is a facile and ephemeral pastime is reiterated poetically in *Beppo:*

> Oh, that I had the art of easy writing,
> What should be easy reading! . . .
> Those pretty poems never known to fail
> How quickly would I paint (the world delighting)
> A Grecian, Syrian or Assyrian Tale,
> And sell you, mix'd with western sentimentalism
> Some samples of the finest Orientalism! (1970: 629)

Leask aptly refers to this attitude as Byron's sense of "artistic shame" (1993: 63). Against this, however, must be set the fact that the East *remained* a positive focal point for Byron and that except on occasions explicitly polemical, he does not indulge in privileging European or classical perspectives.

In a letter to Murray, 21 February 1820, responding to a suggestion that he write a book on the life and customs of the Italians, Byron says:

> I have lived in their houses . . . and in the heart of their families . . . and in neither case do I feel myself authorized in making a book of them. Their morals are not your morals, their life is not your life, you will not understand it. (1984: 227)

This refusal to create a spectacle by exoticising or degenerating is occasionally extended to the Orient also. In his *Eastern Tales,* Oriental customs are detailed painstakingly (Byron was proud of the authenticating circumstance of his having actually visited his locales, unlike Moore or Southey) but rarely are they coupled with value judgments. Customs which may *appear* fanatic from a European perspective are even shown to *have exact parallels* in Christian Europe. The Turkish ruler's murder of a slave girl who was unfaithful to him is revenged by her European lover in *The Giaour,* but he admits that he would have done the same in like circumstances:

> Yet did he but what I had done

> Had she been false to more than one. (1970: 261)

In *The Corsair* the Seyd's intended torture for his European rival Conrad is annotated thus:

> Not much could Conrad of his sentence blame
> His foe, if vanquished had but shared the same. (1970: 291)

Turks and Christians could both be villains, cruel and exacting, and there is nothing particularly Oriental about those vices. It is also possible to argue, as Trivedi has aptly done, that Byron's Oriental descriptions are not overdone; and accounts of sacred objects are presented without an undercurrent of dismissal, unlike, for example in Southey. (Trivedi 1993: 114)

Byron has strongly expressed himself against despotism in all its forms and indicated that he was unlikely to let supposed essential difference serve as a justification for oppression. In his dedication of *The Corsair* to Moore, Byron draws the parallel between oppression in the East and in Ireland quite clearly:

> It is said . . . I trust truly, that you are engaged in the composition of a poem whose scene will be laid in the East; none can do those scenes so much justice. *The wrongs of your own country,* the magnificent and fiery spirit of her sons, the beauty and feeling of her daughters may there be found; and Collins when he denominated his Oriental his Irish Eclogues was not aware how true, was a part of this parallel. (1970: 277, my italics)

The wrongs of oppression are wrongs here, wherever they be perpetrated at home, nearby or far abroad. It is the idea of liberty which prevails over Byron's thought that renders him capable of drawing such parallels and that too, unlike Wordsworth, without emphasizing only the unsavoury aspects of both Ireland and the East as the essential ground of similarity.

"Freedom" was a pervading *Mantra* of Byron's creed. An unambiguous statement of this position is found in the journal entry of January 16, 1814: "The fact is riches are power and poverty is slavery all over the earth and one sort of an establishment is no better or worse for a people than another"[19] (1984: 96). In *Don Juan,* Canto IX, Byron states:

> I wish men to be free
> As much from mobs as kings—from you and me. (1970: 722)

Byron condemns even his admired Napoleon for his change from popular leader to despot and in his "Ode from the French" comments:

> Then he fell—so perish all
> Who would men by man enthrall! (1970: 84)

In keeping with this concept of an ideal freedom, Britain's "glorious ventures" are deflated with the reference to Englishmen as people who "butchered half the earth and bullied the other" (1970: 788).

We may feel that this concept of freedom is qualified, that there is a tinge of prejudice in the 23 November 1813 Journal entry: "The Asiatics are not qualified to be republicans, but they have the liberty of demolishing despots, which is the next best thing" (1984: 88). But we must remember that Byron held a similar opinion of the Greeks, in whose cause he died fighting. In the Notes to *Childe Harold's Pilgrimage* Byron clearly indicates this opinion:

> The Greeks will never be independent, they will never be sovereigns as heretofore, and God forbid they should! But they may be subjects without being slaves. *Our Colonies are not independent but they are free and such may Greece be hereafter.* (1970: 88, my italics)

It must be mentioned that there is an almost incredibly facile optimism regarding Britain's colonies here, in sharp contrast to Byron's usual knowing stance.

An accusation of prejudice can be intensified on account of a letter in which Byron credits the persistent stereotype of the Turks as inveterate homosexuals. He writes to his mother: "you know that boys are not *safe* among the Turks" (1984: 231). As Trivedi points out with reference to Byron's own homosexual proclivity: "it was not only with the Turks that boys were not *safe*" (Trivedi 1993: 108). However, it must be noted that in his *Eastern Tales* Byron does not portray his Orientals in keeping with this stereotype and also that statements which testify to human "sameness" and a universal right to freedom are far more characteristic of him. In a letter to Henry Drury, 3 May 1810, Byron clearly states:

> I see not much difference between ourselves and the Turks, save that we have foreskins and they none, that they have long dresses and we short and that we talk much and they talk little. In England the vices in fashion are whoring and drinking and in Turkey sodomy and smoking. (1984: 36)

Yet another letter to Francis Hogdson in the same vein deflates the rhetoric of Christianity's superior moral claims:

> Talk you of Gallilelism? Show me the effects—are you better, wiser, kinder by your precepts? I will bring you ten Mussalmans shalt shame you in all—good will towards men, prayer to God and duty to their neighbours. And is there a Talpoin or a Bonze who is not superior to a fox-hunting curate? (1984: 53)

The segregation of men based on religion is indicted in Byron's poetry also. In 'The Prayer of Nature' he asks rhetorically:

> Shall each pretend to reach the skies,
> Yet doom his brother to expire
> Whose soul a different hope supplies
> Or doctrines less severe inspires? (1970: 42)

This concept is further enforced in *The Siege of Corinth:*

> But far away
> Scattered over the isthmus lay
> Christian or Moslem, which be they?
> Let their mothers see and say! (1970: 330)

As Trivedi remarks, "with his blithely sceptical temperament, Byron could not under any circumstances have wished to proselytize . . . the one thing Byron as an Orientalist is not is a missionary in disguise" (1993: 118).

In keeping with his main argument, Nigel Leask concentrates on Byron's "Anxiety of Empire," his "regret of imperialism as the harbinger of social and cultural corruption, the nemesis of social order" (Leask 1993: 16-17). According to Leask, the main anxiety in Byron's Oriental works is the fear of "turning Turk"—this does not really hold when we remember that Byron did not have words bad enough for his own country. He was more likely to regard a disruption of his "identity" at that level as a change for the better. To let a Journal entry speak for itself: "I have seen mankind in various countries and find them equally despicable. If anything, the balance is in favour of the Turks" (1984: 47). One who wrote this may be accused of bitterness or snobbery or misanthropy but surely not of an especial fear of or contempt for the orient.

However, it is not possible to endorse an opinion that at an imaginative level, Byron manages to overcome Orientalist binaries in his poetry. Trivedi quite correctly points out that in *The Corsair,* the Christian Byronic hero, Conrad "is not allowed to always prevail over all Eastern Muslim antagonists" without "crucial variations" (Trivedi 1993: 116). But when it is pointed out as a positive feature that in *The Bride of Abydos* in which there are no white characters, the Oriental hero Selim is quite Byronic, one must insist that some emphasis be laid on the fact that *there are no white characters,* a quite necessary condition for the Byronising of the non-western hero.

Leask argues that Byron often overturns the very paradigms within which he operates. For example, in *The Corsair* we have a "brown woman saving a white man from brown men" (Leask 1993: 51) and in both *The Bride of Abydos* and *The Corsair* the hero is defeated precisely because he is *not Oriental enough* due to his troublesome absorption of European chivalric codes (Leask 1993). Leask seems to regard this as a thoroughly positive strategy, but this is a stand which invites argument. It is true that the codes of European chivalry are shown to be grandiose and less than useless when pitted against an Oriental enemy who does not acknowledge these codes. It seems rather far-fetched to argue that if non-European tactics (removed from the honour ideal) are depicted as having to be adopted to succeed in a non-European Oriental world, which does not acknowledge those ideals, such a depiction is in favour of the Orient. The argument that Oriental methods have to be applied for settling Oriental enemies is surely not so much a deflating of European ideals than an indictment of their unsuitability in an Oriental milieu.

Leask identifies a "Utopian moment" in *The Island* where mutineers find solace on a tribal island. Their arrival on the island is described by Byron in ecstatic terms:

> The white man landed! *Need the rest be told?*
> The new world stretch'd its dusk hand to the old
> Each was to each a marvel and the tie
> Of wonder warmed to better sympathy. (1970: 355, my italics)

History would insist that the "rest" *does* need to be told after the "white man lands." We know from sad evidence that such landings are followed by consequences very different from the ideal scenario described by Byron. (The usual sagas of exploitation and appropriation which normally follow the "landing" is brilliantly analyzed *in Marvellous Possessions* by Stephen Greenblatt).

According to Leask, *Lara* in which the Western hero returns from the East thoroughly corrupted and destroyed, sadly represents things as they are; *The Island* "offers a fragile version of hope in terms of the relation between a predatory Europe and its colonial Others . . . in a Utopian space where the violent dichotomies of culture, class and gender are briefly suspended" (Leask 1993: 67). To illustrate this, Leask quotes the lines which depict the "hero," Torquil's education by the simple values of the South Sea islanders who:

> Did more than Europe's discipline had done
> And civilized civilization's son. (Byron 1970: 355)

and describes this as "a reversal of the moral discourse of colonialism" (Leask 1993: 66).

This can be accepted only if we consider the civilizing mission as the sole component of the colonial discourse; a position which is very far removed from the actual state of affairs. The Nature/ Culture dichotomy for instance, the need for over-civilized Europe to be revived by "simpler" colonies—these concepts were equally important parts of the imperial discourse. The dichotomies of culture/nature are not transcended in a vision where simple South Sea Islanders "civilize civilization's son"; in fact, they are reinforced—Europe is civilized, the Orient is closer to nature. It is true that nature is privileged over European civilisation, but (as will be further elaborated in relation to Shelley) changing the locus of power in a binary opposition *does not* force the opposition itself to collapse, it is merely perpetuated with a varying emphasis; difference itself is not reduced, let alone eradicated.

In his 'Ode on Venice' Byron refers to Glory, Empire and Freedom as a "Godlike Triad!" (1970: 105). Empire, if reconciled with freedom (obviously not possible for the colonized countries), was not to be despised. In *Childe Harold's Pilgrimage,* the battle of Marathon is used as a symbol for the East-West conflict and the West is quite clearly identified with Freedom and Asia with despotism.[20]

> The flying Mede, his shaftless broken bow
> The fiery Greek, his red pursuing spear;
> What sacred trophy marks the haliow'd ground
> Recording *Freedom's smile and Asia's tears?*
>
> (1970: 208, my italics)

At the same time, the following lines from *Don Juan,* Canto XII seem to emphasize a conscious opposition to racism and the colour bar as also a belief in positive cultural relativism:

> But if *I had been* at Timbuctoo, there
> No doubt I should be told that black is fair.
> It is. I will not swear that black is white.
> But I suspect in fact that white is black
> And the whole matter rests upon eyesight. (1970: 807)

This does indicate that Byron was perfectly aware that standards of excellence were constructed and relative. We have also seen that Byron far more often welcomed the embrace of the Orient than he feared it. Yet, even this great degree of self-awareness could not render the Orientalist binaries completely redundant in his poetry—a tribute indeed to their in-built strength.

Byron's specific comments with regard to India are few, yet he merits discussion by his significant presence in the imperial context *per se.* To reiterate my opening arguments, we are justified in claiming that Byron did *attempt* transcendence and transgression of stereotypical binaries. Irrespective of the degree of success or failure, one can give credit to an attempt which itself was rare among contemporaries. Byron does manage to turn many colonial stereotypes upside down, the fact that he cannot demolish them may be more indicative of their strength rather than of his weakness. Yet, we should not lose sight of the fact that to expect complete success in such an attempt is Utopian. However, the degrees of conformity did vary and it is greatly to Byron's credit that he displayed practically the widest range of variations conceivable.

E

In a letter to T.J. Hogg dated 22 October 1821, Shelley writes:

> I have some thoughts, if I could get a respectable appointment of going to India or anywhere where I might be compelled to enter into an entirely new sphere of action. But this, I dare say is a mere dream and I shall have no opportunity of making it a reality, but finish as I have begun. (Shelley 1964: II 361-62)

As we know, the dream did remain a dream. But it is interesting to note that Shelley considered India both the source of action and inspiration by virtue of its novelty. As in Byron's case, red-tapism put an end to what could have been one of the most exciting and productive encounters in the history of Indo-British relationships. Shelley had enquired about Indian employment to his friend Thomas Love Peacock, who worked for the East India Company. He received a reply firmly and completely negating the idea. This put an end to Shelley's material and practical Indian aspirations. Apart from his association with Peacock, Shelley's desire to visit India must have been stirred (as Nigel Leask also points out) by the accounts of his cousin, Thomas Medwin who was employed in India. In a letter to Peacock, 12 July 1820, Shelley records that he has "read or written nothing lately, having been much occupied by my sufferings and by Medwin who relates wonderful and interesting things of the interior of India" (1964: I 242). Later, Shelley passes commendatory remarks on Medwin's Indian writings and also writes to a publisher recommending them (1964: I 183, 246). It is reasonably safe to assume that Medwin's descriptions contributed their fair share to Shelley's ideas and images of India.

Apart from such personal contacts, Shelley also seems to have read the most significant works related to India in circulation at that time. In his correspondence, we have references to his having read Edward Moor's *Hindu Pantheon* (1964: I 153); Sir William Jones' *Works* (172); Robertson's *Historical Disquisition* (183); *Lalla Rookh* (191) and Mill's *History* (202). On August 18, 1812, Shelley writes to James Henry Lawrence that "your *Empire of the Nairs* which I read this Spring succeeded in making me a perfect convert to its doctrines" (1964: I 323). He recommends *The Curse of Kehama* to Elizabeth Hitchner (334) and calls it his "favourite poem" (336). Southey's poem obviously had considerable impact on Shelley as we find him quoting from it frequently in his letters. Reference is also made to Sydney Owenson's *The Missionary,* an Indian tale which seems to have impressed Shelley. The work is highly praised in three distinct letters (1964: I 105, 107, 112). In his letters, Shelley also refers to "Brahma" (108) to "Camdeo, the Indian God of mystic love" (123) to "Pariahs" (137), "Hindoos as witnessess" and Arrian's *Historia Indica* (545-46). In *A Philosophical View of Reform,* Shelley uses the idea of caste in India to strengthen his argument:

> Will you render by your torpid endurance this condition of things of permanent as the system of castes in India, by which the same horrible injustice is perpetrated in another form? (1953: 254)

The three specifically 'Indian' poems of Shelley are *Zeinab and Kathema* (which will be analyzed in detail later on), 'The Indian Serenade' and 'Fragments of an Unfinished Drama.' A few other references to India are scattered over his poetic corpus. 'The Indian Serenade' (1970: 580) seems to share with Byron's 'Lines to a Hindoo Air' an idea that assonance, use of alliteration, a surfeit of melancholy and melodrama and repetition had something particularly 'Indian' about them. The poem consists of three stanzas culminating in overflowing sentimental melancholy. One is led to remark that if this was considered a fair specimen of Indian literature, then James Mill's condemnation seems excusable enough. The 'Fragments of an Unfinished Drama' (1970: 482-88) feature as dramatis personae an Indian Enchantress, an Indian youth and lady. References are made to Indian topography to create the necessary ambience.

In "Charles the First," Shelley refers to the "azure depth of Indian seas" (1970: 492) an Indian isle "figures in the "Triumph of Life" (519) and "the tube rose which peoples some Indian dell" is mentioned in 'The Woodman and the Nightingale' (562). A fragment entitled 'I would not be a king' contains the lines:

> Would he and I were far away
> Keeping flocks on Himalay. (649)

In 'The Sensitive Plant' we have references to a "basket of Indian woof" and scented "Indian plants" (562), Brahma figures in Canto X of *The Revolt of Islam* along with "Buddh" and also "Indian breezes," (131, 137) and "Seeva" makes an appearance in *Queen Mab (788). Hellas* contains references to an "Indian slave" (452), "Indian gold" (465) and "Indian superstition" (480). *Prometheus Unbound* is set in "A Vale in the Indian Caucasus" (207) and so there are quite a few references to Indian landscapes. In *Alastor* also, the poet's dream vision takes place in "the vale of Kashmir" (I 8). In a *Letter to Maria Gisborne* there is a reference to Peacock having "turned Hindoo" (360) and in *Peter Bell the Third* "East Indian Madeira" is referred to (354). A very early untitled fragment describes a deer dying among "Indian rocks" (808). There is a reference to Sati in "Rosalind and Helen" where Rosalind asserts her fidelity to her suspicious husband:

> In truth, the Indian on the pyre
> Of her dead husband, half consumed
> As well might there be false, as I
> To those abhorr'd embraces doomed

> Far worse than the fire's brief agony. (175)

It is, of course, evident that these brief references do not justify Quinet's description of Shelley as "completely Indian" (qtd. Schwab 1984: 63). We are led to conclude that Quinet based his statement on something more abstract than specific references to India; on an "Oriental tone" as Nigel Leask calls it (Leask 1993: 71) in Shelley's poetry. John Drew and Leask have undertaken two erudite though widely varying readings of Shelley's Indian dimension in *India and the Romantic Imagination* and *British Romantic Writers and the East* respectively.

Drew's central theme is that of an "ideal image of India used as an organizing principle around which to speculate about the nature of imaginative literature (1987: ix). In keeping with this Drew argues that "in *Prometheus Unbound* Shelley projects on to a 'vale in the Indian Caucasus' a pattern perfectly identical with that elaborated in the mythology of Kashmir" (1987: 233). He also states:

> The Indian setting of *Prometheus Unbound,* faintly discernible as an ultimate veil, serves to indicate that what might pass for an Indian influence is a recognition within the Imagination of India as an appropriate image for that mystical imageless state for which the Imagination is itself but an image. (1987: 281)

It is necessary to state here itself that my analysis holds that Drew's mystic idealism is, to put it mildly, somewhat out of place when we consider the historical fact that Britain *did have* a colony in India, something of which Shelley obviously was not unaware, though it is firmly and completely evicted from Drew's scheme of things.

Nigel Leask notes the curious fact that "nowhere" (practically nowhere, *Zeinab and Kathema* which Leask dismisses as "unremarkable" is an exception) in Shelley's vehement tirades for liberty and against tyranny is the Indian empire referred to specifically and constructs his theory around this omission. He sees in Shelley "a liberal fantasy" which "represents a wish fulfillment of rational universalism exempted from the violence which marks the real *ambivalence* of colonial discourse" (Leask

1993: 78). In other words, Shelley was speaking about India without actually doing so; his Utopianism temporarily gaining the upper hand over both imperial guilt and anxiety though they remain and surface on unexpected occasions. Leask's argument is self-consciously political and well-documented. His insights inform my analysis in many ways, despite disagreements—mainly regarding the sidelining of *Zeinab and Kathema* and specific interpretations of *Alastor* and *Prometheus Unbound.*

Zeinab and Kathema (written in 1811 and included in the *Esdaile Poems*; 1966) is certainly "early." But there is a gap of only 3 years between this work and *Alastor* which Leask analyses in detail. Given the specific Indian content of the poem, this ignoring sets up an uneasy aporia, all the more intensified because it specifically contradicts some of Leask's central assumptions—the lack of direct reference to India and the anxiety of "infection" from India for example.

Zeinab and Kathema is specifically set in India and deals directly with the *violence* of the Imperial enterprise. The narrative concerns the Indian, Kathema, whose lady love Zeinab, along with other women, is carried off to slavery and prostitution in England. After many hardships, Kathema manages to reach England only to be greeted by Zeinab's corpse swinging from the gibbet as a punishment for rebellion. The passionate ire which Shelley directs against the inhuman practices of his countrymen in their colonies as well as the contrasting pictures of England and India, with the balance heavily in India's favour are significant in this poem. The English colonizers are characterized as "Christian murderers."

> The Christian murderers overran the plain
> Ravaging, burning and polluting all.
> Zeinab was reft to grace the robbers' land
> Each drop of kindred blood stained the invaders' brand. (1966: 97)

The claims of colonization contributing to the moral and material upliftment of the colonized people are sharply ridiculed by exposing the depravity and hypocrisy of the colonizers themselves:

> Yes! they had come with their holy book to bring

Which God's own sons' apostles had compiled
That charity and peace and love might spring
Within a world by Gods' blind ire defied
But rapine and war and treachery rushed before
Their hosts and murder dyed Kathema's bower red. (1966: 97)

Shelley also refers to "Christian rapine" and to "gold—the Christian's God"—satisfying his atheistic and reformist tendencies at the same time. It is also interesting to note in passing that India here is obviously fabulously wealthy; Kathema easily and casually hands around "heaps" of gold to gain passage to England.

In his zeal to expose the depravity and hypocrisy of his countrymen colonizers, Shelley idealizes his Kashmir in this poem to serve as a contrast even in topographical and climatic terms:

Yet Albion's changeful skies and chilling wind
The change from Cashmire's vale might well denote
There heaven and earth are ever bright and kind
Here blights and storms and damp ever float
While hearts are more ungenial than the zone
Gross, spiritless, alive to no pangs but their own
There, flowers and fruits are for ever fair and ripe
Autumn there mingles with the bloom of spring
And forms unpinched by frost or hunger's gripe
Here woe on all but wealth has set its foot
Famine, disease and crime even wealth's proud gates pollute
(1966: 99, my italics)

The balance of climatic conditions and of physical and moral advantages, however unrealistically, seems to be totally in India's favour here. It would be a natural assumption at this point that in Shelley's opinion "infection" was more likely to be blown from England to India and not vice versa.

However, Leask argues that "anxiety of Empire" in Shelley manifested itself at the physical level as "the fear of an elephantistic, slave borne disease, returning to infect the masters of space, of the 'external world'" (Leask 1993: 154). Nora Crook and Derek Guiton in *Shelley's Venomed Melody* indicate that Shelley was influenced by William Jones' conception of Elephantiasis/Syphilis as a disease "peculiar to climates," and so occurring in places like India, Africa and the Caribbean from where it could spread into Europe (Crook 1986: 91). The authors append several instances of Shelley's fear of this East/West Indian disease and its manifestations. This well-authenticated physical fear is reworked by Leask into a psychological (psychopathological?) anxiety of Empire. Such an argument seems at odds with the explicit Kashmir—Healthy/Britain—Unhealthy stance of *Zeinab and Kathema.* If Shelley had any such fear at the time, he masks it very successfully in this poem. Yet, the anxiety can be traced in Shelley's later works. It could be either assumed that the pathology of anxiety developed along with increased reading and awareness or that the contradiction is but another aspect of the essential ambivalence of Shelley's stance *vis-à-vis* Empire.

Among Shelley's major poetic works, *Alastor* and *Prometheus Unbound* share at least a nominal Indian setting. *The Revolt of Islam* does not have even that. Yet, it is possible, as Leask has demonstrated, to read all these texts quite convincingly in the light of the colonial enterprise in India. Edward Said has referred to the Orient as an "imaginative geography" and as "a stage on which the whole East is confined" (Said 1978: 59, 63). Using this concept, Leask argues that "we should be prepared to find a certain interchangeability in Romantic representations of the various Asian cultures" (Leask 1993: 75). With specific reference to Shelley:

> The Lebanon of *The Assassins,* the Istanbul of *The Revolt of Islam* or the Kashmir of *Alastor* are easily identifiable one with another, as indeed are terms in which Shelley castigates Islamic, Brahminical (or for that matter, Christian) despotism, superstition and sensuality. (Leask 1993: 75)

This interchangeability enables us to see the colonial context as informing Shelley's references to the East as such.

In Alastor or the Spirit of Solitude the poet protagonist travelling to India from an obstacle ridden Europe is granted a vision of his female prototype; ideal alter ego; which in the denouement proves to be dangerously indeterminate. Shelley traces in detail the path followed by his protagonist on this "Eastward Ho!" mission:

> The poet wandering through Arabic
> And Persia and the wide Carmanian waste
> And o'er the aerial mountains which pour down
> Indus and Oxus from their icy caves
> In joy and exultation held his way
> Till in the vale of Cashmire, for within
> Its loneliest dell, where odorous plants entwine
> Beneath the hollow rocks a natural bower
> Beside a sparkling rivulet he stretched
> His languid limbs. (Shelley 1970: 18)

It is in this "Vale of Cashmire" that the veiled maid—who indicates both insatiate desire and wish fulfillment—makes her appearance.

Joseph Raban has pointed out that the path traced by Shelley's poet:

> closely approximates that of Alexander the Great during the triumphant years between his initial conquests in the Near East and his glorious extension of his empire beyond the borders of the Persian domains.

and also that the other source of Alastor's journey could be the invasion of India by Bacchus/Dionysius (qtd. Leask 1993: 124). The suggestion of penetrating the East, whether in search of a female vision or of territorial expansion, is present in this trajectory. The East, at the very least, is presented as an area open to penetration and exploration. Also, the "vision" provided in India—although temporarily functioning as an ideal—finally leads to the poet's utter disintegration and degeneration.

The presentation of the "vision" as sensuously female is of obvious significance. As Rana Kabbani has pointed out:

> The European was led into the East by sexuality, but the embodiment of it in a woman or a young boy. He entered an imaginary harem when entering the metaphor of the Orient, weighed down by inexpressible longings. (Kabbani 1986: 67)

"Inexpressible longings" are exactly what motivate the *Alastor* poet. And his attempts to express them result in non-poetic terms only in an "Ouboum" effect—an illustration of what Homi Bhabha calls "the archaic nonsense of colonial cultural articulation" (Bhabha 1994: 131).

The vision the *Alastor* protagonist receives in the Orient is both the female other and the Self—"herself a poet" who was singing "themes" and "thoughts most dear to him" (Shelley 1970: 18)—his mouthpiece as Cythna in *The Revolt of Islam* is Laon's. The gender motif here does complicate the issue of ideological and cultural assimilation to a certain extent. In Leask's argument:

> The question of cultural difference becomes entangled with that of sexual difference and a binary opposition, which is almost a cliché in Orientalist discourse is problematized by Shelley's *manifest feminism.* (Leask 1993: 120, my italics)

Manifest feminism? Surely this is too commendatory a term to bestow on the poetic creation of an unutterably sensuous female figure—who in a psychological explanation repeats the poet's thoughts, in Orientalist terms, represents the light of European sensibility through negation of an Oriental identity, and at the crudest Freudian level could (as Leask himself remarks) be a "wet dream?" One should not underestimate the power of clichés—a critical attempt to acclaim their subversive power can easily fall back into cliché itself.

Apart from the debatable claim of "feminism" Leask does argue that Shelley's veiled maid "represents a narcissistic discovery of the *Same*" (1993: 127). [The question of an inevitable coupling of the Other with the Same and narcissism is discussed in the section on Keats.] However, Shelley in Leask's argument is "rescued" from this narcissistic assimilation through recourse to "ambivalence" (128). There are pitfalls in the valourization of ambivalence. At present, the focus is only on analyzing which side of the equation Shelleyan ambivalence ends up in effect.

It is in the context of "manifest feminism" that *The Revolt of Islam* and *Prometheus Unbound* have to be interpreted; also keeping in view the issue of ambivalence. Leask does admit that in *The Revolt of Islam* "a manifest feminism is undone by the poem's investment in a discourse of latent imperialism" (1993: 131). But in the context of a wish fulfillment fantasy of self-motivated revolt in the East, which would establish European values, the very question of feminism is suspect. Even as she initiates the revolution, Cythna is the mouthpiece of Laon, active only when he is incapacitated. The moment he recovers, she all but regresses into passivity; except for an exhilarating moment where she is again the rescuer. In an almost ludicrous switch-over, after the rescue, the two change places and Cythna has to be protected, unable even to find food for herself. Also, her final arrival to burn herself with Laon can definitely be read as a *re-working* of the Sati motif. Reworkings rarely maintain exact parallels with the original and Leask's suggestion that Shelley "suppresses the possibility" (1993: 128) of such a reading—presumably by having Laon alive on Cythna's arrival—is no reason to avoid the reading itself. After all, Shelley suppresses the entire Indian dimension (with *Zeinab and Kathema* being practically the sole exception in his poetic corpus) and all critics who undertake a colonial reading have unanimously ignored *this attempt at suppression*. The ambivalence of the entire process does indicate implication to a large extent—suppression is rarely the psychological outcome of a clear conscience.

Before proceeding to a brief analysis of this aspect in *Prometheus Unbound* it is appropriate to consider two prose texts by Shelley—the fragment entitled *The Assassins* and the tract—*A Philosophical View of Reform.* There is no specific mention of India whatsoever in the former text and the latter contains what is Shelley's most explicit and longest comment on India. Yet, the two are connected by the shared feature of ambivalence.

In *The Assassins* (as figured in Leask's central argument) the same theme as in *The Revolt of Islam* can be seen. The Assassins are Orientals, they are also European revolutionaries. They colonize themselves, breaking away from "human institutions" (Shelley 1951: 160) and find the ideal peace to set up a "colony"—the valley of Bethzatanai which was now empty—"the men of elder days had inhabited this spot" (1951: 162). As Leask brilliantly phrases it: "the valley of the Assassins is conveniently devoid of human habitation, so an egalitarian society can be established without the perennial problem of real colonialism—namely *what to do with the natives*" (Leask 1993: 76, my italics). There is no arguing with the existence of ambivalence here or with the trope of India as "an oxymoronic figure . . . the site of a revolution which is also a form of imperial domination" (Leask 1993: 79). The problem lies in the final valourization of Shelley's ambivalence (especially through *Prometheus Unbound)* into special status. After all, (though perhaps not with anything approaching Shelley's level of suppressed guilt) James Mill had been saying very much the same thing—the necessity for imperial domination to pave the way for progressive reform. As the chapter on Mill indicates, his thesis was not lacking in its own brand of ambivalence.

A Philosophical View of Reform and *Prometheus Unbound* have to be brought forward before the argument can be carried any further. The lengthy passage in the former text, given its explicit reference to India needs to be quoted in full:

> Revolutions in the political and religious state of the Indian peninsula seem to be accomplishing and it cannot be doubted but the zeal of the missionaries of what is called the Christian faith will produce beneficial innovation there even by the application of dogmas and forms of what is here an outworn encumbrance. The Indians have been enslaved and cramped in the most severe and paralyzing forms which were ever devised by man; some of this new enthusiasm ought to be kindled among them to consume it and even if the doctrines of Jesus do not penetrate through the darkness of that which those who profess to be his followers call Christianity, there will yet be a number of social forms modelled upon those European feelings from which it has taken its colour substituted to those according to which they are at present cramped and from which when the time for complete emancipation shall arrive, their disengagement may be less difficult and under which their progress to it may be the less imperceptibly slow. Many native Indians have acquired, it is said, a competent knowledge in the arts and philosophy of Europe, and Locke and Hume and Rousseau are fa-

> miliarly talked of in Brahminical society. *But the thing to be sought is that they should as they would if they were free to attain a system of arts and literature of their own.* (Shelley 1953: 224-25, my italics)

One can hardly ask for a better example of ambivalence. The entire passage is tortured between the awareness that imperialism is domination and the equally strong conviction that the East *has* to be "reformed." Leask sums up the ideological impasse:

> But perhaps the most remarkable thing about Shelley's passage is the awkwardness of its last sentence, and in particular the faltering unpunctuated conditional 'as they would if they were free.' The main body of the text has described a 'revolutionary' liberation from the straightjacket of Brahmanism, albeit a gradual one, the last sentence is forced, surreptitiously to admit that the European values which are to free them are also those which enslave them. Phrases like 'complete emancipation' become by this token problematic, emancipation from Brahmins or from the British? *What are we to think of a revolution which enslaves rather than liberates* or a discourse of revolution which admits that it is *also a* discourse of domination? (Leask 1993: 119, my italics)

Again, there is no question regarding the ambivalence and the encapsulation of it is sharply focused. There is an elision here however which has to be noted. Shelley would have had no problem with "a revolution which enslaves *rather* than liberates." He would have easily declared it no revolution at all. The problem lay in the fact that from Shelley's European though radical perspective, the colonial process enslaved *as it* liberated. The process was seen as simultaneous, the dichotomy from that perspective, inbuilt.

At this point, a certain other brief reference in the same *A Philosophical View of Reform* merits mention. Speaking of the necessity of not postponing reform, Shelley writes:

> The strongest argument, perhaps for the necessity of Reform is the inoperative and unconscious abjectness to which the purposes of a considerable mass of the people are reduced. They neither know nor care—they are *sinking into a resemblance with the Hindoos*

> *and the Chinese who were once men as they are.* (Shelley 1953: 257)

Unfortunately, this is clear enough; the defense of ambivalence is inadmissible. "Who were once men"—the question of what the "Hindoos and the Chinese" now are is better left unasked. There is an awareness here of the "truth" of imperialism—a constructed, unstable, biased "truth" and yet a powerful one—and it is the fight against this "truth" that gives rise to the ambivalence. If one did not believe in this truth—part of which is the inferiority myth—at all, there would be no problem. But since there is belief, however unwilling—there is an almost unavoidable tinge of bad faith in the denials. "As they would if they were free" —Shelley "knows" this is false—if the Indians were free—i.e., from the British—they *could not,* within his framework, develop their own "system of arts and literature" which would in any way be comparable to that which could be offered by the enslaving liberation of Empire. As long as this conviction persists, the ambivalence prefigures not guilt but subconscious complicity in hiding/denying what is actually held to be "true."

"And the Celt knew the Indian" runs a powerful line in *Prometheus Unbound*—optimistic and encompassing at first glance. The bad faith, the denial—even this poem—which along with Byron's the *Island* Leask singles out for its Utopian moments is not free from them. The stereotypes may be seen to have been reversed—not dismantled—in *Prometheus Unbound.* The male European figure Prometheus has a more "passive" role as opposed to the "active" presence of Asia, especially in the visit to Demogorgon. [Drew points out the resemblance between Shelley's Demogorgon and the Indian Seshnaga and also that Shelley follows the Indian method of "describing" Demogorgon and through him the supreme Being entirely in negatives (1987: 264).[21]

It is true enough as Leask points out that Prometheus' presence in the East is one of captivity and bondage and not one of conquest (1993: 143). But the whole question of "action" has to be rethought in the context of this poem. Prometheus' revoking of the curse *is* action, it is the one positive action which can set the chain of events leading to Jupiter's deposition in motion. Asia's 'action' on the other hand consists primarily of "being educated," of "receiving knowledge." The active/passive dichotomy has so many shades here that it cannot be used to suggest that the female/male; Asia/Europe binaries have been overthrown.

Leask clearly states that Shelley was an advocate of liberal imperialism which he describes as "displaced revolution" (1993: 6). But he still insists that though "much of Shelley's writing is carried by the force of the stereotypical binary oppositions, West/East, male/female, reason/imagination, it is apparent that to reverse the power current in any one pair upsets the general economy of equivalences" (Leask 1993: 121-22). It needs to be insisted on (as has already been done in the case of Byron) that a reversal (that too theoretical) of the structure does *not* collapse binary oppositions or even "upset" them; it merely represents them in a more subtle fashion. If *Prometheus Unbound* does attempt to carry its argument without resorting to the stereotypical passive female Orient, the attempt is in itself subverted by the ambivalence regarding the very concept of action within the poem. A simple active/passive binary would have been much easier to handle than what we actually have.

It is possible to agree, that Shelley, with his undoubted radicalism was "*searching* for a voice to say what no other contemporary British writer even dreamed of saying. Namely that the colonial encounter need not exhaust the possibilities of the meeting of different cultures" (Leask 1993: 169, my italics). But the point is that the search *stays* at the level of a search, precisely because Shelley was fighting against what he unfortunately "knew"; the unsavoury "truth" of the need for colonialism. "And the Celt knew the Indian" (Shelley 1970: 238)—the term "know" is invested with a boundless optimism. But the optimism is forced against the clear knowledge that it is hardly justified by any actual scenario which resulted when the West came to "know" the East. The parallel with Byron's "And civilized civilization's son" (1970: 355) and "The white man landed! Need the rest be told?" (1970: 355) is glaringly obvious.

Prometheus Unbound ends on a highly idealistic note where forgiveness, endurance, love and courage are eulogized by Demogorgon as follows:

> This, like thy glory, Titan is to be
> Good, great and joyous, beautiful and free
> This is alone, Life, Joy, *Empire* and Victory.
>
> (Shelley 1970: 268, my italics)

Unfortunately, what is described above is *not* Empire, as is well exemplified by Britain's Indian Empire, and as Shelley could not but have known, it could never be Empire and no amount of poetical idealism would suffice to make it so. To transcribe "Empire" so as to subvert its actual effect is also to elide its material reality for the sake of poetical consistency. Shelley's search for an alternative vision can be commended, but it has to be borne in mind that one has to stop short of valourizing ambivalence since the *acceptance* of the structural imperatives of the imperial discourse was the factor responsible for self-subversion.

F

When it comes to discussing the effect of political realities on literary production, Keats has often been treated as a special case. Nigel Leask, in this context, qualifies Keats with the term "even": "History is once again on the agenda and the political and ideological concerns of poets like Wordsworth, Byron, Shelley and *even* Keats are now read as being constitutive of their poetry than merely background material" (Leask 1991: 11, my italics). Of course, the 'even' is justified to a certain extent when we consider that the explicit dismissal of history as distinct from mythology was a significant part of Keats' poetic credo. Whether it is completely justified is a question I will return to at the end of this section.

Paul A. Cantor in *Creature and Creator* draws attention to the following lines from *Endymion* as indicating that "Keats was not temperamentally suited to traditional epic themes and he explicitly rejected the subject of war in favour of the more lyric theme of love (Cantor 1985: 166):

> Hence, pageant history! Hence gilded cheat!
> Swart planet in the universe of deeds! . . .
> But wherefore this? What care though owl did fly
> About the great Athenian admiral's mast?
> *What care though striding Alexander past*
> *The Indus with his Macedonian numbers?*
> Though Ulysses tortured from his slumbers
> The gutted Cyclops, what care?—Juliet leaning
> Amid her window flowers, sighing—weaning
> Tenderly her fancy from its maiden snow
> Doth more avail than these—the silver flow
> Of Hero's tears, the swoon of Imogen
> Fair Pastorella in the bandits den,
> Are things to brood on with more ardency
> *Than the death day of empires.* (Keats 1873: 80, my italics)

These lines may also be interpreted as a conscious negation of history and withdrawal from it as a source of poetic creation. In the light of such avowed attitudes and given the fact that mythical and legendary climes beyond 'lived' history framed the basis of most of Keats' themes, it is tempting to conclude that the world was *not* "too much with" him. There is a case to be made out for the school of criticism which argues that history and the political facts of day-to-day life, including Empire and overseas trade did not have much to do with Keats' poetics.

However, a total acceptance of this position would amount to giving too much credit altogether to the intentional fallacy. This is surely one of those contexts where we must go beyond what the author *seems* to say on a subject and base our conclusions on more detailed analysis.

Keats' *Collected Letters* provide a good starting point for an examination of his relationship with the East and India in particular. Of course, Keats' letters do not prove to be the kind of treasure trove of references to India that for example, Coleridge's Notebooks do. There are no references to either Indian philosophy or explicit statements regarding the perusal of any

Indian work. But we do find that Keats had considered a far more immediate and intimate relationship with India than the abstruse realms of metaphysics and philosophy could provide.

In a letter dated 31 May 1819 (the despondent period following the reviewers' savaging of *Endymion*), Keats writes: "I have the choice as it were of two poisons—the one is voyaging to and from India, the other is leading a feverous life alone with poetry" (1970: 257). Further letters of 9 June and 15 July of the same year record the idea of going as a surgeon on an India-bound ship and the final rejection of the idea because the poet could not "bear to give up my favourite studies" (1970: 269). These letters, apart from a couple of references to Hinduism, Vishnu and elephants form the sum total of Keats' epistolary references to India. But the fact that Keats was seriously considering India related employment does justify us in at least assuming that he was not unaware of the economic and semiotic associations attached to India.

When we examine Keats' poetic corpus from this perspective, we find that India had indeed made her contribution to his muse. *Endymion* with which Keats practically started his poetic career as well as the fragmented "The Cap and the Bells" which ended it contain references of varied length and significance to India. References to India/Asia can also be found in *Isabella, Hyperion,* some of the sonnets and in *The Fall of Hyperion.* Besides these, the sonnet 'To the Nile' as well as the doggerel 'Song to Myself' help us in figuring out Keats' way of adjusting to the concept of the Other, partly Oriental in its manifestations. Rana Kabbani in *Imperial Fictions* remarks:

> The Orient provided the Romantics with a set of hazy images, a florid landscape through which their heroes could move. Shelley's heroes visit ruins, voyage up the valley of the Nile, pass through Persia and Arabia, climb the Himalayas, arrive at the most solitary valley in Kashmir—illustrating the master theme of the major Romantic poems—the theme of travel. (1986: 30)

This theme is indicated by Keats also in a wistful remark in the 'Sonnet to J.H. Reynolds':

> O to arrive each Monday morning from Ind
> To land each Tuesday from the rich Levant. (1973: 367)

The motif is further elaborated in a letter dated 16 December 1818 where travel is presented as predominantly an exotic imaginative activity:

> My thoughts are very frequently in a foreign country. I live more out of England than in it—the mountains of Tartary are a favourite lounge if I happen to miss the Allegbany ridge or have no whim for Savoy. (1970: 179)

With the exceptions of *Endymion, Hyperion* and 'The Cap and the Bells' the use of Indian images in Keats' poetry can be seen largely as casual borrowings from the storehouse of contemporary poetic imagery. In *Isabella* we have references to a body "embalm'd in warm Indian clove" and a maiden who "withers like a palm/cut by an Indian for its juicy balm" (Keats 1973: 193). A poignant image in the same poem indicates an awareness of economic ground realities. Discussing the far reaching money grubbing activities of Isabella's brothers, Keats adds:

> For them the Ceylon diver held his breath
> And went all naked to the hungry shark
> For them his ears gushed blood. (1973: 182)

There are also a few references in other poems to the Lama, to Asian poppy and to missionary Churches in India. These are scattered and isolated instances which add nothing more than a little numerical strength to any sustained study.

The situation is different in *Endymion, Hyperion* and 'The Cap and the Bells.' First, however, it is worthwhile to examine Keats' sonnet 'To the Nile' as a microcosm of his attitude to the image of the Other provided by imperial exploration. Though the setting is specifically Egyptian, the reference to

> Such men . . . who worn with toil
> Rest for a space 'twixt Cairo and Deccan (1973: 380)

clearly justify us in bringing the Indian aspect into consideration. Keats rejects the narrow Orientalising which he characterizes here as the "ignorance that makes a barren waste of all beyond itself." He extends the acceptance of similarity to the Other represented by the Nile:

> thou dost bedew
> Green rushes like our rivers and dost taste
> The pleasant sunrise, green isles has thou too
> And to the sea as happily dost haste. (1973: 380)

Such a "homogenizing transformation" of the other into the same is seen in Keats' most sustained references to India also. The other is "dignified" by being divested of its non-human or exotic trappings, but this "dignity" comes at the cost of its identity.

The figure of the "Indian Maid" in Book IV of *Endymion* is open to various interpretations. In the first place, the maid is in Greece as a result of the Bacchic/Dionysian invasion of India. The legend of Bacchus' invasion was, as we have seen, obviously of great interest to the Romantic poets. Leask remarks that for Shelley, "Dionysius' conquest represented a civilizing mission or synonymously a Hellenising mission against which to set for either positive or negative comparison, Britain's 'revolutionary' impact on India" (1993: 123).

The imperial motif is present in Keats also as far as the basic idea of conquest goes. There is not the slightest sign however of a civilizing mission to be traced. The maid has followed Bacchus back from India, but finds that his promises of freedom from woe were false. She is satiated with the sensuality associated with Bacchus and appeals to Endymion—who by rights is dedicated to the divine Phoebe—for protection. It is precisely at the point where Endymion is most distressed with the shadowy and unobtainable nature of his divine mistress that he hears the maids lament:

> Ah, woe is me: that I should fondly part
> From my dear native land!
> Ah, foolish maid:
> Glad was the hour when with thee, myriads bade
> Adieu to Ganges and their pleasant fields
>
> Yet I would have, great Gods! But one short hour
> Of native air, let me but die at home. (Keats 1973: 132)

The narrator rebukes Endymion for his interest in the Maid, which is presented as a lapse in faithfulness to Phoebe:

> See not her charms! Is Phoebe passionless?
> Phoebe is fairer far: O gaze no more. (1973: 133)

But the maid with "curls of glossy jet" and "lively eyes in swimming search" (133) is presented in such a way as to render Endymion's "transgression" quite understandable. Despite his dedication to the ideal figure of Phoebe, Endymion falls in love at first sight with the Indian maid also. She is ambiguously addressed as:

> . . . young angel, fairest thief
> who stolen hast away the wings wherewith
> I was to o'ertop the heavens. (1973: 134)

It is possible to interpret the role of the Indian maid here as the conventional "seductive Orient" stereotype, with Phoebe as the ideal from which the Indian maid is luring Endymion away. However, the discourse of human/real vs. ideal/unreal with which Endymion justifies his passion for the maid complicates the issue:

> Thou swan of Ganges, let us no more breathe
> This murky phantasm! (1973: 143)
>
> There never lived a mortal man who bent
> His appetite beyond his natural sphere
> But starv'd and died. My sweetest Indian, here
> Here will I kneel, for thou redeemed hast
> My life from too thin breathing: gone and past
> Are cloudy phantasms.
> . . . My Indian bliss!
> My river lily bud! One human kiss!
> One sigh of real breath (1973: 148)

The Indian maid is human and real here, a union with her being 'natural.' Phoebe, the Greek Goddess on the other hand is a visionary ideal, a phantasm which cannot be grasped, an unnatural choice for union. This was a bold position to take (if conscious) at a time when racial discourses were crystallizing and representations of successful miscegenations studiously avoided by most contemporaries.

India is definitely a conquered land in the context of *Endymion.* The paraphernalia is arranged behind the description of Bacchus' overwhelming conquest:

> The Kings of Inde their jewell'd sceptres vail
> And from their treasures scatter pearled hail
> Great Brahma from his mystic heaven groans
> And all his priesthood moans
> Before young Bacchus' eyewink turning pale. (1973: 138)

The maid is representatively feminine and submissive, seeking protection, unlike the powerful, protective Phoebe. But a union with the maid is presented as possible, while Phoebe is a "phantasm." The affair takes an unexpected turn with the maid's presence leading Endymion to a self-examination and a final (though temporary) spiritualization—a most appropriate role for a representative of mystical/spiritual India! Once Endymion achieves this spiritualization and vows himself to celibacy, the Indian maid undergoes what Leask describes as a "racial transformation into a blonde Greek Goddess" (1993: 125). The process:

> At which that dark eyed stranger stood elate
> And said in a new voice, but sweet as love
> To Endymion's amaze . . .
> And as she spake, into her face there came
> Light as reflected from a silver flame
> Her long black hair swell'd ampler, in display
> Full golden, in her eyes a brighter day
> Dawn'd blue and full of love. Aye, he beheld
> Phoebe, his passion! (1973: 156-57)

Apparently, the union with the Goddess was not possible unless the human was thus spiritualized. The Indian maid merges into the Greek Goddess, a fit disguise, a not improper mate. She suffers no actual *loss of dignity;* but no longer retains the distinct identity which was earlier attributed to her.

Concentrating on this transformative aspect, Leask is abruptly dismissive of Keats' use of India: "For Keats' poem unlike Shelley's Orientalism is primarily a question of style, an imperial heraldry uncomplicated by the anxiety of Empire. India is merely an appendage to classical Greece; the exotic imagery on a Corinthian column (Leask 1993: 125). This is too swift a judgment. The choice of India as the locale for a figure which combined both allure and an impulse to "spiritualization" cannot be dismissed as incidental or insignificant.

Leask himself has suggested that when "the other strikes fear into the heart of metropolitan culture, therapeutical or assimilative agencies struggle to restore homeostasis, the healthful ease of the same" (1993: 8). The literal inch-by-inch transformation of the Indian stranger into the traditional Goddess figure deserves to be seriously considered as a homeostatic transformation, one of Leask's assimilative devices.

In *Hyperion* Asia is one among the fallen Titans. She is like the others insofar as she too is a Titan at present dispossessed by the Olympians. She is however, unlike them in that while they bewail their fate, she looks ahead with a prophetic vision to future glory:

> . . . Nearest him
> Asia, born of most enormous Caf . . .
> More thought than woe was in her dusky face
> For she was prophesying of her glory;
> And in her wide imagination stood
> Palm shaded temples and high rival fanes
> By Oxus or in Ganges sacred isles.
> Even as Hope upon her anchor leans
> So leant she, not so fair, upon a tusk
> Shed from the broadest of her elephants (1973: 231)

There is distinction here; Asia's "dusky face" and the fact that she is "not so fair" as Hope are mentioned. But there is also integration. The temples of Oxus and Ganges are traced back to a Titanic ancestor, sharing their origins with relics of classical antiquity. The anxiety of India's past stretching beyond that of Empire is overcome by accommodating Asia into a common mythical heritage. Asia is accepted, *with dignity, as* one, indeed a prominent one among Titans like Saturn and Hyperion. But this acceptance is at the cost of her distinct identity as a presence extrinsic to Europe's classical past. The "disturbing" Orient is transformed into the same for Europe.

A vignette from "The Cap and the Bells," Keats' final verse production (in the mock heroic style) encapsulates this transformational tendency successfully. The Indian girl in this context is literally a changeling. The Fairy Emperor, Elfinan is in love with a human female, Bertha. He is compelled to marry a fairy princess, but plans to be with Bertha somehow. For this, he seeks the help of an old soothsayer called Hum, who informs him that the improbably fair haired Bertha is actually a changeling of Indian birth:

> Good! Good! Cried Hum, I've known her from a child.
> She is a changeling of my management
> She was born at midnight on an Indian wild;
> Her mother's screams with the striped tiger's blent
> While the torch bearing slaves a halloo sent
> Into the jungle; and her palanquin
> Rested amidst the deserts dreariment
> Shook with her agony, till fair were seen
> The little Bertha's eyes opened on the stars serene (1973: 327)

The transformational process is complete here. The Indian girl born in such stereotypically Oriental circumstances is an unsuspected changeling, a full human being, a desirable and fit mate for the Fairy King.

Differences are elided in Keats' transformations of the Oriental Other into the Same. Of course, it is possible to connect this with the anxiety of Empire, with the assimilationist processes of the Indologists, with what Leask calls the "narcissistic discovery of the Same" (1993: 126).

But there are differences to be noted between the homogenizations of Keats and Shelley, or Keats and Jones for that matter. In the first place, anxiety is not a pervasive issue, so far as we can judge, in Keats' conception of the Other. Keats does not seem to be remarkably *disturbed.* Is this due to a lack of awareness? Indifference? Absorption in a mythical universe? These questions are of course speculative. But the fact does remain that anxiety if extant, is considerably muted in Keats. So the bizarre, frenetic necessity for homogenization which spurs Shelley does not drive Keats, his transformations are more in keeping with *poetic* demands and with a more assured (though unproblematised) acceptance of similarity.

More important, for better or worse, Keats was not a reformist. That also meant that he was not a civilisation spreader—he obviously was quite content to take the Orient poetically, grant its difference, underline his concept of essential oneness and let the matter rest. His transformations are based on the conception of oneness, *preexistent, not to be created* by the reforms of imperialism which had to negotiate between the Scylla and Charybdis of radicalism and domination. We may accuse Keats of political apathy, of indifference, but we have to admit the relative lack of "ambivalence" in its overburdened, over valourized, over-positivized sense in his works. Empire for Blake in his universal condemnation of System is *more,* theoretically (if *less,* materially) than what actually is—but he is consistent in condemnation of 'his' Empire; free from the bad faith which pursues other radical attempts fated to end in equivocation. At perhaps the opposite end of the spectrum, with perhaps considerable naivete, Keats maintains the same consistency in an openness towards oneness which is comparatively untouched by the planned machinations of assimilation. This is not meant to valourize Blake or Keats—it is perhaps matter for regret that only in a symbolic universe or in a stance of poetic withdrawal can there be some freedom from the insistent, pervasive, insinuating, inculpating bad faith of Imperialism. The idea is only to point out the possibility of "different" positions, which if in one sense they signal a withdrawal from the arena, in another perhaps indicate valuable "freedom" for the imagination without the suspect adjunct of ambivalence.

To conclude, I would wish to indicate the possibility that there may be a kernel of awareness in the "naive" doggerel "Song to Myself" by Keats:

> There was a naughty boy

And a naughty boy was he
He ran away to Scotland
The people there to see.
Then he found
That the ground
Was as hard
That a yard
Was as long
That a song
Was as merry
That a cherry
Was as red
That lead
Was as weighty
That four score
Was as Eighty
That a door
Was as wooden
As in England
So he stood in his shoes
And he wondered
He wondered
He stood in His
Shoes and he wondered. (1973: 258, my italics)

To link "theory" to "naiveté," perhaps, just perhaps "the discovery of wonder that is latent in our own practices, a wonder that has become flattened by familiarity" could lead to the "realization that what is most unattainably marvellous, most desirable, is what you almost already have, what you could have—if you could only strip away the banality and corruption of the everyday—at home" and lead to the ownership "by virtue of a *refusal of possession,* as if *wonder could be prolonged* into an ebb and flow of delight" (Greenblatt 1991: 25, my italics).

NOTES

1. The reference is to "role-playing" in its historical sense, but there is a sense of "acted on" by history also involved.
2. Records indicate that this painting by Blake is lost now.

3. "Everywhere in reality, Boheme finds oppositions and contradictions. There is no good without evil, no light without darkness, no quality without its difference. . . . Significant in Boheme's world view are the teachings that the universe is a union of contradictions, that life and progress imply opposition" (Thilly 1993: 249).
4. As mentioned later on, a reference to this concept in more jocular vein can be found in Byron's *Don Juan* also.
5. The statement gains enormously in significance given the contemporary urgings of colonialism as the natural and legitimate means of national advancement. The Torrens' comment quoted in the Conclusion is a case in point.
6. The view of the professional soldier as the most subjugated form of humanity is echoed by Shelley in *A Philosophical View of Reform* (1953: 232).
7. The echoes in colonial discourse of this idea are patently obvious. The concept of "free trade" where subject nations were educated into new "wants" and then made to obtain them at high prices is distinctly foreshadowed.
8. The phrase "later imperialist" in relation to Urizen is borrowed from Erdman's *Blake: Prophet against Empire* (1977: 52).
9. Is it possible to see a connection with Keats' notion of "negative capability?"
10. The plural is used advisedly, Coleridge's vacillations are almost paranoiac.
11. The implicit suggestion was that the *potential* for growth also was exhausted, raising the need for an "outside" source of inspiration.
12. In the 3rd issue of *The Friend* Coleridge urges his countrymen to count their blessings "by reflecting on the direful effects of caste in Hindostan and then transfer yourself in fancy to an English cottage" (1970: IV 20).
13. These reasons are as follows:
    a) The happier and freer the mother country, the more reluctant the better sort of people will be to leave it. Only the refuse therefore, will go to the colonies.
    b) The love of money is greater in free countries because wealth gives more advantages in such an atmosphere.
    c) In base minds, the possession of freedom intensifies the lust of power over others.

d) The laws of property are more secure in free countries and hence humane regulations are more difficult to enforce as interfering with property.

e) The influence of men of property which furnishes a strong motive to get rich by any means is strongest in free countries.

14. A note of later edition adds: "I have said savages—not natives with what we may deem less perfect forms of government and civil and religions institutions than our own." Obviously, as long as the choice lies with the imperialist, this qualification is not much of a safeguard.
15. Britain's commercial prosperity due to her global trade is referred to in Book VIII of *The Excursion:*

    Hence is the wide sea peopled—hence the shores
    Of Britain are resorted to by ships
    Freighted from every climate of the world
    With the world's choicest produce. (Wordsworth 1936: 683)

16. The Irish/Oriental connection motif is stressed by Byron also in his dedication of *The Corsair* to Thomas Moore.
17. Homi Bhabha states that many statements apparently dismissible as "imperialism's double think" are in fact "sheer" desperate acknowledgement of an aporia in the inscription of empire" (1994: 129).
18. Is the emphasis on "ineradicable" or on "distinction"? If on the former, a suggestion that Byron has managed "eradication" is problematic in itself.
19. It may apear that Byron is arguing here that any government is as bad as any other and so imperial rule is no better/worse than any other system. But it must be noted that he *does* later concede a slight advantage to the Turks.
20. This does seem to stand against Trivedi's assertion in *Colonial Transactions* that the East/West dichotomy was not a major part of Byron's championing of the Greek cause. Of course, the time gap between the Marathon war and Byron's personal knowledge of contemporary Turks cannot be denied its significance.
21. Demogorgon is "described" as:

    I see a mighty darkness
    Filling the seat of power, and rags of gloom
    Dart round, as fight from the meridian sun

> Ungazed upon and shapeless, neither limb
> Nor form, nor outline yet we feel it is
> A living spirit. (Shelley 1970: 236)

22. In answer to Asia's questions on the Supreme Being, Demogorgon replies:

> If the abysm
> Could vomit forth its secrets
> . . . but a voice
> Is wanting, *the deep truth is imageless.* (1970: 238, my italics)

Chapter 8

Conclusion: Constitutive Contradictions

It has become a commonplace of postcolonial criticism today that the notion of imperial edifices being either impermeable or monolithic is but a convenient myth. The shades of ambiguity found among contemporary colonial representations of India indicate that a monolithic structure did not exist. However, it does appear as though postcolonial criticism has on occasion over-valourized ambivalence, made it into *the* distinct feature of the imperial edifice and thrust practically the entire burden of "weakening" the edifice onto these ambivalences. In Section B of this chapter, the line of argument indicated above is pursued further. In Section A below, I shall briefly go over the earlier chapters, emphasizing the ambivalences traced.

A

In the Introduction the importance as well as the existence of ambivalence was practically "taken on trust." The analysis to follow, it was indicated, would consciously search for ambivalences, ambiguities and instabilities within colonial representations. Certain attitudes towards India were identified as the parameters within which the analysis would function. The texts taken up for detailed examination were those produced by Englishmen and women between 1757 and 1857. Chapter 2 provided a background by surveying several earlier Western (not necessarily British) representations of India. The political process whereby British power in India (wielded at this stage by the East India Company) was consolidated up to 1857 was also examined in some detail. The major ideological trends of Conservatism, Utilitarianism, Evangelicalism, Imperialism, Commercialism and

Romanticism, which naturally influenced representations of the colony, were sketched in outline.

In Chapter 3, the pictures of India set up by the Conservative rhetoric of Burke and the Indologism of William Jones were examined in detail. The discursive networks here were seen to be extremely ambivalent, with many illogical pronouncements and self-contradictions enabling diverse alternative interpretations. As the occasion demanded, India's position swung from victim to corrupter. Indians were simultaneously innocent and devious; the Empire boon and curse for England at one and the same time. All these could be traced in the public rhetoric itself; the dichotomy between public pronouncements and utterances considered private was even more marked.

Chapter 4 undertook a study of James Mill's *History of British India* as a representative text for the Utilitarian perspective. Despite Mill's "admirable" steadiness of purpose in belittling India, his discourse is in no way free from gaps and fissures. India was necessary as a laboratory for Utilitarian experiments, but going by keen economic commonsense, the notion of Empire was problematic. The pressures of championing representative rule at Home and logically advocating complete subjection abroad can be seen in Mill's writing, which reveals both overkill and a reluctance to explain or substantiate his statements.

Chapter 5 surveyed the works produced by certain British travellers in India, male and female, from different social and professional strata. These differences of gender and class produce their own types of ambivalence across and also within individual texts. The ambiguous representations of *Sati* are taken as a primary example of this trend. The questions of the "femininity" of the native, of religion and conversion—all these reflect the same trend in varying ways.

Chapter 6 takes up three texts, specifically located in India for individual analysis—*The Curse of Kehama, Lalla Rookh and The Surgeon's Daughter*. Perhaps it is not very remarkable that the Gothic and idealized versions of India co-exist in these texts. Of greater significance is the contradiction the representation of India entails with separately avowed liberal attitudes and the fear, which borders the exoticization. Also, the question of whether Indians are the victims or the devilish tempters is far from being resolved. Romanticism calls for praise to be bestowed on Hyder Ali, while Imperialism insists that his downfall should be not only portrayed but also justified and welcomed. The tension set up by this and similar contradictory demands pervade the texts.

Chapter 7 undertook a survey of Imperial attitudes and reflections in the works of five "major" Romantic poets—Blake, Coleridge, Wordsworth, Shelley and Keats. The main reference is of course to representations of India, but any statement which aids in understanding attitudes towards Empire are taken up for consideration. It is seen that in a majority of cases, Empire is the one area where constantly articulated political or even poetical principles do not hold. It is a territory (where sometimes in blatant and illogical self-contradiction) different standards, rules and principles apply. [Exceptions, if they exist, may seem suspiciously dependent on overarching mysticism and aestheticism. That there could be some other, maybe more positive explanation is only hinted at very tenuously in the chapter, much more as a hope than as a conviction.]

B

In the final analysis, there is evidently no shortage of ambivalence, or incongruity in colonial representations. They can be found practically everywhere, in Conservative as well as Utilitarian pronouncements, in history and in poetry. However, after listing these ambivalences, one has to consider their actual *effect,* which is a problematic area. It is tempting to expect that with all the gaps and fissures it clearly contained, the colonial paradigm should have collapsed in a few decades. (The reference of "collapse" here is to be understood in a rhetorical sense. The fact that rhetorical fragility in no way necessarily entails *practical* collapse is accepted.) But we know for a fact that it went from strength to strength for centuries. The *presence* of ambivalence is undeniable, but it would seen that its *effect* needs to be rethought—a process that I now briefly and tentatively attempt.

Rey Chow points out that the trap of ambivalence could confine us to perpetually "study/deconstruct" colonial texts; which would be seen as all the richer for that very ambivalence:

> All we would need to do would be to continue to study—to deconstruct the *rich and ambivalent* language of the imperialist! . . . In the masquerade of deconstruction and 'difficult' theory [is revived] an old functionalist notion of *what a dominant culture permits in the interest of maintaining its own equilibrium.* (My emphases; Chow 1997: 128)

"permits"—with this word, one feels that Chow has hit on the *mot juste.*

It is of course, evident that at an ontological or epistemological level, strategic textual discourses which aim at domination *cannot* totally succeed in being complete. But it does seem that the inconsistencies or ambivalences within the colonial paradigm were not extraneous "mistakes" which weakened the system. At a practical level, I believe these *contradictions* were actually *constitutive* elements of the structure itself. Far from weakening the *working* force of the imperial network, they may even have furthered its efficiency. They would have made it possible to accommodate divergent, even conflicting political and theoretical positions without any external, enfeebling incongruity.

In a way, the ambivalences were *expected,* in fact, even *provided for.* It is not very likely that until under the tremendous impetus of an 'event' like the Mutiny, national greed or hatred would be aired openly. Ambivalence or euphemism can be seen to be almost inevitably present in practically any expression of national or class justification of self-aggrandizement, and that not just in imperial contexts.

For example, Malthusian economics, which in plain terms implies "the right of the rich to starve the poor" (Hazlitt 1998: 50) is, as we know stated as scientific and objective rationality. To take an example closely linked to Imperialism, the hardly altruistic scheme of shipping convicts and the starving poor forcibly to colonies is presented as a welfare measure: "For the immediate relief of actual distress, there remains no remedy except an extension of colonialism" (Torrens 1998: 51).

A cry of "Exterminate the Brutes" *in clear accents* cannot be heard very often in the history of imperialism. Either acute shrewdness or unresolved conscience qualms would step in to mute the tones.

Also, when a Burke or a Shelley, who in most affairs championed justice, endorsed (however reluctantly) the colonial enterprise, would that not be a positive thrust for imperialism? The fact that Mill appears doubtful in regard to Britain's economic advantage from imperialism would make his plan of action seem all the more unselfish and rationally Utilitarian. When *Wordsworth* himself decries "nature" *in India* the need of immediate "civilization" seems to be underscored. At this stage of consideration, I find it difficult to maintain any serious belief in the "weakening" effect of ambivalence.

The value of ambivalence remains but more in an internal sense. Obviously Byron cannot be equated with Southey, or Jones and Mill unproblematically conflated. Indeed, ironically enough, the "richness" of these texts is enhanced by their ambivalence. There would be no point or interest in reading them if they all said the same things in the same way.

I do not suggest that imperialism should be credited with some uncanny prescience. At the same time, underestimating its discourse will not help matters. It is possible and even desirable in postcolonial analysis to deploy internal contradictions for unravelling purposes. But it has to be kept in mind that during the epoch of imperialism, during the period when these texts had their most significant presence (in an imperial context) these contradictions were precisely those aspects, which contributed *psychological coherence* to the entire project.

The Colossus of Imperialism *is* cracked. And since they were not easily visible, due credit has to be given to those who pointed out the cracks. But these cracks in the Colossus did not, as we know cause any quick collapse. On the contrary, the *Cracks and the Colossus* stood together; maybe they even stood *because* they were together.

Works Cited

Acland, Charles. *A Popular Account of the Manners and Customs of India.* London: John Murray, 1847.

Adams, Percy. *Travel Literature and the Evolution of the Novel.* Kentucky: University of Kentucky Press, 1983.

Ahmed, Aijaz. *In Theory.* Delhi: OUP, 1994.

Anglo-Saxon Chronicle. Trans. Garmon Sway. London: J.M. Dent, 1962.

Arrian. *Historia Indica. Ancient India as Described by Megasthenese and Arrian.* Ed. J.W. McCrindle. London: Traheme, 1877.

Aschroft, Bill. "Excess: Postcolonialism and the Verandahs of Meaning." *De-scribing Empire: Post-Colonialism and Textuality.* Chris Tiffin and Alan Lawson, ed. London: Routledge, 1994.

——, et al, ed. *The Post-Colonial Reader.* London: Routledge, 1995.

Asiatic Researches. 20 vols. New Delhi: Cosmo, 1979.

Banerjee, C.R. "India in Shakespeare." *Indian Journal of English Studies.* (1964): 55-67.

Barrell, John. *The Infection of Thomas De Quincey: A Psychopathology of Imperialism.* Yale: Yale University Press, 1991.

Batten, C. *Pleasurable Instruction: Form and Convention in Eighteenth Century Travel Literature.* Berkeley: University of California Press, 1978.

Bearce, George. *British Attitudes to India 1754-1858.* London: OUP, 1961.

Bernier, Francois. *Travels in the Mogul Empire. A.D. 1656-1668.* New Delhi: S. Chand, 1979.

Bhabha, Homi K. *The Location of Culture.* London: Routledge, 1994.

Blake, William. *Complete Works with Variant Readings.* Geoffrey Keynes, ed. London: OUP, 1972.

Brantlinger, Patrick. *Rule of Darkness: British Literature and Imperialism.* London: Carnell University Press, 1988.

Bratton, et al, ed. *Acts of Supremacy: The British Empire and the Stage: 1790-1930.* Manchester: Manchester University Press, 1988.

Broughton, Thomas Duer. *Letters from a Mahratta Camp during the Year 1809.* Calcutta: K.K. Bagchi, 1977.

Bronowski, J. *William Blake and the Age of Revolution.* London: Routledge, 1972.

Burke, Edmund. *Speeches on the Impeachment of Warren Hastings.* 2 vols. New Delhi: Discovery Publishing House, 1987.

——. *The Writings and Speeches of Edmund Burke.* Vol. 5. P.J.M. Marshall, ed. Oxford: Clarendon Press, 1981.

——. *Writings and Speeches.* Ed. P.J. Stanlis. New York: Anchor, 1963.

Burton, Richard Francis. *Goa and the Blue Mountains.* London: Dent, 1851.

Byron, Lord George Gordon. *Byron's Letters and Journals.* Ed. Leslie A.M. Marchand, ed. London: Picador, 1984.

Byron's Poetical Works. Frederick Page ed. London: OUP, 1970.

Camoens. *Luciad.* Trans. Atkinson. London: Stratton, 1952.

Cantor, Paul A. *Creature and Creator: Myth Making and English Romanticism.* Cambridge: Cambridge University Press, 1985.

Carey, W.H. *The Good Old Days of Honourable John Company.* 2 vols. Calcutta: Riddhi, 1980.

Carnall, Geoffrey, ed. *Impeachment of Warren Hastings: Papers from a Bicentenary Commemoration.* Edinburgh: Edinburgh University Press, 1989.

Cheng, Vincent J. *Joyce, Race and Empire.* Great Britain: Cambridge University Press, 1995.

Chow, Rey. "Where Have All the Natives Gone?" *Contemporary Postcolonial Theory.* Ed. Padmini Mongia. Delhi: OUP, 1997.

Colebrooke, H.T. *Essays on the Religion and Philosophy of the Hindus.* New Delhi: Ashok, 1976.

Coleridge, Samuel Taylor. *Biographia Literaria.* Ed. George Watson. London: J.M. Dent, 1971a

——. *Collected Letters of S.T.C.* Ed. Earl Leslie Griggs. Oxford: OUP, 1971.

——. *Collected Works of S.T.C.*, ed. Kathleen Coburn. 14 vols. Great Britain: Routledge 1970a.

——. *Complete Poetical Works of S.T.C.* 2 vols. Ed. Hartley Coleridge. London: Routledge, 1970.

——. "Lay Sermon" and "Citizen's Manual." *Political Tracts of Wordsworth, Coleridge and Shelley.* Ed. R.J. White. Cambridge: Cambridge University Press, 1953.

——. *Notebooks of S.T.C.*, ed. Kathleen Coburn. New York: Panther Books, 1957.

Cooke, Katherine. *Coleridge.* London: Routledge, 1970.

Crook, Nora and Derek Guiton. *Shelley's Venomed Melody.* Cambridge: Cambridge University Press, 1986.

Damrosch, Leopold. *Symbol and Truth in Blake's Myth.* New Jersey: Princeton University Press, 1980.

Derrida, Jacques. *Of Grammatology.* Trans. Gayatri Spivak. Baltimore: John Hopkins University Press, 1976.

Dodwell, Henry. *Nabobs of Madras.* New Delhi: Asian Educational Series, 1986.

Dow, Alexander. *History of Hindustan.* New Delhi: Today & Tomorrow Publishers, 1973.

Drew, John. *India and the Romantic Imagination.* Delhi: OUP, 1987.

Dryden, John. *Amboyna. Collected Dramatic Works.* Ed. V.A. Dearing. Vol. 5. Oxford: OUP, 1961.

Dyson, K.K. *A Various Universe.* Delhi: OUP, 1978.

Eden, Emily. *Up the Country.* London: Curzon Press, 1930.

Edwardes, Michael. *Glorious Sahibs.* London: Eyre Press, 1968.

Edwardes, Michael. *The Nabobs at Home.* London: Constable, 1957.

Embree, Ainslie T. *Imagining India.* Delhi: OUP, 1989.

Erdman, Davis. *Blake: Prophet against Empire.* New Jersey: Princeton University Press, 1977.

Fane, Isabella. *Miss Fane in India.* Ed. John Pemble. Gloucester: Allan Sutton, 1985.

Fanon, Frantz. *Black Skin, White Masks.* New York: Grove Press, 1968.

——. *The Wretched of the Earth.* New York: Harmondsworth, 1977.

Fay, Eliza. *Original Letters from India (1779-1815).* London: Hogarth Press, 1986.

Fisher, Michael H. *The Politics of the British Annexation of India 1757-1857.* Delhi: OUP, 1996.

Forbes, James. *Oriental Memoirs.* New Delhi: Gian, 1988.

Forster, William ed. *Early Travels in India 1583-1619.* London: OUP, 1921.

Forster, William. *The East India House: Its History and Associations.* Delhi: Mittal, 1987.

Foucault, Michael. *Power/Knowledge.* Ed. Colin Gordon. New York: Pantheon, 1980.

——. *The Foucault Reader.* Ed. Paul Rabinow. New York: Pantheon, 1984.

Furber, Holden. *The John Company at Work.* Cambridge: Cambridge University Press, 1948.

Fussel, Paul. *Abroad: British Literary Travelling between the Wars.* Oxford: OUP, 1980.

Goethe. *Selected Verse.* Trans. David Luke. England: Penguin, 1964.

Green, Martin. *Dreams of Adventure, Deeds of Empire.* London: Routledge, 1980.

Greenblatt, Stephen. *Marvellous Possessions: The Wonder of the New World.* Oxford: Clarendon Press, 1991.

Hazlitt, William. "A Reply to the *Essay on Population* by the Rev. T.R. Malthus." *Romantic Period Writing 1798-1832: An Anthology.* Ed. Zachary Leader and Ian Heywood. London: Routledge, 1998.

Heber, Reginald. *Narrative of a Journey through the Upper Provinces of India.* 3 vols. Delhi: B.R., 1985.

Herodotus. *History.* Ed. Mc Griggle. Cambridge: Cambridge University Press, 1954.

Holder, Heidi J. "Melodrama, Realism and Empire on the British Stage." *Acts of Supremacy.* Ed. Bratton et al. Manchester: Manchester University Press, 1991.

Inden, Ronald. *Imagining India.* London: Basil Blackwell, 1990.

Jackson, J.R., ed. *Coleridge: Critical Heritage.* London: Routledge, 1970.

Jameson, Frederick. *The Political Unconscious.* New York: Current University Press, 1981.

Jones, Sir William. *Works of Sir William Jones.* 13 vols. Ed. Lord Teigmnouth. Delhi: Agam Prakashan, 1976.

Kabbani, Rana. *Imperial Fictions.* Britain: Harper Collins, 1994

Kaul, H.K. ed. *Traveller's India.* Delhi: OLTP, 1997.

Keats, John. *Letters of John Keats.* Ed. Robert Gittings. Oxford: OUP, 1970.

——. *Keats' Poetical Works.* Ed. H.W. Garwood. Oxford: OUP, 1973.

Lawrence, Honoria. *The Journal of Honoria Lawrence: India Observed 1837-1854.* London: Hodder, 1980.

Leask, Nigel. *British Romantic Writers and the East: Anxieties of Empire.* New Delhi: Cambridge University Press, 1993.

Mahajan, V.D. *British Rule in India and After.* Delhi: S. Chand, 1969.

Majeed, Javed. "James Mill's *The History of British India* and Utilitarianism as a Rhetoric of Reform." *Modern Asian Studies,* 24.2 (1990): 209-24.

Malcolm, Sir John. *Political History of India.* 2 vols. London: Dent, 1826.

Mandeville, Sir John. *Voyages of Sir John Mandeville—Fourteenth Century Verse and Prose.* Ed. Kenneth Sisam. London: OUP, 1921. 94-104.

Mani, Lata. "Cultural Theory, Colonial Texts: Reading Eyewitness Accounts of Widow Burning." *Cultural Studies.* Ed. Grosberg et al. New York: Routledge, 1992.

Mannoni, O. *Prospero and Caliban.* Trans. Pamela Powerland. London: Methuen, 1956.

Martyn, Rev. Henry. *Journals and Letters of the Rev. Henry Martyn.* Ed. Rev. S.W. Wilberforce. 2 vols. London: Constable, 1837.

Maurice, Thomas. *Indian Antiquities or Dissertations on Hindustan.* 8 vols. Delhi: Concept, 1984.

Megasthenese. *Indica: Ancient India as Described by Megasthenese and Arrian.* Ed. J.W. McCrindle. London: Traherne, 1877.

Mill, James. "Essay on Government." *Utilitarian Logic and Politics.* Ed. Jack Lively and John Rees. Oxford: Clarendon Press, 1978a.

_____, *The History of British India.* 3 vols. New Delhi: Associated, 1978.

Mills, Sara. *Discourses of Difference.* London: Routledge, 1993.

Minh Ha, Trinh T. "Writing Postcoloniality and Feminism." *The Postcolonial Reader.* Ed. Ashcroft et al. London: Routledge, 1995.

Moor, Edward. *The Hindu Pantheon.* Delhi: Indological Book House, 1968.

Moore, Thomas. *Lalla Rookh: An Oriental Romance.* London: Dare 1936.

Mukherjee, S.N. *Sir William Jones: A Study of Eighteenth Century British Attitudes to India.* Bombay: Orient Longman, 1987.

Muirhead, John. *Coleridge as Philosopher.* London: Allen & Unwin, 1930.

Nandy, Ashis. *The Intimate Enemy.* Delhi: OLJP, 1989.

Nightingale, Pamela. *Trade and Empire in Western India: 1784-1806.* Cambridge: Cambridge University Press, 1970.

Niranjana, Tejaswini. *Siting Translation.* Los Angeles: University of California Press, 1992.

Oaten, E.F. *European Travellers in India.* New Delhi: Asian Educational Services. 1991.

Orme, Robert. *A History of the Military Transactions of the British Nation in Indostan.* 2 vols. New Delhi: Today and Tomorrow Publishers, 1981.

——. *Historical Fragments of the Mughal Empire.* New Delhi: Associated, 1982.

Panikkar, Chitra. "Joyce's India." Unpublished Paper. 1996.

Periplus of the Erythrean Sea. Trans. Wilfred. H. Schoft. New Delhi: Munshilal Manoharlal, 1974.

Polo, Marco. *The Travels of Marco Polo.* Ed. Milton Rugoff. New York: Signet Classics, 1961.

Porter, Dennis. "Orientalism and its Problems." *The Politics of Theory.* Ed. Francis Barker. Colchester: University of Essex, 1982. 179-93.

Pratt, Mary Louise. "Scratches on the Face of the Country or what Mr. Barrows Saw in the Land of the Bushmen." *Critical Enquiry,* Autumn 12: 1 (1985): 119-43.

Reardon, Bernard. *From Coleridge to Gore: A Century of Religious Thought in Britain.* London: Longman, 1971.

Richards, Thomas. *The Imperial Archive.* London: Verso, 1993.

Ridley, Hugh. *Images of Imperial Rule.* New York: St. Martin's Press, 1983.

Robertson, William. *A Historical Disquisition Concerning Ancient India.* Delhi: Goyal Offset Printers, 1981.

Roterio. Trans. (into Malayalam) Manu. *Malayalam Varika.* May 15 (30-33). May 22 (46-47). 1998.

Said, Edward. *After the Last Sky.* London: Vintage, 1993

——. *Culture and Imperialism.* London: Vintage, 1993

——. *Orientalism.* London: Routledge, 1978.

Schwab, Raymond. *The Oriental Renaissance.* New York: Columbia University Press, 1984.

Scott, Sir Walter. *The Surgeon's Daughter.* London: J.M. Dent, 1920.

Sedlar, J.W. *India and the Greek World.* New Jersey: Rowan and Littlefield, 1980.

Sencourt, Robert. *India in English Literature.* Gurgaon: Vintage, 1990.

Sharpe, Jenny "The Violence of Light in the Land of Desire or How William Jones Discovered India." *Boundary* 2. 20.1 (1993): 35-48.

Shelley, P.B. *Esdaile Poems.* Ed. Neville Rogers. Oxford: Clarendon Press, 1966.

——. *Letters of Percy Bysshe Shelley.* Ed. Frederick L. Jones. London: OUP, 1964.

——. "Philosophical View of Reform." *Political Tracts of Wordsworth, Coleridge and Shelley.* Ed. R.J. White. Cambridge: Cambridge University Press, 1953.

——. *Selected Poetry and Prose.* Ed. Kenneth Neil Cameron. New York: Rhineheart, 1951.

——. *Shelley: The Poetical Works.* Ed. Thomas Hutchinson. London: OUP, 1970.

Sleeman, Sir William. *The Rambles and Recollections of an Indian Official.* Karachi: OUP, 1915.

Southey, Robert. *Poetical Works of Robert Southey.* London: Longman, Green, 1873.

Spivak, Gayatri Chakravorty. "Can the Subaltern Speak?" *Marxism and the Interpretation of Culture.* Ed. Cary Nelson, Lawrence Grosberg. London: Macmillan, 1988.

Stanford, J., ed. *Ladies in the Sun: The Memsahib's India: 1790-1860.* London: Galley Press, 1968.

Stokes, Eric. *The English Utilitarians and India.* Delhi: OUP, 1982.

Teltscher, Kate. *India Inscribed.* Delhi: OUP, 1995.

Thapar, Romila. "Interpretations of Ancient Indian History." *History and Theory.* 7: 3 (1979): 317-29.

Tharu, Susie and K. Lalitha. Introduction. *Women Writing in India.* Vol. I. Delhi: OUP, 1991.

Thilly, Frank. *A History of Philosophy.* New Delhi: SBW, 1993.

Torrens, Major Robert. "A Paper on the Means of Reducing the Poor Rates and of Affording Permanent and Effective Relief to the Labouring Classes." *Romantic Period Writings 1798-1832: An Anthology.* Ed. Zachary Leader and Ian Heywood. London: Routledge, 1998.

Trivedi, Harish. *Colonial Transactions.* Calcutta: Papyrus, 1993.

Tytler, Harriet. *An Englishwoman in India: The Memoirs of Harriet Tytler: 1828-1858.* Ed. Anthony Sattin. Oxford: OUP, 1986.

Varthema, Ludovico. *Travels in India: Early Travels in India.* Ed. J. Talboys Wheeler. Delhi: Desi Publications, 1974.

Viswanathan, Gauri. *Masks of Conquest.* London: Faber and Faber, 1989.

Ward, Rev. William. *View of the History, Literature and Religion of the Hindoos.* 2 vols. London: Black, Parbury and Allen, 1817.

Williamson, Thomas. *Oriental Field Sports.* London: Edward Orme, 1810.

Wilson, H.H. *Hindu Fiction.* New Delhi: Nag Publishers, 1979.

Wordsworth, William. *Letters of William and Dorothy Wordsworth.* Ed. Ernest de Selincourt. London: OUP, 1937.

——. *Wordsworth: Poetical Works.* Ed. Ernest de Selincourt. London: OUP, 1936.

Select Bibliography

Adams, Percy. *Travellers and Travel Liars: 1600-1800*. Berkeley: University of California Press, 1978.

Anderson, Benedict. *Imagined Communities: Reflections on the Origin and Spread of Nationalism*. London: Verso, 1983.

Asad, Talal. *Anthropology and the Colonial Encounter*. London: Ithaca Press, 1973.

Aschroft, Bill, et al. Ed. *The Empire Writes Back*. London: Routledge, 1989.

Auerbach, Eric. *Mimesis: The Representation of Reality in Western Literature*. Trans. Willard R. Trask. New Jersey: Princeton University Press, 1953.

Baldick, Chris. *The Social Mission of English Criticism 1848-1932*. Oxford: Clarendon Press, 1983.

Balhatchet, Kenneth. *Race, Sex and Class under the Raj: Imperial Attitudes and Policies and their Critics: 1793-1900*. New Delhi: Vikas, 1979.

Barker, F. Ed. *Europe and its Others*. Vol. 1. Colchester: University of Essex, 1984.

——, ed. *The Politics of Theory*. Colchester: University of Essex, 1982.

Barr, Pat. *The Memsahibs*. London: Sears and Warburg, 1976.

Behdad, Ali. *Belated Travellers*. U.S.A.: Duke University Press, 1994.

Bhabha, Homi K. Ed. *Nation and Narration*. London: Routledge, 1994.

Breckenbride, Carol A. and Peter Van der Veer. Ed. *Orientalism and the Postcolonial Predicament*. Delhi: OUP, 1994.

Buchnan, Francis. *The Journal of Francis Buchnan*. Patna: Vikas, 1930.

Chakravorty, Dilip. *A Passage to the Orient*. Delhi: Amar, 1988.

Chatfield, Robert. *Historical Review of the Commercial, Political and Moral Status of Hindostan*. London: Muirhead, 1808.

Chatterjee, Partha. *Nationalist Thought and the Colonial World: A Derivative Discourse?* New Delhi: OUP, 1986.

——. *The Nation and its Fragments: Colonial and Postcolonial Histories*. Princeton: Princeton University Press, 1993.

Clifford, J. and G.E. Marcus, ed. *Writing Culture: The Poetics and Politics of Ethnography*. Berkeley: University of California Press, 1986.

Cowasjee, S. *Women Writers of the Raj*. London: Grafton, 1990.

Cronin, Richard. *Imagining India*. New York: St. Martin's Press, 1989.

Donaldson, Laura. *Decolourizing Feminisms: Race, Gender and Empire Building*. London: Routledge, 1993.

Edwardes, Michael. *British India 1772-1947*. New Delhi: Rupa, 1993.

——. *The West in Asia* 1850-1914. London: Batsford, 1967.

Franklin, Michael J. *Sir William Jones*. Cardiff: University of Wales, 1995.

Gore, P. *The Imaginary Voyage in Prose Fiction: A History of its Criticism and a Guide to its Study*. New York: Columbia University Press, 1983.

Grant, Charles. *Bombay Cotton and Indian Railways*. London: Longman, 1850.

Greenberger, Allen. *The British Image of India: A Study in the Literature of Imperialism 1880-1960*. London: OUP, 1969.

Guha, Ranajeet. "The Prose of Counter Insurgency." *Subaltern Studies*. II. Delhi: OUP, 1983.

Gupta, R.K. *The Great Encounter: A Study of Indo-American Literature and Cultural Relations*. New Delhi: Abhinav, 1986.

Hemenway, Stephen. *The Novel of India: The Anglo-Indian No*vel. Calcutta: Writers' Workshop, 1975.

Hilton, Brown. *The Sahibs*. London: Hodge, 1948.

Hobsbaum, Eric and Terence Ranger. Ed. *The Invention of Tradition*. Cambridge: Cambridge University Press, 1983.

Hockley, William. *Pandurang Hari or Memoirs of a Hindoo*. London: Chatto and Windus, 1883.

Hutchins, F.G. *The Illusion of Permanence: British Imperialism in India*. New Jersey: Princeton UP, 1967.

Hyam, R. *Empire and Sexuality: The British Experience*. Manchester: Manchester University Press, 1982.

Joshi, Krishnanand. *The West Looks at India*. Bareilly: Prakash, 1969.

Lucas, Samuel. *Dacoitee in Excelsis or the Spoilation of Oudh by the East India Company*. Allahabad: Universal Press, 1974.

Mack, Robert. Ed. *Oriental Tales*. Oxford: OUP, 1992.

Mason, Philip. *The Men who Ruled India*. New Delhi: Time Books, 1987.

Maurya, Abhai. Ed. *India and World Literature*. Delhi: ICCR, 1990.

Misra, Udayon. *The Raj in Fiction: A Study of Nineteenth Century British Attitudes to India.* Delhi: B.R., 1987.

Moorhouse, Geoffrey. *The Governor-Generals of British India.* 4 vols. Delhi: Discovery Publishers, 1984.

Morris, J. Pax. *Britannica: The Climax of an Empire*. Harmondsworth: Penguin, 1963.

Mukherjee, Sujit. *Forster and Further: The Tradition of Anglo-Indian Fiction.* Bombay: Orient Longman, 1993.

Narayanan, Gomati. *The Sahibs and the Natives.* Delhi: Chanakya, 1986.

Newman, Judy. *The Ballistic Bard. Postcolonial Fictions*. Great Britain: Arnold, 1995.

Ngugi, T. wa. *Decolonizing the Mind.* London: Heinemann, 1986.

Niranjana, Tejaswini, et al. Ed. *Interrogating Modernity: Culture and Colonialism in India.* Calcutta: Seagull, 1993.

Parry, Benita. *Delusions and Discoveries: Studies on India in the British Imagination 1880-1930.* Bombay: Orient Longman, 1974.

Pennant, Thomas. *The View of Hindostan.* 2 vols. London: Henry Hughes, 1878.

Pratt, Mary. *Imperial Eyes*. London: Routledge, 1995.

Praz, Mario. *The Romantic Agony*. Oxford: OUP, 1970.

Princep, James. *Essays on Indian Antiquities: Historical, Numismatical and Paleographic.* New Delhi: Indological Book House, 1971.

Pritchard, Iltudus. *Chronicles of Budgepore.* Delhi: Manohar Reprints, 1972.

Singh, Bhupal. *A Survey of Anglo-Indian Fiction.* London: Curzon Press, 1975.

Singh, Shailendra. *Novels on the Indian Mutiny.* New Delhi: Arnold Heinemann, 1973.

Spear, Percival. *The Nabobs*. Calcutta: Rupa, 1991.

Spivak, Gayatri Chakravorty. *In Other Worlds*. London: Methuen, 1987.

Steadman, John. *The Myth of Asia.* London: Macmillan, 1970.

Thapar, Romila. *Past and Prejudice*. New Delhi: National Book Trust, 1979.

Trelawny, Edward. *Records of Shelley, Byron and the Author*. Great Britain: Hazel Watson and Viney, 1973.

Trevelyan, Sir George Otto. *The Competition Wallah*. New Delhi: Swapna, 1991.

Trotter, L.J. *Warren Hastings*. London: J.M. Dent, 1918.

Vernede, R.V. ed. *British Life in India* Delhi: OUP, 1995.

Vishwanatham, K. *India in English Fiction.* Waltair: Andhra University Press, 1971.

Visweswararn, K. "First Europeans in Malabar: Heteroglossia in the Opening up of India." Unpublished paper. 1992.

Young, Robert. *White Mythologies: Writing History and the West.* London: Routledge, 1990.

Index